Arts in the Key of Joy

THIRD EDITION

Aesthetic Excellence in Action

Allen Schantz

Aesthetic Arts Press

Aesthetic Arts Press

Arts in the Key of Joy: Aesthetic Excellence in Action, 3rd Edition
Published by *Aesthetic Arts Press*
Copyright © 2015 by Allen Schantz. All rights reserved. (Portions previously published, © in 2014 second edition, © in 2013, © in 2010 as *Arts in a New Key: Aesthetic Imageination in Action,* 5th edition, © in 2007 as *A New Key for the Arts: Aesthetic Power in Action* and © in 2006 as *The Arts in a New Key: Aesthetic Power in Action*.) No parts of this publication may be reproduced or distributed in any form or by any means, or stored in a database or retrieval system, without the prior written consent of Aesthetic Arts Press, including, but not limited to, mechanical, photocopying, recording, any network or other electronic storage or transmission, or broadcast for distance learning.

This book is printed on acid-free paper.

Every effort has been made to contact the copyright holders, but should there be any errors or omissions, Aesthetic Arts Press would be pleased to insert the appropriate acknowledgement in any subsequent printing.

ISBN: 978-0-9635275-8-5

1 2 3 4 5 6 7 8 9 0

S. D. G.

To

My University Students

and

Thoughtful People Everywhere

*May this book
be the beginning of
a journey of responsibility and joy!*

Contents

PART I—AESTHETIC EXPERIENCE IN ACTION • 1

INTRODUCTION • 3

1. **TAKING TIME TO TASTE AESTHETIC EXCELLENCE • 5**

   Aesthetic Excellence in Music **8** ▪ Extra-Aesthetic—Other Aspects of Life Outside the Aesthetic **8** ▪ Confusing Aesthetic and Extra-Aesthetic Concerns **9** ▪ Artistic (Aesthetic plus Extra-Aesthetic Aspects of the Arts) **10** ▪ Actions for Practice and Delight **11**

2. **IDENTITY, THE ARTS, AND HISTORY • 13**

   The Palindrome of the Human Story **14** ▪ The Many Uses of the Arts **16** ▪ Folk Art: Participation (Lucy) **16** ▪ Fine Art [Classical Art]: Aesthetic Study and Delight (Schroeder) **18** ▪ Popular/Commercial Art: Mass Consumption **20** ▪ Blurred Edges **20** ▪ Folk Participation as a Prelude to Fine and Popular Arts **21** ▪ Actions for Practice and Delight **22**

3. **UNLOCKING THE ARTS WITH THE MUSICAL KEY • 23**

   Music without Words (The Key to Aesthetic Experience) **23** ▪ GOD SAVE THE KING (AMERICA) **24** ▪ Music and the Other Arts Compared **25** ▪ Isolating the Aesthetic Aspect of Music **26** ▪ Levels of Listening (and Viewing) **26** ▪ Aesthetic Raw Elements of all the Arts **27** ▪ Actions for Practice and Delight **28**

4. **MUSIC IN BLACK AND WHITE • 29**

   FRÉRE JACQUES **29** ▪ The Aesthetic Raw Elements of Music **30** ▪ Rhythm (Time) **30** ▪ Rhythm Itself **30** ▪ Beat **31** ▪ Meter **31** ▪ Even Meter **31** ▪ Odd Meter **31** ▪ Ground Rhythm **32** ▪ *Tempo* **32** ▪ Melody **33** ▪ Special Insight 4-1: *Give Me the Do-Re-Mi* **33** ▪ Sailing the Ivory *C* **34** ▪ Half Steps and Whole Steps in the Major Scale **34** ▪ ODE TO JOY **35** ▪ FRÉRE JACQUES **35** ▪ ANTIOCH **36** ▪ BEETHOVEN 5th (Movement IV, Theme A) **36** ▪ The Difference between Major (brighter) and Minor (darker) **36** ▪ ODE TO SORROW, FRÉRE JACQUES, and BEETHOVEN 5th (I) in Minor **37** ▪ Harmony and Bass **39** ▪ Three Primary Chords **39** ▪ Major Chord Chart for Keyboard and Ukulele by Fifth Down **42** ▪ Minor Chord Chart for Keyboard and Ukulele by Fifth Down **43** ▪ Texture (Layers) **43** ▪ Monophonic Texture **44** ▪ Homophonic Texture **44** ▪ Polyphonic Texture **44** ▪ Listening for Layers in Music **46** ▪ Actions for Practice and Delight **47**

5. **THE COLORS OF SOUND ▪ 49**

   Dynamics (Soft/Loud) 49 ▪ Instrument Pitch Range (Low/High) 51 ▪ The Piano 51 ▪ The Guitar (Ukulele) 53 ▪ The Voice 53 ▪ Timbre (Quality of Sound) 55 ▪ Illustrations of Vocal Sound Colors 55 ▪ The Speaking Voice 55 ▪ The Singing Voice 55 ▪ Wind, Percussion, and Stringed Instruments 57 ▪ Wind Instruments 58 ▪ Percussion Instruments 59 ▪ Stringed Instruments 60 ▪ The Symphony Orchestra 60 ▪ Guide to the Orchestra 62 ▪ The Concert Band 64 ▪ Interactive Guide for *Stars and Stripes Forever* (1896) 64 ▪ The Jazz Band 66 ▪ The Rock/Pop Band 66 ▪ Actions for Practice and Delight 67

6. **DRAWING THE LINE ▪ 69**

   Drawing 69 ▪ Printmaking 70 ▪ Painting 71 ▪ Architecture 71 ▪ Sculpture 73 ▪ Applied Design 73 ▪ The Aesthetic Raw Elements of Art 74 ▪ Line 74 ▪ Shape 75 ▪ Perspective 75 ▪ Drawing the Way the Eye Sees and Adding Additional Vanishing Points 77 ▪ Space (Positive and Negative) 77 ▪ Texture 78 ▪ Actions for Practice and Delight 79

7. **THE COLORS OF LIGHT ▪ 81**

   Value (Shadow and Light, Black and White/Soft and Loud) 81 ▪ Hue Range (Palette/Instrument Pitch Range) 82 ▪ Primary Pigment Colors 82 ▪ Traditional Color Wheel 83 ▪ Secondary, Complementary, and Intermediate Colors 83 ▪ Warm and Cool Colors (Complementary Pairs) 84 ▪ Saturation (Dull to Vivid/Timbre: Mellow to Piercing) 85 ▪ The Interaction between Value, Hue Range (Palette), and Saturation 85 ▪ Putting the Colors of Sound and Light Together 85 ▪ Actions for Practice and Delight 86

8. **DANCING IN THE STREET ▪ 87**

   Ballet 87 ▪ The Five Basic Positions 88 ▪ Modern Dance 88 ▪ Jazz 88 ▪ Hip-Hop 88 ▪ Tap Dance 88 ▪ The Raw Elements of Dance 89 ▪ Body Shape 89 ▪ Energy 89 ▪ Action 90 ▪ Rhythm (Time) 90 ▪ Space 90 ▪ The *Nutcracker* 91 ▪ Actions for Practice and Delight 93

9. **YOU'RE A POET AND DON'T KNOW IT ▪ 95**

   The Raw Elements of Poetry 98 ▪ Line 98 ▪ Packed Word Pictures 99 ▪ Packed Word Sounds (Rhyme in General) 100 ▪ Poetic Rhythm 101 ▪ A Metrical Index for Setting Poetry to Music and Vice Versa 102 ▪ Poetic Colors of Sound 102 ▪ Form in Poetry 103 ▪ Guide for Shakespeare's Sonnet 18—*Shall I Compare Thee to a Summer's Day* 103 ▪ The Translated Song Poetry of the Bible 104 ▪ Enjoying Poetry 105 ▪ Actions for Practice and Delight 107

10. PUTTING SOME ENGLISH ON THE DRAMATIC STORY • 109

Special Insight 10-1—*The Key to the Aesthetic Development of English: The Two Williams* **110** ▪ Bringing the Stories of the Bible to Life for the English Reader **112** ▪ The Raw Elements of Story **112** ▪ *Samson and Delilah* **113** ▪ Guide to *Samson and Delilah* **116** ▪ Story and the Other Arts **116** ▪ The Raw Elements of Theatre **117** ▪ *Much Ado About Nothing* **119** ▪ The Story of Musical Theatre **123** ▪ Common Genres in Story, Theatre, and Musical Theatre **124** ▪ Actions for Practice and Delight **125**

11. CREATING FORM • 127

Dramatic Shape **127** ▪ Form in Art and Music **128** ▪ NEW BRITAIN (*Amazing Grace*) **128** ▪ Variation Form **129** ▪ SIMPLE GIFTS **130** ▪ Guide for Variations on SIMPLE GIFTS from *Appalachian Spring* **131** ▪ Alternating Form **131** ▪ Ritornello Form **132** ▪ Guide for the First Movement of *La Primavera* [*Spring*] **132** ▪ The Form of the Whole Concerto **134** ▪ Guide for *Spring*, Movement 2 **135** ▪ Guide for *Spring*, Movement 3 **135** ▪ The Whole Set of Four Concertos (*Four Seasons*) **136** ▪ Form in Dance **138** ▪ Pointed Toward Aesthetic Excellence **138** ▪ Actions for Practice and Delight **139**

12. THE GOAL: AESTHETIC EXCELLENCE • 141

The Idea of Image*i*nation **142** ▪ Unity **142** ▪ Diversity **143** ▪ "Fittingness-Intensity" **143** ▪ Aesthetic Excellence Summarized **145** ▪ Creating, Discovering, and Practicing Aesthetic Excellence **145** ▪ Becoming Part of a Practicing Community **145** ▪ The Aesthetic Excellence of a Performance and the Aesthetic Excellence of a Work **146** ▪ Face to Face with *Combatooka*, *Thi*, and *Jabberwocky* **146** ▪ Evaluating the Aesthetic Excellence of Three Works of Art **148** ▪ Three Selections of Music **151** ▪ Beethoven's Fifth **151** ▪ Central Motive and Other Themes for Beethoven's Fifth Symphony **153** ▪ Actions for Practice and Delight **155** ▪ Listening Guides for Beethoven's Symphony No. 5 **157**

PART II—AESTHETIC AND EXTRA-AESTHETIC INTERACTION • 163

13. AESTHETICS, FUNCTION, ETHICS, AND WORLDVIEW • 165

The Painting of a Hero **165** ▪ A Symphony Picturing a Hero **166** ▪ A FEW Criteria for Artistic Excellence **167** ▪ Aesthetic Excellence as the First Criterion for Artistic Excellence **167** ▪ Functional Fit as the Second Criterion for Artistic Excellence **167** ▪ Ethical Integrity as the Third Criterion for Artistic Excellence **168** ▪ Worldview Fit as the Fourth Criterion for Artistic Excellence **168** ▪ Trying Your Hand at Evaluating Two Paintings **170** ▪ "Going the Extra Mile" with a Christian View of Ethics **173** ▪ *Special Insight 13-1—An Eye for an Eye, the Ten Commandments, and the Radical Ethics of Jesus (Going the Extra Mile and Loving Your Enemies)* **174** ▪ Guide to the Words of Pärt's *Credo* **175** ▪ Artistic Excellence Summarized **176** ▪ Actions for Practice and Delight **177**

14. A SHORT HISTORY OF STYLE • 179

Artistic Styles in History **181** ▪ Ancient Styles (to 1450) **182** ▪ Common-Practice Style (ca. 1450–1900) **182** ▪ Avant-Garde [Modern] Styles (ca. 1900–1975) **182** ▪ Mixed [Postmodern] Period (ca. 1975–present) **182** ▪ Art History in Six Paintings **183** ▪ Poetic History in Six Poems **186** ▪ Music History in Fifteen Minutes **188** ▪ Mixed [Postmodern] Style **189** ▪ Special Insight 14-1: *The Natural Harmonic Series—The Key of Joy* **190** ▪ The Amazing Pentatonic **191** ▪ Joy to the World! **191** ▪ Actions for Practice and Delight **193**

15. IT'S YOUR MOVE • 195

APPENDIXES • A1

APPENDIX A—A CREATIVE PROJECT IN THE ARTS • A3

APPENDIX B—GUIDE TO *JOSEPH AND HIS BROTHERS* • B1

APPENDIX C—TUNES AND TEXTS • C1

PART I—AESTHETIC EXPERIENCE IN ACTION

INTRODUCTION ▪ 3

1. TAKING TIME TO TASTE AESTHETIC EXCELLENCE ▪ 5
2. IDENTITY, THE ARTS, AND HISTORY ▪ 13
3. UNLOCKING THE ARTS WITH THE MUSICAL KEY ▪ 23
4. MUSIC IN BLACK AND WHITE ▪ 29
5. THE COLORS OF SOUND ▪ 49
6. DRAWING THE LINE ▪ 69
7. THE COLORS OF LIGHT ▪ 81
8. DANCING IN THE STREET ▪ 87
9. YOU'RE A POET AND DON'T KNOW IT ▪ 95
10. PUTTING SOME ENGLISH ON THE DRAMATIC STORY ▪ 109
11. CREATING FORM ▪ 127
12. THE GOAL: AESTHETIC EXCELLENCE ▪ 141

INTRODUCTION

What do you think of when you hear the phrase, *the arts*? Many people think about an elitist activity with which they feel uncomfortable. They suppose that the arts are confined to a concert hall, an art museum, or a dusty library. For these people, the arts seem separated from life. However, the arts actually grow out of ordinary experience:

> the events and scenes that hold the attentive eye and ear of man, arousing his interest and affording him enjoyment as he looks and listens: the sights that hold the crowd—the fire-engine rushing by; the machines excavating enormous holes in the earth; the human-fly climbing the steeple-side; the men perched high in air on girders, throwing and catching red-hot bolts. The sources of art in human experience will be learned by him who sees how the tense grace of the ball-player infects the onlooking crowd;… the zest of the spectator in poking the wood burning on the hearth and in watching the darting flames and crumbling coals.[1]

What are these arts with their roots in ordinary experience? They include music, art[2] and dance—poetry, story, and theatre. The arts are universal to humankind. In every society, people sing lullabies, draw pictures, dance dances, and tell stories. The arts in all of their diversity have played a significant role in all cultures of every time and every place. Across the world, the arts continue as a powerful force.

Yet, many people seem oblivious to the significant impact of the arts in their daily lives. They live unaware of the beauty that surrounds them. In your own experience, think about this question: What would your life be like without music, colors, words, and actions? How deeply do the arts touch your life?

Whatever your experience with the arts, I invite you to join me on an intriguing journey intended for thinking people of all ages. In this book you will not only learn to think *about* the arts, you will learn to think *in* the arts, and you will even learn to think *up* the arts: plays, stories, poems, dances, drawings, paintings, carvings, and music!

---

[1] John Dewey, *Art as Experience*, Reprint (New York: Capricorn Books, 1958), p. 5.
[2] Including Architecture, Sculpture, Applied Design, Drawing, Painting, and Printmaking.

CHAPTER 1
TAKING TIME TO TASTE AESTHETIC EXCELLENCE

The arts "present what the narrow and desperately practical perspectives of real life exclude."[1]

Renaissance (1450–1600) *Bowl of Vegetables* or *The Gardener* (upside down)

The *arts* focus on the *aesthetic* aspect of living (engaging the perceptions) as opposed to *an*aesthetic (a drug dulling the perceptions). An **aesthetic** (noun, from Greek *aisthetikos*—sense perception) is the structural and perceptual "principles… for clarifying and confirming critical statements"[2] about works of art. To understand the aesthetic aspect of works of art takes sustained perceptual focus on the work of art itself. Take some time to study the painting on the right.[3] Observe how it is put together, the use of light and color, the lines, the shapes, the brushstrokes, the textures, etc. Now turn the painting on the right upside down! Can you see the gardener? When you are thoroughly experiencing the *perceptual qualities* of this artwork because of the way it is put together (*structural qualities*), you are focusing on its aesthetic aspects. Now take some time to study the paintings on the following pages in a similar way. Observe the use of light and color, the lines, the shapes, the textures, etc. How do they exhibit unity, variety, and dramatic shape (tension, climax, and release) in the way they are put together? The arts heighten our senses, stir our emotions, stimulate our minds, engage our bodies, and lift our spirits. They focus on the aesthetic aspect of human experience.

---

[1] C. S. Lewis (Ed. Walter Hooper) *On Stories and Other Essays on Literature* (New York: Harcourt Brace Jovanovich, 1982), p. 10.
[2] Monroe Beardsley, *Aesthetics: Problems in the Philosophy of Criticism* (New York: Harcourt, Brace & World, Inc., 1958), p. 4.
[3] Giuseppe Arcimboldo (1527–1593) *Ortaggi in una ciotola o L'ortolano* [*Bowl of Vegetables* or *The Gardener*] (1590), 30 x 50 cm (11.9 x 19.7 in.), oil on panel, Museo Civico Ala Ponzone, Cremona.

Baroque (1600–1750) Frans Snyders (1579–1657) *Dogs Fighting in a Wooded Clearing* (date unknown) oil on canvas, 173.4 × 241.9 cm (68.3 × 95.2 in), museum unknown.

Neo-classical (1750–1825)—Jacques-Louis David (1748–1825) *Napoleon Crossing the Alps* (1800) oil on canvas, 261 x 221 cm (102 1/3 x 87 in), Château de Malmaison, Rueil-Malmaison, France.

Romantic (1825–1900)—Eugene Delacroix (1798–1863) *Lion Hunt* (1860/1861) oil on canvas 76.5 x 98.5 cm (30 x 38½ in), Potter Palmer Collection, 1922.404, Art Institute of Chicago.

Avant-garde [Modern] (1900–1975)—Marc Chagall (1887–1985), *Paris Through* the *Window* [*Paris par la fenêtre*] (1913) oil on canvas, 136 x 141.9 cm (53 9/16 x 55 7/8 in) Solomon R. Guggenheim Museum, New York.

What did you discover about these paintings? Did you notice the different styles throughout history from the Renaissance onward? Were you able to distinguish between the way they were put together, the style, and the subject matter?

Now, take some time over several days to listen intently a number of times to the musical selections below [with particular attention to instruments, tone colors, volumes, melodies, harmonies, layers, etc.]. Observe how they are put together. Again, breathe deeply, and notice how your interaction with these elements brings your senses, your emotions, your mind, your body, and your spirit to life.

Aesthetic Excellence in Music through History (Renaissance–Present)

The Cricket Renaissance (1450–1600)	*Spring, I* Baroque (1600–1750)	*A Little Night Music, III* Classical (1750–1825)	*Ride of the Valkyries* Romantic (1825–1900)	*The Moor's Room* Avant-Garde (*Modern*) (1900–1975)
The Cricket Is a Good Singer [*El grillo*] (pub. 1505), attr. Josquin des Prez (ca. 1450–1521)—(Playlist Arts Key 01 [1]) or http://youtu.be/62-aBOZrqh8?t	Antonio Vivaldi (1678–1741) *Spring* [*La Primavera*] 1st movt. from *Four Seasons* (1725)—(Playlist Arts Key 01 [2]) or http://youtu.be/cQgd0vx3nYM	Wolfgang Amadeus Mozart (1756–1791) *Eine kleine Nachtmusik*, III Menuetto (Playlist Arts Key 01 [3]) or http://youtu.be/en6MzTZuiVQ	Richard Wagner (1811–1886) *Feuerzauber*, last scene of *Die Walküre* (1854–1856), 2nd opera in *The Ring* (Playlist Arts Key 01 [4]) or http://youtu.be/P73Z6291Pt8?t	Igor Stravinsky (1882–1971), *Scene III: The Moor's Room* from *Petrushka* (1911), (Playlist Arts Key 01 [5]) or http://youtu.be/esD90diWZds?t=14m3s [to 17:01]

What did you discover? Did you hear the unity, variety, and dramatic shape (tension, climax, and release) of each selection? Were you able to distinguish between aesthetic appreciation of the music, the styles, and your likes or dislikes?

Although the aesthetic aspect of living has been present throughout human history, its use for its own sake came into full flower during the Renaissance (*Rebirth*) period. The use of the arts primarily for their aesthetic value continues through the present, as shown in the five style periods on the previous pages and above.

Extra-Aesthetic—Other Aspects of Life Outside the Aesthetic

The arts also impact (and are impacted by) other modes of living. Each of the other dimensions of life has an aesthetic aspect, and the arts have **extra-aesthetic** (outside the aesthetic) aspects. For example, the works cited previously have personal, geographical, and historical aspects. Marc Chagall (Russian) painted *Paris through the Window* in Paris in 1913 near the beginning of the 20th century, and each of the other paintings and musical selections has different personal, geographical, and historical/stylistic characteristics. "Taking time to stop and taste" the aesthetic dimension can have an impact on the way in which we relate to other human beings, play basketball, prepare a meal, or even the way we do business.

So what are these aspects of human life? They are the **humanities** or the **liberal arts**—those branches of knowledge that are concerned with human life. These humanities or liberal arts (from the Latin for *liberating studies*) are a part of our human history. They were taught in the Middle Ages as the trivium (grammar, rhetoric, and logic) and the quadrivium (arithmetic, music, geometry, and astronomy). Although the liberal arts are sometimes associated almost exclusively with high schools and colleges, in actuality they are dimensions learned in every area of culture including elementary and middle schools, homes, and human life in general. The Dutch philosopher Herman Dooyeweerd provides one helpful way of thinking through this. He sketches the following fifteen modes of living (on the left). Each of these modes may be correlated with a particular discipline in the liberal arts (on the right).

Modes of Living	**Disciplines**
1. Belief [Faith]	[Theology/Philosophy]
2. Ethical	[Ethics]
3. Juridical [Legal]	[Law]
4. Aesthetic	[The Arts]
5. Economic	[Business]
6. Social	[Sociology]
7. Lingual	[Languages]
8. Historical	[History]
9. Logical	[Logic]
10. Psychical	[Psychology]
11. Biotic	[Biology]
12. Physical	[Physical Sciences]
13. Kinetic	[Motion Sciences]
14. Spatial	[Spatial Sciences]
15. Numerical	[Mathematics]

Leonard Meyer, the musical philosopher, lists these areas of life in a different way: Ideas, Arts, Social, Economic, Political, Individual, Inanimate, Animate, Human, and Numerical relationships.[1]

Today, an education in the liberal arts includes the disciplines mentioned above (with variations depending on the particular institution). Each liberal arts discipline has its particular focus. Whereas arts focus on the *aesthetic*, biology focuses on *organic life*. In addition, each discipline interacts with the other modes of living. In the case of biology, the impact of other modes of living on biology would be called *extra*-biotic.

Confusing Aesthetic and Extra-Aesthetic Concerns

In making critical judgments about a work in the arts, it is easy to confuse aesthetic aspects and extra-aesthetic concerns: to confuse aesthetic aspects with likes and dislikes, with subject matter, with style, with function, with truth, and with a whole host of other extra-aesthetic concerns. It is the thesis of this text that aesthetic excellence must

---

[1] Leonard Meyer, "Concerning the Sciences, the Arts—AND the Humanities" in *Critical Inquiry* (September, 1974), p. 204.

be judged independently and that it serves as the linchpin for the broader category of artistic excellence, which includes extra-aesthetic concerns as they relate to its aesthetic excellence (or lack of it).

Artistic (Aesthetic plus Extra-Aesthetic Aspects of the Arts)

The term **artistic** (everything that happens in the arts) includes both the aesthetic and the extra-aesthetic aspects of the arts. Notice in the following chart that the *aesthetic* mode, [#4 on the chart] has been pulled to the left so that we may consider its concentrated role in the arts (chapters 3–12). We will also explore the interaction of aesthetic and extra-aesthetic aspects, including social function and human identity [chapter 2], worldview and ethics [chapter 13], and historical style [chapter 14].

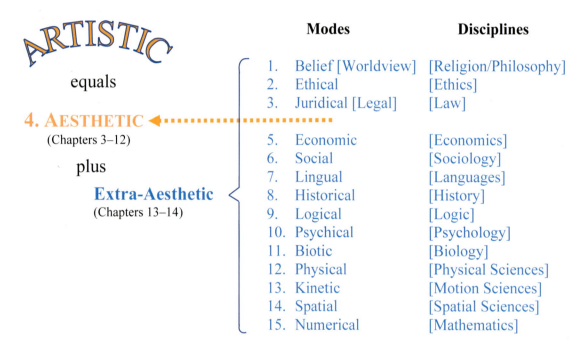

Discovering the aesthetic impact of the arts provides a start, but there is more. The arts, in and of themselves, will not make us more ethical or more loving. Knowing and doing the arts is no guarantee that we will be responsible in their use. It is only when aesthetic excellence and ethics meet that the full impact of the arts takes hold. We will explore the arts as both *objects* and *instruments* of duty and delight, taking the time to create and appreciate aesthetic and extra-aesthetic excellence and to practice using our creative *image*-ination responsibly (ethically) and joyfully.

Actions for Practice and Delight

1/1. Take time to carefully sample the five paintings at the beginning of the chapter on pages 5–7 and the five musical selections listed on page 8 (*Naxos* playlist Arts Key 01) numerous times over numerous days. Then, write down your observations about the structure (unity, variety, and dramatic shape) you perceive in each painting and in each musical selection. Discuss how your observations above help you to focus on the aesthetic aspects rather than on the extra-aesthetic aspects such as subject matter, likes and dislikes, style, etc. Which two of the 10 selections (one in art and one in music) are your aesthetic favorites and why? [Notice that these examples cover a wide variety of historical styles in order to give a variety of choices for varying tastes.]

1/2. In a short essay (thesis, support, conclusion) of 250–300 words, discuss the importance of a well-rounded education. What role do music, art, and dance—poetry, story, and theatre have in such an education?

1/3. Study several college and university catalogs (online for most) and discuss the requirements for general education. Which of the fifteen components of a holistic liberal arts education (discussed in this chapter) are emphasized at each university? Are there disciplines in the general education requirements that are not in the list of fifteen? Do all include the arts as a part of a general liberal arts education?

Chapter 2
Identity, the Arts, and History

Family Tree[1]

Take some time to observe the painting *Family Tree* by Norman Rockwell above. In this painting, the boy is shaped and inspired by past generations—his family tree. It is because of them that he has a place in history (in this illustration, American history with all

---
[1] Norman Rockwell (1894–1978), *Family Tree* (1959) from *The Saturday Evening Post*, October 24, 1959 (cover).

its social diversity). This painting, on the cover of the *Saturday Evening Post* in 1959, illustrates the use of the arts for extra-aesthetic purposes. It leads us to the relationship of the aesthetic to the extra-aesthetic and the questions "Who am I, what do the arts have to do with my human identity, and what is the use of the arts in the human story," as illustrated below. Because of their pervasive influence on the arts, the stories of the Bible are cited as the pedagogical flip side of the stories of American history. For example, the Story of Abraham (2000 B.C.) is the flip side of the Story of *Me* (2000 A.D.).

The Palindrome of the Human Story

FOLK-ART FUNCTIONS

The Beginning—Story of Creation of Human Beings in the Image of God

ca.2000$^?$ B.C.—Story of Abraham (Father of Arabs, Hebrews, and All People of Faith[1]) from Ur, Mesopotamia [Iraq] (Near Eastern Civilizations: Sumerian/Akkadian/Babylonian)

ca.1776$^?$ B.C.—Story of Joseph, Abraham's Great Grandson (Egyptian Civilization)

ca.1492$^?$ B.C.—Story of Moses and the Arts[2]

1000 B.C.—Story of King David (Psalms) and the Arts[3]

 1 A.D.—The Hinge of History: the Stories of Jesus (storyteller and poet)

1000—Story of Leif Eriksson (Viking [Erik's son]), who discovered America (first)

FINE-ART FUNCTIONS (on a separate track from *FOLK ART FUNCTIONS*)
Fine-Art Periods: Renaissance (1450–1600), Baroque (1600–1750), Classical/Neo-Classical (1750–1825), Romantic (1825–1900), Avant-garde [Modern] (1900–1975)

1492—Story of Columbus, who sailed the ocean blue and discovered America (again)

1776—Story of the Declaration of Independence
    Thomas Jefferson (Neo-Classical architect, principal author of the Declaration, and third president)

FOLK-ART, FINE-ART, AND POPULAR/COMMERCIAL-ART FUNCTIONS MIX
Mixed Period [Postmodern] (1975–present)

2000—**The Story of *Me*** (user of the arts and rookie musician, artist, dancer, poet, storyteller, and/or playwright), created in the image of God

The Consummation

[?] Exact dates not historically verifiable. Setting the Exodus at traditional dates of 1446 B.C. or 1260 B.C., gives the traditional dates for Abraham at 2166–1991 B.C. or 2000–1825 B.C.; for Joseph 1915–1805 B.C. or 1749–1639 B.C.; and for Moses' birth at 1526 B.C. or 1340 B.C. respectively.

[1] Father of many nations, Genesis 17:4, father of Arabs (Genesis 16:15); father of Hebrews (Genesis 21:3), and father of all people of faith (Galatians 3:6–7).

[2] Moses and music (Exodus 15), art (Exodus 25 ff.), dance (Exodus 15:20–21), poetry (Exodus 15), story and theatre (the first five books of the Bible including Exodus).

[3] David as musician (lyre player, 1 Samuel 16:14–23), architect (I Chronicles 28), dancer (2 Samuel 6:14), poet (many of the Psalms, including Psalm 23), and storyteller and actor (1 Samuel 21:10–15).

Renaissance (1450–1600) Michelangelo Buonarroti (1475–1565) *The Creation of Adam* (ca. 1511–1512) fresco, 4.8 x 2.30 m (15 ft 9 in x 7 ft 7 in) Sistine Chapel Ceiling, Rome.

In the beginning, the ancient Hebrew story of creation ties human identity to the creation of human beings in the *image* of God (Latin, *imago dei*).

> And God said, "Let us make a human in our image, by our likeness; to hold sway over the fish of the sea, and the fowl of the heavens and the cattle and the wild beasts and all the crawling things that crawl upon the earth."
>
> And God created the human in his image,
> in the image of God he created him,
> male and female he created them.
>
> And God blessed them, and God said to them, "Be fruitful and multiply, and fill the earth and conquer it, and hold sway over the fish of the sea and over the fowl of the heavens and over every beast that crawls upon the earth."[1]

The "male and female" relationship and "be fruitful and multiply and fill the earth" part of this "image" suggests that we as human beings are responsible to bear, nurture, and care for each other, including the children of current and future generations. The "holding sway" part implies that human beings are God's representatives on earth, entrusted with developing and caring for the rest of the created world.

In this story, the overarching aspect of human uniqueness lies in *our responsibility as active agents in the world*—taking the time to nurture and to care for animals, plants, our earth, and its people. In this view, *being a human being* means *being a humane being* (characterized by kindness, mercy, and compassion) rather than being *inhuman or inhumane* (characterized by unkindness, reprehension, and indifference). This suggests that the process of learning to be human is the process of becoming a responsible human

---

[1] Genesis 1:26–28 as translated by Robert Alter, *The Five Books of Moses*.

being in *every* area of life, including the arts. This includes our capacity for the arts, but this capacity receives its fundamental significance from our *responsibility*.[1] In this view, human beings are responsible in every dimension of life (see previous chapter) including the arts in both aesthetic and extra-aesthetic aspects. In caring for our world, this story suggests that we have the responsibility for both aesthetic excellence and extra-aesthetic diligence in using arts for the glory of God and for the good of others including the children of present and future generations.

The Many Uses of the Arts

In a comic strip from *PEANUTS*,[2] Schroeder has just purchased a recording. As he walks out of the store, he encounters Lucy.

Lucy: What's that Schroeder? (*Pointing to the recording in his hands*)

Schroeder: This is a new recording of Brahms' Fourth Symphony… (*As he looks at the recording with admiration*)

Lucy: What are you going to do with it?

Schroeder: I'm going to take it home and listen to it…

Lucy: You mean you're going to dance to it?

Schroeder: No. I'm just going to listen to it…

Lucy: Are you going to march around the room while you listen to it?

Schroeder: No. I'm just going to sit and listen to it…

Lucy: You mean you're going to whistle or sing while you listen to it?

Schroeder: No. I'm just going to listen to it… (*As he turns and walks away*)

Lucy: That's the most ridiculous thing I've ever heard! (*She shouts after him*)

The arts have many uses. Music may be used for dancing, marching, whistling, or singing along (as is Lucy's description above) or it may be used for its own sake (as in Schroeder's use above). There are three primary social functions of music and the other arts throughout history: 1) folk art, 2) fine art, and 3) popular/commercial art.

Folk Art: Participation (Lucy)

Folk art (art of the people) is participatory art that is intended for faith, family, and community. Until the dawn of the Renaissance (ca. 1450), the arts were virtually inseparable from religious, family, and community purposes and associations. The Bible illustrates the folk arts. It is comprised of dramatic stories (approximately 2/3) and poetry (approximately 1/3) and verbally describes the use of all the other folk arts. It begins with

---

[1] For this entire argument, see Wolterstorff, *Art in Action* (Grand Rapids: Eerdmans, 1980), pp. 72–78.
[2] Charles M. Schulz, *PEANUTS* from *Play It Again, Schroeder* (New York: Ballentine Books, 2007), p. 37.

the story of creation in theme and variation form. Music is associated with God's creative activity: "Where were you when I laid the foundation of the earth, when the morning stars sang together and all the sons of God shouted for joy." The first mention of instruments other than voice in the Bible is in Genesis 4:21—"His brother's name was Jubal. He was the father of all those who play the lyre (*kinnor*) and pipe (*ugav*)." The pipe is the oldest musical instrument known except for the human voice. Prehistoric pipes (flutes) and artworks from the Paleolithic Period have been found in caves in France and Germany. As an example of the use of the human voice in ancient style, listen to a male overtone singer from Tuva in central Asia (*Naxos* playlist Arts Key 02 [1]), and as an example of the ancient pipe (flute), listen to a Ney [pipe/flute] player (*Naxos* playlist Arts Key 02 [2]). Writing and the consequent writing of history began in Mesopotamia ca. 3000 B.C., followed closely by Egypt. Abraham (ca. 2000? B.C.), father of Arabs, Hebrews, and all people of faith,[1] was from Ur, Mesopotamia and represents Mesopotamian culture for pedagogical purposes. Joseph (ca. 1776?), the great grandson of Abraham who became a ruler in Egypt, represents Egyptian culture.

Reproduction of Jewish High Priest's garments as described in Exodus 28

The story of the Exodus of the Hebrews (ca. 1492? B. C.) from Egypt covers all the arts. Chapters 1–14 recount the ***dramatic story*** of Moses' birth, his years as a young man as a prince of Egypt, his exile, return, and the ten plagues, culminating with the parting of the Red Sea in Exodus, chapter 14. The story of the Red Sea crossing is commemorated in ***poetry, music, and dance*** in Exodus 15 with the Song of Moses, sung by Miriam and other women in call-and-response form, accompanied by hand drums and dancing (verses 20–21). Exodus 16–24 continues the ***dramatic story*** with the Hebrews journey in the desert, the giving of the Ten Commandments, accompanied by the sound of the ram's horn (*yobel, shofar*) [19:13, 16, 19; 20:18] (*music again*). Exodus 25–40 describes the ***art*** in the construction of the tabernacle (tent of meeting) with all of its furnishings and the high priest's garments, illustrated on the right.[2] Unlike art, which can be preserved, folk music is an unnotated, oral tradition passed on from generation to generation, so the only idea we have of how the music of the Bible might have sounded comes from verbal descriptions and traditions recorded after the advent of sound recording (in the late 1800s). Listen to an example of the sounding of the ram's horn (*shofar*) with its various signals (*Naxos* playlist Arts Key 02 [1] or *Naxos* keywords shofar blessings [1]).

---

[1] Father of many nations, Genesis 17:4, father of Arabs (Genesis 16:15); father of Hebrews (Genesis 21:3), and father of all people of faith (Galatians 3:6–7).
[2] Illustration from the *ESV Study Bible* (Wheaton, Illinois: Crossway Bibles, 2008), p. 208.

The *dramatic story* of David (1000 B.C., reigned 1010 to 970 B.C.) also covers all the arts. David is first introduced as a handsome shepherd lad and skillful **lyre player** (1 Samuel 16). He is an **architect** (I Chronicles 28, plans for the temple) and **dancer** (2 Samuel 6:14). He is a **singer** and lyric **poet** (who wrote many of the Psalms, including Psalm 23, "The Lord is my shepherd"). He is even a **storyteller** and **actor** (1 Samuel 21:10–15).

Creators of folk art include religious communities, children, fathers, mothers, grandmothers, grandfathers, uncles, aunts, friends, and other cultural communities. Typically, folk artists are not formally trained, and many are self-taught. Folk art is understood by the community of participants within a particular cultural group and reflects the lives of the people who produce it, use it, and value it. It is spontaneous and heart-felt art that reflects joys and sorrows, relationships and romances, and events and circumstances.

In folk art, one's focal awareness is on the communal aspect in which everyone participates in one way or another (for example, congregational singing). The aesthetic aspects play a *subsidiary* or *accompanying* role. In a hymn or praise song (also used in Sub-Saharan Africa to praise a powerful leader), the focus is on the *function* of the music rather than on the music itself. The well known praise song *Amazing Grace*, with lyrics (1779) by the British hymn writer John Newton, was set to its traditional American folk melody in the 1800s, titled appropriately as NEW BRITAIN (words and music on pages C2, C3). Folk art includes lullabies and singing around the piano and the campfire. It includes quilting bees, Easter egg coloring, sweater knitting, family drama, and paintings by family members. In a patchwork quilt, the focus is on the function of the quilt to keep one warm with the aesthetic excellence or mediocrity of the quilt serving to give delight or a headache. In religious services, the focus is on worship with the aesthetic excellence or mediocrity of the arts serving as a ringing reinforcement or a disturbing distraction. Music is often used as an aid to memory, as in the ABC song to help children to memorize the alphabet. In reverse fashion, sometimes a poem is used to help memorize music. Most of the songs in Appendix C of this text are folk songs. You may wish to participate with others in singing and/or playing NEW BRITAIN (*Amazing Grace*) [pages C2 and C3] with words by John Newton in 1779, later set to the 19th century American folk tune that we know so well today, and *My Country 'Tis of Thee* (AMERICA or GOD SAVE THE KING) on pages C2/C3 and page C13.

Fine Art [Classical Art]: Aesthetic Study and Delight (Schroeder)

Fine Art (sometimes called "classical art" or "high art") is art that is intended primarily for aesthetic study and delight. Fine art grows out of folk art and is often based upon it. This use of art began to factor out during the Renaissance (1450–1600) when "Columbus sailed the ocean blue in 1492." This art may have a subject, carry a message, or tell a story, but its primary purpose is to serve as a paragon of perceptual contemplation and delight, with special physical conditions to enhance the perceptual experience (for example, a concert hall, a museum, a gallery, a theatre, or a small intimate space). Whether or not this art is absolute (a Mozart or Brahms Symphony, for example) or whether it tells a story (Mozart's *The Marriage of Figaro*, for example),[1] the primary emphasis is on its aesthetic excellence. Fine art is used primarily by an educated elite. This cultural elite is open (not tied to wealth, heredity, or occupation), and it has close ties to an intellectual elite (to achieve membership, one attends a college or university).[2] This art is practiced by highly skilled artists who have worked many years to perfect their art. Thomas Jefferson (1743–1826) designed his own neo-classical Virginia home, *Monticello* (his "essay in architecture"), modeling it after the Renaissance artist Palladio's *Villa Rotunda*.

Neoclassical (1750–1825) Thomas Jefferson (1743–1826) *Monticello* 110' long, 87' 9" wide, 44' 7" high, near Charlottesville, Virginia.

Although often thought of as art in the educated European and American tradition, fine art also occurs in other cultures. In Indian fine-art music (classical music), for example, both the performers and the audience typically sit on rugs or mats on the floor. Concerts are more informal and relaxed than in fine-art music (classical) concerts in the west. People converse about the music during the performance and sometimes get up in the middle of the two to three-hour concert to get refreshments. (It should be noted that in Indian classical concerts, there is no intermission.) You may wish to listen to *Gat Kirwani*

---

[1] Art that has a subject, carries a message, or tells a story may also be intended primarily for aesthetic contemplation and delight. The story, message, or subject matter weds propositional meaning to aesthetically excellent art adding impact to the message and meaning to the art that neither would have by itself. An example of this would be Mozart's opera, *The Marriage of Figaro*. The interest of the opera lies in the way that Mozart's musical genius shows off the satirical meaning of the story.

[2] Nicholas Wolterstorff, *Art in Action* (Grand Rapids: Eerdmans, 1980) and *Art, Religion, and the Elite* (an unpublished paper, 1981). In this text, Nicholas Wolterstorff argues that many of us in Western culture have been "blinded by high art." We mistakenly believe that all art is created solely for the purpose of aesthetic contemplation. As opposed to this predominant idea, he has convincingly demonstrated that art is multi-functional and should be appreciated in action. There are a variety of actions that artists perform by means of their works.

composed by George Harrison of the Beatles in the style of fine-art music of India (although much shorter) and arranged by Ravi Shankar (*Naxos* playlist <u>Arts Key 02</u> [3] or keywords: <u>*Gat Kirwani* Genius</u> [6]). Listen for the solo sitar (stringed instrument), accompanied by drone (fixed pitch), and tabla (hand drum).

Popular/Commercial Art: Mass Consumption

Popular art (sometimes called "commercial" art) is art that is intended to be sold (or be used to sell something else) to the largest number of people possible. Thus, by definition, popular art is art that is used by the largest number of people. (Popular music had its genesis in the United States around 1776 with inexpensive sheet music becoming widely available.)[1] Because it is marketed for mass use, popular art is usually not as challenging or complex as fine art, although it is based on the language of that art. Popular art is permeated with extra-aesthetic values and associations: the personality and life-style of celebrities, the social activities that are part of artistic activities, social/economic/political associations, and memories of friendships and romance. In popular art, one's focal awareness is on the immediate value of the product being presented. Like fast food, it is intended to be immediately purchased and consumed by as many people as possible. As in folk art, the aesthetic component plays a *subsidiary* or *accompanying* role. In popular dance music, for example, the focus is on the appropriateness of the beat for dancing with the aesthetic excellence of the music playing an accompanying role. In many movies, for example, the focus is primarily on box office receipts rather than the aesthetic aspects.

Much popular art is intended primarily for accompanying or adding strength to some other function. There is visual art that has the sole purpose of advertising a particular product or group of products (sometimes termed "advertising art"). The culinary arts, fashion design, interior decorating, and computer animation are also designed to add strength to other functions. There is music for dancing, dining, driving, movies, studying, shopping, therapy, exercise, and a whole host of other things.

Blurred Edges

These categories of art overlap, blur into each other, and exchange functions, especially in today's society. Headphones become a virtual concert hall, the Internet becomes a virtual art gallery, and the home becomes a virtual stage. Any of the categories above (folk, fine, and popular) may function in another category.

Much folk and fine art has become popular art, sold to and appreciated by large numbers of people in the marketplace. Some tunes from fine art music have become folk art, for example, the tune of ODE TO JOY set to the words *Joyful, Joyful* or a tune from FINLANDIA set to the words *Be Still, My Soul*. What was originally intended as art music is now used for dozens of activities other than contemplation and study. A sampling of a

---

[1] See Charles Hamm, *Yesterdays: Popular Song in America* (New York: W. W. Norton, 1979).

myriad of current CD titles confirms this trend: *Bach for Barbeque, Baroque at Bathtime, Chopin and Champagne, Commuter Classics, Mozart for Your Morning Workout, Music for the Morning Commute,* and *Tune Your Brain for Stress Relief.*

Some popular and folk art is raised to the level of fine art, used primarily for the study of its aesthetic excellence. Many folk artifacts are placed in museums and contemplated as fine art. Amish quilts are now hung in museums for their aesthetic beauty rather than being used to keep one warm on a cold winter night. A similar pattern occurs with Native American clothing, African masks—the list goes on and on.

Musical examples include the piano compositions in Fantasies and *Delusions* by Billy Joel or the album *True Love Waits* by classical pianist Christopher O'Riley playing the music of Radiohead (keywords: O'Riley True Love Waits). The popular song *Bohemian Rhapsody* by Queen is known and listened to today primarily for its aesthetic excellence with scant attention given to the message regarding social justice. Many students know it so well that they can sing along with the words. To focus on the aesthetic value of the music itself, listen to the music with panpipes substituting for voices (*Naxos* playlist Arts Key 02 [4] or keyword: *Bohemian Rhapsody* Relaxing Pan Pipes [1]). [This piece, composed in 1975 by Freddie Mercury (Frederick Bulsara), is in Mixed Style with panpipes, electric guitars, and amplified instruments in the style of a Romantic opera.]

Jazz is an example of a popular art that has now shifted categories and has become fine-art music, studied in universities and colleges and listened to in concert halls all over the world. The jazz pianist, Dr. Billy Taylor calls jazz "America's classical music." In 1983, Wynton Marsalis won Grammy Awards both as the best jazz performer and the best classical performer on trumpet. For his performances in both genres, see *YouTube* keywords: 1983 Grammy Performance and Acceptance Speech or http://youtu.be/YHytOMuSnUA. In 2014, Jazz at Lincoln Center (JALC) under the direction of Wynton Marsalis formed a strategic partnership with the National Association for Music Education (NAfME) to provide education resources that will enhance the ability to teach jazz and to understand the importance of jazz as part of America's collective history.

Folk Participation as a Prelude to Fine and Popular Arts

Following the lead of history, participation in the folk arts serves as a prelude to the aesthetic appreciation of the fine arts and to the ethical use of the popular arts. We move from thinking *about* the arts to thinking *in* the arts.

Actions for Practice and Delight

2/1. Learn the palindrome dates surrounding the hinge of history and how they relate to the functions of the arts (page 14).

2/2. Participate with others in singing and playing the following songs in the songbook at the back of this text (*Appendix C*) until you know them thoroughly: *Heart and Soul* (page C1) and NEW BRITAIN [*Amazing Grace*] (pages C2 and C3).

2/3. Tell the story of your family tree and your use of the arts (including your use of folk, fine, and popular arts) from your birth to the present time (including, for example, whether anyone sang lullabies to you as a baby).

2/4. Using *Naxos* playlist Arts Key 02 [tracks 1–6], and sitting (or lying) in a quiet place (you may wish to use headphones) with your eyes closed, listen to the following examples again and again as you think about what you are hearing. Do this several times in spaced intervals over the course of two or more days [minimum three times]. After each complete hearing, record your experience in writing and how you progress on the following:
   a. Diagram and describe the dramatic shape (rising tension, climax, and release) for each selection.
   b. Discuss how each of the selections fulfills its function.
   c. Discuss which selection is your favorite and why.

[The information for accessing these individually is also listed below in case you wish to listen to more of each album.]
   1) Folk Function: Overtone singing from Tuva—voice, the oldest instrument (*Naxos* playlist Arts Key 02 [1], *Naxos* 8.570316 [17], or keywords: overtone singer)
   2) Folk Function: Pipe [flute], the next oldest instrument (*Naxos* playlist Arts Key 02 [2], keywords: song of the ney dashti [9])
   3) Folk Function: Ram's horn (*shofar*) [first mentioned in Exodus 19:13] (*Naxos* playlist Arts Key 02 [3], *Naxos* keywords: shofar blessings [1] or shofars call)
   4) Folk Function: Amazing Grace (*Naxos* playlist Arts Key 02 [4] or keywords: Amazing Grace Folk Mushet [14])
   5) Fine-Art Function in Indian Music (mixed style with ancient flavor): *Gat Kirwani* composed by George Harrison of the Beatles in the style of fine-art music of India and arranged by Ravi Shankar (*Naxos* playlist Arts Key 02 [5] or keywords: Gat Kirwani Genius [6]). Listen for the solo sitar (stringed instrument), accompanied by drone (fixed pitch), and tabla (hand drum).
   6) Popular/Commercial Function (mixed style): *Bohemian Rhapsody* with panpipes (*Naxos* playlist Arts Key 02 [6], *Naxos* keyword: BARDD35 [1]), or keywords bohemian rhapsody bar de lune.

2/5. List the items you have spent money on in the past year that relate to your use of music: money for concerts, albums, an iPod, an iPhone, etc., and detail which of these gave you the most bang for the buck.

Chapter 3
Unlocking the Arts with the Musical Key

Music is the wordless key that unlocks all the arts: **M**usic, **A**rt, and **D**ance—**P**oetry, **S**tory, and **T**heatre (**MAD PoST**). **M**usic is the organization of sound in time. **A**rt is the organization of images in space. **D**ance is the organization of the body in time and space (usually accompanied by music). **P**oetry is the organization of packed word pictures and sounds in time. **S**tory is the organization of events in time. **T**heatre is story acted out in time and space. **M**usical **T**heatre combines all the arts. This chapter gives an overview of the arts and their *elements*, the raw ingredients for creating aesthetic experience.

mi   re   do   la   so

Music without Words (The Key to Aesthetic Experience)

It is easy to confuse aesthetic and extra-aesthetic concerns. The worded arts of poetry, story, and theatre are inextricably intertwined with the fabric of their extra-aesthetic subject matter. Even art and dance are usually tied to subject matter, although some art and dance are non-representational. Music, on the other hand, is not inextricably tied to its subject matter or text. Different words and subject matter are often put to the very same tune. For example, notice that texts and tunes on facing pages from C2–C11 in Appendix C are interchangeable. For example, the words to *Amazing Grace, Joy to the*

World [Psalm 98], and *Gilligan's Island* (in Appendix C on page C2) may be sung to any of the tunes that are usually used to set these words on page C3. [Any text in ballad meter may be set to any tune in ballad meter.]

Another easily understood example is the traditional tune used for the words *God Save the King* [*Queen*] and a variety of other words including *My Country 'Tis of Thee*, for the same tune, usually titled GOD SAVE THE KING (QUEEN) or AMERICA [page C13].[1] Although this tune had existed much earlier, its first definitive publication appeared in 1745. (This folk tune GOD SAVE THE QUEEN may be found on *Naxos* playlist Arts Key 03 God Save the King [1].)

GOD SAVE THE KING (AMERICA)

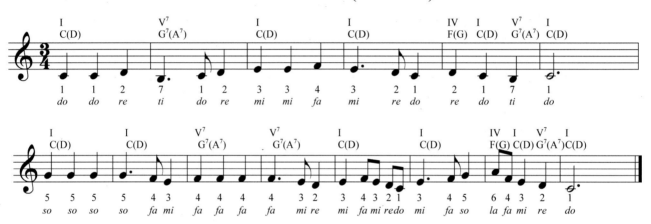

United Kingdom National Anthem	American Counterpart
God save great _____ (name) our king [queen], Long live our noble king [queen] God save the king [queen]. Send him [her] victorious Happy and glorious Long to reign over us God save the king [queen].	My country 'tis of thee Sweet land of liberty Of thee I sing Land where my fathers died Land of the pilgrim's pride From every mountainside Let freedom ring.
Words, 1745, Traditional	Words, 1831, Samuel Francis Smith
King Christian's Anthem **English Translation**	**Lichtenstein Anthem** **English Translation**
Heil dir im Siegerkranz, Hail thou in victor's crown, Herrscher des Vaterlands! King of the fatherlands! Heil, Christian, dir! King Christian, hail! Fühl in des Thrones Glanz Feel in the throne's warm glow Die hohe Wonne ganz, High ecstasy to know, Liebling des Volks zu sein! To be the peoples' favorite! Heil, Christian, dir! King Christian, hail!	Oben am deutschen Rhein Above the German Rhine Lehnet sich Liechtenstein Lies peaceful Liechtenstein, An Alpenhöh'n. On Alpine heights. Dies liebe Heimatland, This well-loved native land, Das teure Vaterland, This precious fatherland Hat Gottes weise Hand God's wise and gracious hand Für uns erseh'n. Gave us these sites.
Words, 1790, Heinrich Harries Translation, 2009, Allen Schantz	Words, 1850, Jakob Josef Jauch Translation, 2009, Allen Schantz

Music is independent from words. Music that is married to a particular set of words may be divorced from them and married to a different set of words (as above), or it

---

[1] The names of tunes are notated in capital letters in this text.

may be used for its own sake, as illustrated by a plethora of musical variations on this tune by *well over one hundred different composers*. The following two are representative: 1) Variations on *God Save the King*[1] by Beethoven in 1802–1803 (*Naxos* playlist Arts Key 03 [2], and 2) Variations on *America* by Charles Ives in 1892, orchestrated by William Schuman in 1963 (*Naxos* playlist Arts Key 03 [3]. These instrumental variations on this tune allow us to concentrate on the aesthetic experience of the music itself without reference to any particular set of words.

Music and the Other Arts Compared

As an example of the difference between the independent nature of music (which can be used by itself or hold different subject matter) and the interdependent nature of representational art and its subject matter, consider the previous tunes compared to Goya's *Los Fusilamientos del 3 de Mayo* [*The Executions of the Third of May*]. In Goya's painting, the subject matter (soldiers, guns, innocent victims, pool of blood) is part of the way the artwork is put together. It would be extremely difficult, if not impossible, to overlay the same painting with different subject matter or with no subject matter at all.

Francisco de Goya y Lucientes (1746–1828), *Los Fusilamientos del 3 de Mayo* [*The Executions of the Third of May*] 1814–1815, Oil on canvas, 267 x 345 cm., 8 ft. 9 in. x 11 ft. 4 in., Prado, Madrid.

---

[1] Seven Variations for Piano in C major: on the English folk song "God Save the King." Full score at imslp.org/wiki/7_Variations_on_%27God_Save_the_King%27%2C_WoO_78_%28Beethoven%2C_Ludwig_van%29.

In contrast (as previously outlined), one may overlay music with different subject matter, different sets of words, or with no words at all. Music is an *aesthetic vessel* that may stand on its own or carry a variety of different contents. This led Walter Pater to exclaim, "All art constantly aspires to the condition of music."[1] Suzanne Langer agrees: "It is easier to grasp the *artistic* import of music than of the older and more model-bound arts... Its artistic mission is more visible because it is not obscured by meanings belonging to the represented object."[2]

Isolating the Aesthetic Aspect of Music

To isolate the aesthetic aspect of music, an acoustically well-designed concert space provides an ideal place for listening to instrumental music itself without extraneous aural or visual distractions. When that option is unavailable, good earphones (or headphones) provide a virtual concert hall. When using earphones, it is helpful to sit (or lie) in a quiet place with eyes closed (and/or lights out) with the volume set at 50% or below. In that way, it is easy to concentrate on the aural cues without interference from any of the other senses.

Listening intently and intentionally to instrumental music provides a helpful first step in exploring the aesthetic experience that is the focus of all the arts. During our extended discussion of music, we will encounter many different types and styles of music, from the Western classical tradition and the music of other cultures throughout history to jazz and popular music of our time. This will serve to introduce us to the amazing variety that is present in all of the arts. In addition to standing alone, music is also used to accompany or be accompanied by the other arts: music and dance, music in architectural spaces, music and story, music and poetry, and music and theatre. This does not mean, however, that music is more important (or less important) than the other arts that follow it.

Levels of Listening (and Viewing)

In his classic work, *What to Listen for in Music*, Aaron Copland distinguishes three levels of listening: "1) the sensuous plane, 2) the expressive plane, 3) the sheerly musical plane."[3] He describes the sensuous plane as "the plane on which we hear music without thinking, without considering it in any way." Many people "use music as a consolation or an escape. They enter an ideal world where one doesn't have to think about the realities of everyday life... Music allows them to leave it, and they go off to a place to dream, dreaming because of and apropos of the music yet never quite listening to it."[4]

---

[1] Walter Pater, *The Renaissance*, 5th ed. (London: MacMillan and Company, 1901), p. 135. [In the reprint by Random House Publishers (New York) in their Modern Library of the World's Best Books, this quote appears on p. 111.]
[2] Suzanne Langer, *Philosophy in a New Key*, 3rd ed. (Cambridge, Massachusetts: Harvard University Press, 1957), p. 257.
[3] Aaron Copland, *What to Listen for in Music* (New York: McGraw-Hill, 1939), p. 7.
[4] Ibid., pp. 7–8.

The second plane, the "expressive plane," is synonymous with "fittingness-intensity" in Chapter 12 of this text. Aaron Copland writes, "Listen, if you can, to the forty-eight fugue themes of Bach's *Well Tempered Clavichord*. You will soon realize that each mirrors a different world of feeling…"[1]

The third plane that Aaron Copland describes is the "sheerly musical plane:

> It is very important for all of us to become more alive to music on its sheerly musical plane… The intelligent listener must be prepared to increase his awareness of the musical material and what happens to it. He must hear the melodies, the rhythms, the harmonies, the tone colors in a more conscious fashion. But above all he must, in order to follow the line of the composer's thought, know something of the principles of musical form.[2]

All three levels work together. Aaron Copland concludes:

> "Actually, we never listen on one or the other of these planes. What we do is to correlate them—listening in all three ways at the same time… What the reader should strive for, then, is a more active kind of listening. Whether you listen to Mozart or Duke Ellington, you can deepen your understanding of music only by being a more conscious and aware listener—not just someone who is listening, but someone who is listening *for* something.[3]"

The aesthetic (structural and perceptual) elements—what to listen *for* and what to look *for* in each of the arts—are shown below.

Aesthetic Raw Elements of All the Arts

Worded or Wordless	Wordless Arts		Worded Arts		
Music[4]	*Art*	*Dance*	*Poetry*	*Story*	*Theatre*
Melody	Line	Body	Line	Characters	Characters
Harmony	Shape	Energy	Packed Word Pictures	Word Choice	Word Choice
[Bass]	[Perspective]	Action	Packed Word Sounds	Setting	Artistic Setting
Rhythm (Time)	Space	Rhythm (Time) Space	Rhythm (Time)	Rhythm (Time)	Rhythm (Time) Space
Texture (Layers)	Texture				

Colors of Sound
  Volume (Dynamics)
  Pitch Range
  Timbre
	Colors of Light
	  Value
	  Hue Range
	  Saturation
		Colors of Sound and Light	Colors of Sound
			  Volume (Dynamics)
			  Pitch Range
			  Timbre
				Colors of Sound
				  Volume (Dynamics)
				  Pitch Range
				  Timbre
					Colors of Sound and Light, and
					  Body
					  Energy
					  Action

FORM	FORM	FORM	FORM	FORM	FORM

---

[1] Ibid., p. 11.
[2] Ibid., p. 13.
[3] Ibid., pp. 14–15.
[4] A mnemonic device for musical elements follows: Mel *Hart's* Bass *Rh*y*thm pLa*y*ers Col*or *Farm*.

Actions for Practice and Delight

3/1. Learn the elements of music as listed on the previous page. If you wish, you may use the mnemonic device in footnote four on the previous page. Think about how the elements of music relate to the elements of the other arts.

3/2. Participate with others in singing and/or playing the following folk song in the songbook at the back of this text (*Appendix C*, page C13) until you know it thoroughly: *My Country 'Tis of Thee* (GOD SAVE THE QUEEN or AMERICA).

3/3. From Folk-Art to Fine-Art Function. Sitting (or lying) in a quiet place (you may wish to use headphones) with your eyes closed, listen to the song GOD SAVE THE QUEEN (*Naxos* playlist Arts Key 03 God Save the King [1]). Then, listen many times either to Beethoven's *Variations on God Save the King* [2 on the playlist] or to Charles Ives' *Variations on America* [3 on the playlist] in spaced intervals over the course of two or more days (**minimum three times**). Label clearly which selection you have chosen (Beethoven or Ives). After each complete hearing, record your experience in writing and how you progress on the following:

1) Listen for the melody. [In the Beethoven variations, each half of the melody is repeated twice.] How soon are you able to hear when each variation begins (the beginning of the melody), and how many variations can you count?
2) Describe the mood of each variation.
3) Which variation is your favorite, and why? [*This may change over the course of your listening.*]
4) What other elements of music can you hear beside the melody?
5) Conclude your written comments by discussing how Beethoven's or Ives' variations allow you to concentrate on the music itself rather than on any words associated with it. Describe how your listening has changed and what you have learned over the course of this assignment.

Chapter 4
Music in Black and White

"With his ebony hands on each ivory key
He made that poor piano moan with melody."[1]

FRÉRE JACQUES [ARE YOU SLEEPING]

Music, as we know it today, has four essential layers: melody, harmony, bass, and ground rhythm.[2] In a musical ensemble, the higher-pitched instruments play the melody (lead), the middle-pitched instruments play the harmony, the lower-pitched instruments play the bass, and the percussion instruments (sometimes unpitched) play the ground rhythm. In a four-member band, these functions are usually filled by lead guitar (and vocals), rhythm guitar (with harmony) and back-up vocals, bass guitar (playing both bass and rhythm), and drum set. In a purely vocal ensemble there is no percussion section, so

---

[1] Langston Hughes (1902–1967), *The Weary Blues* (1923), lines 9 and 10.
[2] Since earliest times, melody and rhythm have been an essential part of music. Functional harmony and its corresponding bass line came into being during the Baroque period (1600–1750).

the ground rhythm is sung by the bass and harmony parts. The keyboard and guitar are instruments that can play all these layers at once. Melody begins the cycle of the aesthetic raw elements of music followed by harmony/bass, rhythm, and texture (layers). Colors of sound, and form will be covered in later chapters.

The Aesthetic Raw Elements of *Music*—Organized Sound
Melody—series of single pitches set to a rhythm (pentatonic/modal/major/minor)
Harmony—series of simultaneous pitches set to a rhythm (dissonant/consonant)
[Bass]—the lowest note of a chord; foundation of harmony from 1600 on
Rhythm—pattern of sounds/silences in time: <u>Beat</u>—steady pulse; <u>Meter</u>—organization of the beat (even/odd); and *Tempo*—speed of the beat (slow>fast)
Texture (Layers)—number, type (melody, harmony/bass, rhythm), and relationship

Colors of Sound
   Volume [Dynamics] (soft<loud)
   Instrument Pitch Range (low<high)
   Timbre—quality of sound (mellow<piercing, legato<staccato, etc.)

Form—structure of a work with central theme (A), development, (A^1, A^2, etc.), contrast (B, C, etc.), and dramatic shape (rising tension, climax, and release)

Rhythm (Time)

Although melody is the first of the aesthetic raw elements, rhythm is the engine at the back that drives the musical train and will be covered first. It may be divided into four basic parts: 1) rhythm itself, 2) beat, 3) meter, and 4) *tempo* (pace).

<u>Rhythm Itself</u>. A **rhythm** is a pattern of sounds and silences through time. A lead rhythm is the pattern of sounds and silences in the melody, as in the example FRÉRE JACQUES [ARE YOU SLEEPING]. Notes represent the duration of individual sounds. A *whole note* serves as the basis for the notation of duration (as in the first line below). A *half note* is one-half the duration of the whole note; a *quarter note* one-fourth the duration of the whole note; and an *eighth note* one-eighth the duration of the whole note. A rest (an upside down hat, 2 right side up hats, 4 squiggly lines, and eight 7s below) is a symbol indicating silence.

Beat. The **beat** is a regular pulse underlying the rhythm. It may be implied, or it may be explicit, as played by the drums in a rock band.

Meter. **Meter** is the *organization* of the beat into regular groups (even or odd) of accented and unaccented beats. In musical notation, vertical bars (see below) organize the meter. The space between each bar is called a **measure**. The accented beat is always the first beat in the measure.

Even Meter. In music, even meter may be either 2 beats or 4 beats per measure. (See measures below with four beats for each measure.) The first beat after each bar line is accented. (There is a secondary accent on beat three if there are four beats per measure. However, rhythm in much popular music and jazz emphasizes the second and fourth beats. This is called a **backbeat**.) Even meter beginning on a strong beat is shown below. A **meter signature** (time signature) indicates the number of beats per bar (top number) and the kind of note receiving one beat (bottom number). 2/4 meter means 2/quarter notes per measure, and 4/4 meter means 4/quarter notes per measure. Try saying the words of the lead rhythm as you tap or strum the beat. (Be sure to stress the first beat.)

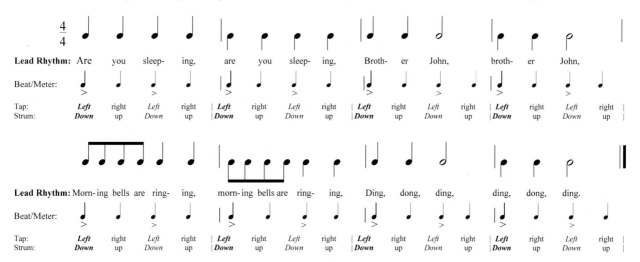

Odd Meter. 3/4 meter means 3/quarter notes per measure. Try saying the words of the lead rhythm as you tap or strum the meter below. (Be sure to stress the first beat.)

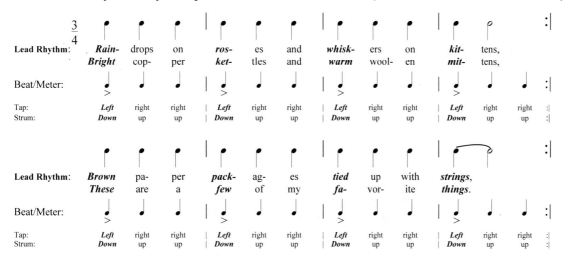

Ground Rhythm. A **ground rhythm** is a rhythm based on the beat that accompanies a lead rhythm. If there is a bass instrument, it will sometimes play on every beat or sometimes emphasize just the accented beats. Percussion instruments may play a different background beat such as the one below.

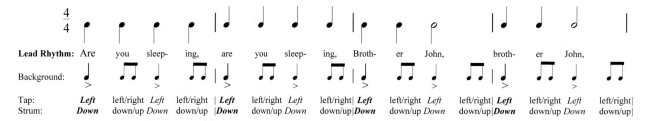

Tempo. **Tempo** (Italian for "pace") is the rate of speed of the beat. *Tempo* is related to a biological sense of pace: the heartbeat, the breath rate, or bodily motion at rest or in a vigorous state of exercise. As an expressive element, slower tempos are generally fitting for more restful events, whereas faster tempos are usually used for festive occasions. After the Renaissance began in Italy, Italian gradually became the international language for musical terms. Interestingly, *Italic* is a style of printing that was also first used in Renaissance Italy. Thus, Italian musical terms are written in *italics*. Italian terms for *tempo*, their pronunciations, and their abbreviations are summarized as follows:

Tempo (slow<fast)	
Italian	English
largo	very slow
adagio (ä -dä'zhō)	slow
andante (än-dän' tā)	moderately slow
moderato (mŏd-ə-rä'tō)	moderately fast
allegro	fast
presto	very fast
accelerando (ä-chěl-ə-rän'dō)	gradually faster
ritardando	gradually slower
a (ä) *tempo*	back to the original pace

In the previous examples, try saying the words for *Are You Sleeping* in rhythm, while tapping very slowly to the beat. Then, gradually increase the pace (*tempo*) of the beat and words each time you do this until you cannot tap or say the words any faster. Likewise, try saying the words for *Raindrops on Roses* (MY FAVORITE THINGS) in rhythm, while tapping very slowly to the beat. Then, gradually increase the pace (*tempo*) of the beat and words each time you do this until you cannot tap or say the words any faster. To hear the difference between odd and even meter, listen to an intriguing instrumental version of the Beatles' *Lucy in the Sky with Diamonds* (*Naxos* keywords: Beatles Baroque Lucy [15]). As a helpful introductory example to the intriguing rhythms of Indian fine-art music, you may wish to listen to *Tabla Solo in Ektal* by the virtuoso tabla player Alla Rakha (Naxos keywords: Monterey Tabla [2]).

Perhaps the most famous rhythm of all time is the following. Try tapping the rhythm with the left hand (stems down) and the right hand (stems up). Can you guess which famous work this is?

Melody

Melody (lead) is a series of single *pitches* set to a rhythm. The rhythm of a melody without its pitches resembles a straight line, whereas the melody itself resembles a curved line. Harmony resembles a series of vertical lines. (See illustrations at the beginning of the chapter.)

Some instruments (such as the voice or trumpet) are melody instruments that can sound only one tone at a time. Other instruments (such as the keyboard, guitar, or ukulele) can either play one tone at a time or more than one tone at a time, thus producing chords. These instruments frequently play melody, harmony, and bass simultaneously, or they may add harmony and/or bass to a tune sung or played by another instrument.

Special Insight 4-1
Give Me the Do-Re-Mi

The *sol-fa* (*do-re-mi*) system was originally developed by Guido Arentino (Guido d'Arezzo [Guido from Arezzo], c. 990–1050), a Benedictine monk and music theorist who developed the four line staff, the precursor of our five line staff. He set the Latin poem *Ut queant laxis* to music in order to teach his choirboys to sight sing music previously unknown to them (*Naxos* keywords: Guido ut queant laxis [3]). From Guido's teaching practice has come our *sol-fa* (*do-re-mi*) system. The Latin word *ut* has been replaced by the Italian term *do*, and the European fixed-*do* system (i.e., *do* refers to C, *re* refers to D, etc.) has become a movable *do* system (i.e., *do* may begin on any note) in many countries. The *sol-fa* (*do-re-mi*) system has been popularized today by *Do-Re-Mi* from *The Sound of Music* by Richard Rodgers and Oscar Hammerstein II. This song, on the right, gives the English pronunciation for the *do-re-mi* syllables.

Ut quéant láxis	Doe [*do*, *1*], a deer, a female deer,
*re*sonáre fíbris	Ray [*re*, *2*], a drop of golden sun.
*Mí*ra gestórum	Me [*mi*, *3*], a name I call myself,
*fá*mulituorum,	Far [*fa*, *4*], a long, long way to run.
*Sól*ve pollúti	Sew [*so*, *5*], a needle pulling thread,
*lá*bii reátum,	La [*la*, *6*], a note to follow sew.
Sáncte Joánnes.	Tea [*ti*, *7*], a drink with jam and bread,
	That will bring us back to ***do***-oh-oh oh!

Sailing the Ivory C. A helpful way to learn melodies, chords, and bass is to begin on the keyboard and ukulele (or guitar) in the range of men's voices (from **C** on the left through the higher ranges of boys' and women's voices on the right). Notice that the black keys are grouped in twos and threes with a skip between the groups. Notice also that the note **C** is labeled as **1** and that each letter after it is numbered consecutively until the next **C** is reached. This is an example of a major scale. Numbers are assigned to each key to match the scale degrees of the major scale beginning on the note **C** (to the left of the two black keys). **Tablature** (pictures of the keyboard and fretted fingerboard) is used to help in playing tunes. For ukulele (or guitar), the designation "o" indicates an open string whereas the designation "●" indicates that a finger is to be pressed against the string. Try playing each of these pitches on the keyboard and matching each pitch with your voice in your voice range. Then, try singing and playing the corresponding tunes. [If you wish, you may use the *do-re-mi* syllables. See special insight on the previous page for pronunciation. If you don't have a keyboard that is readily accessible, try the following online keyboard: http://www.bgfl.org/custom/resources_ftp/client_ftp/ks2/music/piano/. Click the instruction button to learn how to play the piano keyboard using the computer keyboard.]

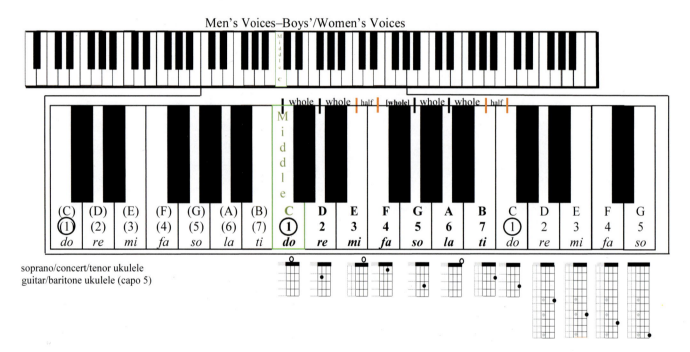

Half Steps and Whole Steps in the Major Scale. From one key (fret) to the very next key (fret) on the keyboard (guitar/ukulele) is a **half step**. A **whole step** skips one key (fret). A **major scale** consists of the following pattern of whole and half steps: whole-whole-half-[whole]-whole-whole-half. Notice that both halves of the major scale are exactly the same (whole whole half), separated by a whole step (a half-step between scale degrees 3–4 [*mi–fa*] and 7–8 [*ti—do*]). [A major scale may begin on any tone so long as the same order of whole and half steps is maintained.] The name of scale degree *1* (one) is called the **key**, in this case the key of C (major). The major scale above begins on Middle C (the open 3rd string [counted from the right above] of the soprano/concert/tenor ukulele).

Learn to sing and play the following melodies on both keyboard and ukulele (or guitar) in the key of **C** major. (Play in the higher range of boys' and women's voices. Men will sing one octave lower.) The Roman numerals and letter names on top indicate chords as well as the bass line.

ODE TO JOY
(from Beethoven, 9th Symphony, 4th Movement, 1822–24)

FRÉRE JACQUES [ARE YOU SLEEPING]
(*Naxos* keywords: Marianne8672248 [Disc 5, #19])

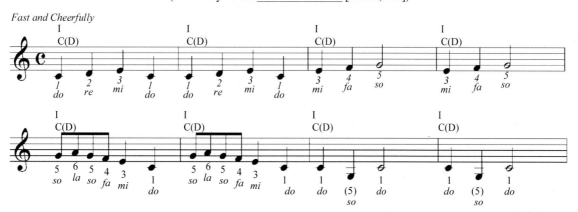

ANTIOCH
(Lowell Mason, 1848; based on G. F. Handel, 1742)

BEETHOVEN 5th (Movement IV, Theme A)
(*Naxos* keywords: Beethoven 5 Leibowitz Leonore [9])

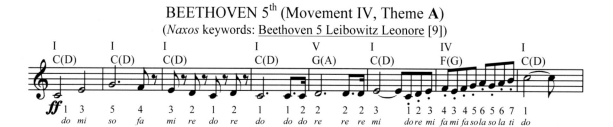

The Difference between Major (brighter) and Minor (darker). The Latin words *major* and *minor* are commonly used to indicate the larger and smaller portions of something (for example a major and a minor in a degree program). The **minor** (smaller) **scale** differs from the major scale in that the distance between scale degrees *1* and *3* is always one half step smaller in minor than in major. This means that the 3rd scale degree is always lowered in pitch by one half-step. Usually the 6th degree is also lowered in pitch by one half-step. A symbol called a flat (♭) is used to indicate a pitch that is lowered one half-step. Minor is more compressed and closed-in than major. Combined with slower tempos, it suggests darker, sadder images for most people. The following example shows **C** major with its parallel minor (**C** minor) as the paradigm for other scales. [A **parallel scale** begins on the same scale degree.] The *do-re-mi* syllables *me* and *le* are pronounced "may" and "lay" respectively (just as *re* is pronounced "ray").

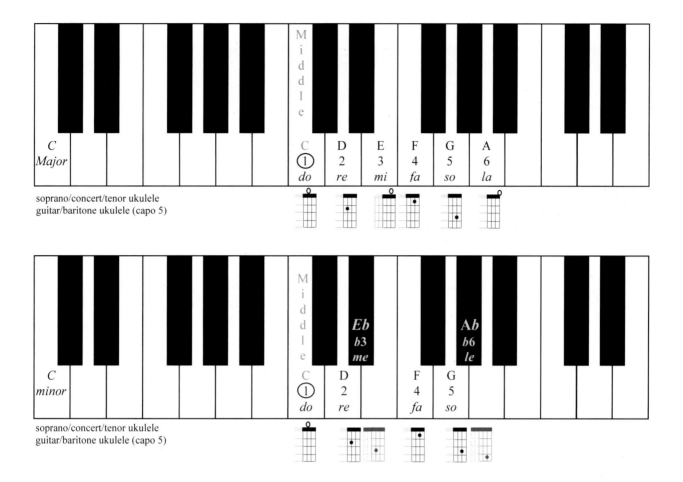

ODE TO SORROW, FRÈRE JACQUES, and BEETHOVEN 5th (I) in Minor. ODE TO SORROW, FRÈRE JACQUES, and BEETHOVEN 5th (movt. 1) provide helpful examples of the differences between major and minor melodies and harmonies. Sing these melodies as you play them on the keyboard, ukulele, or guitar to experience the difference between major and minor. Notice that minor sounds more dissonant (clashing) than major.

ODE TO SORROW
(parody of Beethoven, 9th Symphony, 4th Movement, 1822–24)
(Keywords: Lumiere Ode to Sorrow [1])

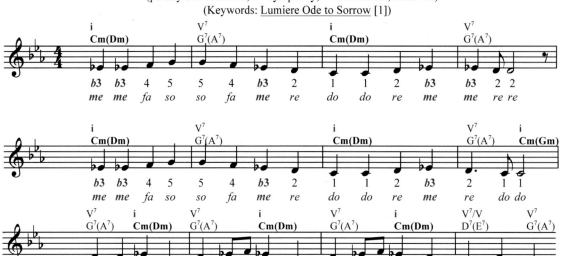

FRÈRE JACQUES in Minor
(1st part of Mahler, 1st Symphony, *Titan*, 3rd Movement)
(*Naxos* keywords: Titan Cinema Classics [3])

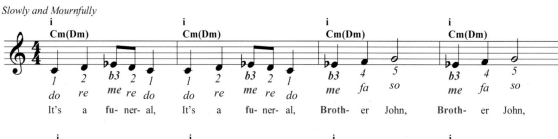

BEETHOVEN 5th SYMPHONY in C Minor (Movement 1, Theme 1)
(*Naxos* keywords: Beethoven 5 Leibowitz Leonore [6])

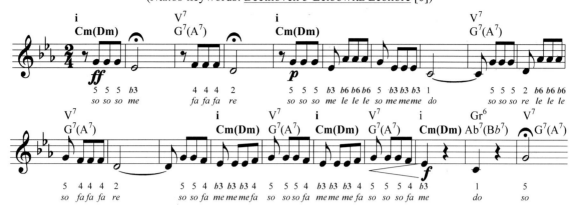

Harmony and Bass

Harmony is a series of simultaneous *pitches* set to a rhythm, implying or forming chords. **Bass** is the lowest note of a chord. A **chord** is a combination of three or more tones sounded at once, usually three notes such as the 1st, 3rd, and 5th degrees, skipping other notes of the scale. The first six tones of the harmonic series outline a major chord built on the fundamental (a C chord on the ivory keys when built on the C fundamental). The **equal-tempered scale** (dividing the octave into twelve equal parts) allows harmonies to be generated beginning on any bass note. A major chord is a 3-tone chord with 4 half steps between the first two tones and 3 half steps between the second two tones, for example, scale degrees *1/3/5* (C/E/G) of the major scale. Minor reverses what happens in major. A **minor chord** is a 3-tone chord with *3* half steps between the first two tones and *4* half steps between the second two tones, for example, scale degrees *1/b3/5* (C/Eb/G) of the minor scale.

Three Primary Chords. Most songs can be accompanied with the **three primary chords** (the chords built on scale degrees *1*, *4*, and *5* respectively). The chord built on the 1st degree contains scale degrees *1/3/5*, the chord on the 4th degree *4/6/1*, and the chord on the 5th degree *5/7/2*. Roman numerals designate the whole chord rather than just the scale degree, thus **I** (one), **IV** (four), and **V** (five) chords in a major key. Minor chords are noted by lower case Roman numerals ("I" becomes "i"), thus **i** (one), **iv** (four), and **V** (five) containing the scale degrees 1/b3/5, 4/b6/1, and 5/7/2. Notice that the V chord is a major chord in both major and minor keys. Popular symbols use a lower case "m" after the name of the chord for minor chords ("C" becomes "Cm"). Following are some of the most common chords for keyboard and ukulele in the keys of **C**, **G**, **D**, **A**, and **E** major and minor (major on the left, minor on the right).

I (i), IV (iv), and V Chords in the Key of C (Cm)

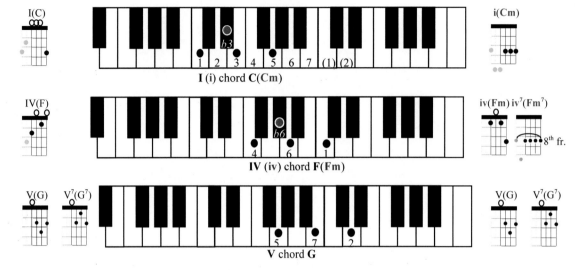

I (i), IV (iv), and V Chords in the Key of G (Gm)

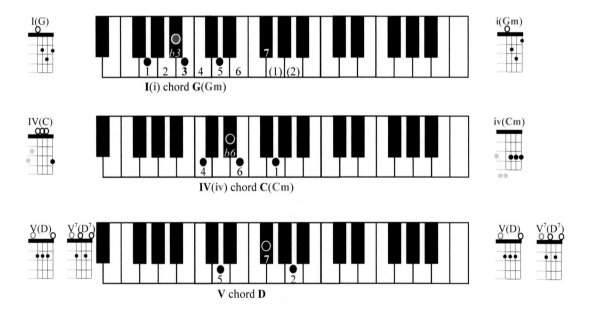

I (i), IV (iv), and V Chords in the Key of D (Dm)

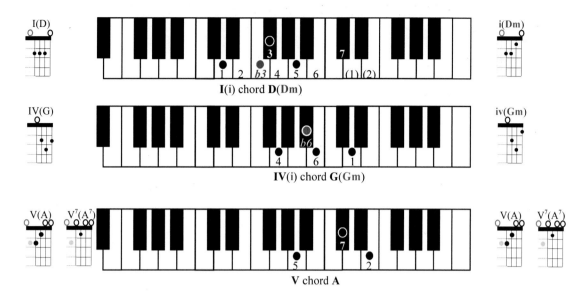

I (i), IV (iv), and V Chords in the Key of A (Am)

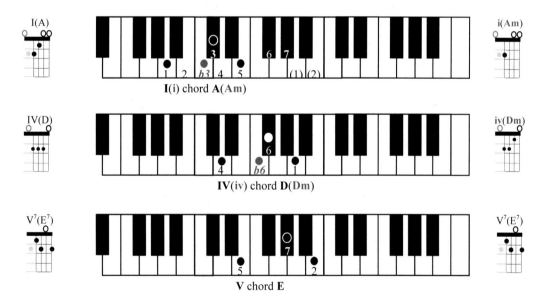

I (**i**), IV (**iv**), and V Chords in the Key of E (**Em**)

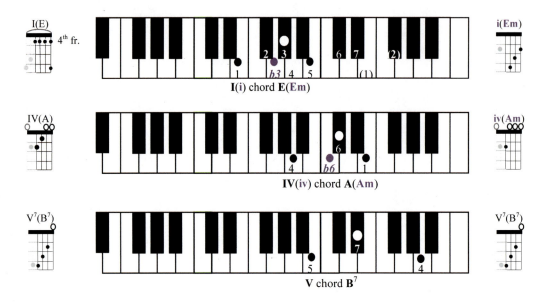

Major Chord Chart for Keyboard and Ukulele by Fifth Down
(Chord chart by scale degrees of C major in APPENDIX C, pages C1 and C23)

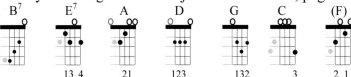

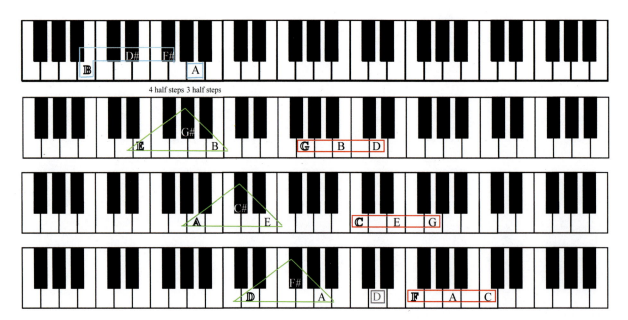

Minor Chord Chart for Keyboard and Ukulele by Fifth Down
(Chord chart by scale degrees of C major in APPENDIX C, pages C1 and C23)

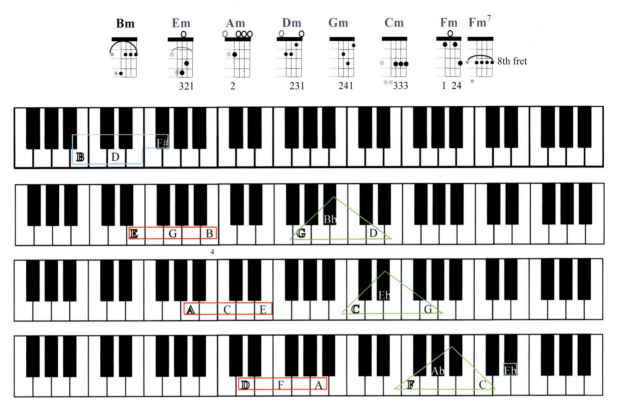

Texture (Layers)

Texture is the number, type, and interrelationship of melodic, harmonic, bass, and ground rhythm layers. Many musical works begin with one layer and gradually build interest by adding more and more layers, for example the Beatles *Lucy in the Sky with Diamonds* (*Naxos* keywords: Beatles Baroque Lucy [15]).

The interrelationship of layers is based on how various layers relate to the lead melody. This interrelationship may be monophonic (one lead melody only), homophonic (one lead melody only with accompaniment), or polyphonic (two or more rhythmically independent lead melodies with or without additional accompaniment).

Monophonic Texture. **Monophonic** (*mono*=one, *phonic*=sounding) is *one* lead melody layer without other layers.[1] The melody may be played or sung by one person or a hundred—it is still monophonic as long as everyone is sounding the same melody together and there are no other layers.

FRÈRE JACQUES (monophonic)

Homophonic Texture. **Homophonic** (*homo*=together, *phonic*=sounding) is *two or more layers* with only one lead layer.[2] As long as there is only one melody layer with accompaniment, the texture is homophonic whether only one or a hundred additional layers of accompaniment are added.

FRÈRE JACQUES (homophonic)

Polyphonic Texture. **Polyphonic** (*poly*=many, *phonic*=sounding) is *two or more rhythmically independent melody layers*. This includes the same melody played against itself starting at different places (as in a round, see below). Different melodies in addition to the first are called countermelodies. They must be equal in importance to the primary melody, i.e., a bass line repeated over and over does not count as a countermelody.

FRÈRE JACQUES (as a round, with rhythmic independence)

Gustav Mahler (1860–1911) uses monophonic texture (2 bars), homophonic texture (6 bars), and polyphonic texture (remainder) in his treatment of this melody in the third movement of his 1st Symphony (*Titan*). Notice how Mahler begins with the background-bass rhythm of the timpani, adds the tune in the contrabass and then keeps adding

---

[1] **Heterophony** (different-sound) is two or more voices elaborating and improvising on the same tune simultaneously. Heterophonic texture occurs most frequently in non-western music.

[2] **Biphonic** (two-sounds) is one lead melody accompanied by a drone.

additional layers (*Naxos* keywords: Titan Cinema Classics [3]). Red arrows indicate when a new instrument enters with the FRÈRE JACQUES melody.

Listening for Layers in Music

In summary, listen for the following layers (texture) in music: 1) melody (plus countermelodies, if any); 2) harmony, 3) bass (often sounds only on the downbeat rather than on every beat), and 4) ground rhythm.

Actions for Practice and Delight

4/1. As outlined in this chapter, try each tune on the keyboard and/or on the ukulele, and sing along as you match the pitches. [If you don't have a keyboard readily available you can find one online.[1]] Learn to sing *Joy, You Glorious Spark* (ODE TO JOY) [Appendix C8] and FRÈRE JACQUES [Appendix C13] in major and to accompany them with bass line or chords. Choose one of these or another favorite tune (or tunes) from this chapter and learn the melody (with chords if you wish) so that you can sing it and/or play it on the keyboard and/or on the ukulele. Write about your experience. Plan to share your experience and be prepared to play and/or sing the tune you have learned (with chords if you wish) with a group, with one other person, or even by yourself.

4/2. Listen to the Beatles' *Lucy in the Sky with Diamonds* (*Naxos* playlist <u>Arts Key 04A Layers</u> [1] or keywords: <u>Beatles Baroque Lucy</u> [15]) from their classic 1967 album *Sgt. Pepper's Lonely Hearts Club Band*. Create and fill in a chart or an outline similar to the following. (The first answers are filled in for you.)

Times	Sections	*Tempo*	Meter (even, or odd)	Texture (# of layers, and type of layer—melody (countermelody if present), harmony, rhythm, or bass (every beat or 1st beat of the bar only)
00:00	Intro	*moderato*	Odd	1. background harmony
00:06	A	*moderato*	Odd	1. melody 2. background harmony 3. bass—1st beat of the bar only
00:30	B			
00:49	C			
01:07	A			
01:33	B			
01:51	C			
02:08	A			
02:31	C repeated			

Then, listen to the first minute of each of the following selections of music several times and see if you can figure out how layers are added and hear the difference between monophonic, homophonic, and polyphonic textures as they enter. Create and fill in a chart or an outline similar to the following.

Selections—Listen to the first minute	*Tempo*	Meter (even or odd)	Describe the texture as each layer enters—# of layers, type of layer [melody, countermelody (if present), harmony, rhythm, or bass] and relationship (monophonic, homophonic, or polyphonic)
Saxophone—My Favorite Things (*Naxos* playlist <u>Arts Key 04A Layers</u> [2] or keyword: <u>CAMCD-1089</u> [14])			
Wind Ensemble—My Favorite Things (*Naxos* playlist <u>Arts Key 04A Layers</u> [3] or keyword: 75442260792 [4])			
Ode to Joy (*Naxos* playlist <u>Arts Key 04A Layers</u> [2] or keyword: 8.201001 [Disc 4, #5])			

---

[1] <u>http://www.virtualpiano.net/</u> See ? for help as to how to play the keyboard.

4/3. Work on the minor melodies in this chapter, and learn to sing FRÈRE JACQUES in minor (either with numbers, *do-re-mi* syllables, or words) [accompanied with bass and/or chords if possible] on page C13. Then, listen to Gustav Mahler's treatment of FRÈRE JACQUES [*Are You Sleeping*] (*Naxos* playlist: Arts Key 04B Major and Minor [3] or keywords: Titan Cinema Classiques [3]) as you follow the score on page 45 until you have memorized the entrance of each layer both visually and aurally. Write about your experience. How many listenings did it take before you could follow everything?

4/4. Listen to how composers have emphasized the difference between minor and major. In a short essay, discuss the differences in mood between major and minor in each pair of examples and then the differences between major and minor in general. Create and fill in a chart or an outline similar to the following.

Selections—Listen to the first minute	Major or Minor?	Describe the mood in detail.
1. *Wolferl's Schmankerl* (after W. A. Mozart) (*Naxos* playlist Arts Key 04B Major and Minor [1] or keyword: *Wolferl's Schmankeral Opera String Quartet* [12])		
2. Variations on Ah, vous dirai-je, maman, K. 265, variation 6, (*Naxos* playlist Arts Key 04B Major and Minor [2] or keyword: Mozart *Ah Vous* 6 Tewes)		
3. Mahler 1st Symphony, 3rd movt. (*Naxos* playlist Arts Key 04B Major and Minor [3] or keywords: Titan Cinema Classiques or Spotify: Mahler Titan Feierlich Bernstein Adagio)		
4. Frère Jacques (*Naxos* playlist Arts Key 04B Major and Minor [4] or keyword: Marianne8672248 [Disc 5, #19]		
5. Beethoven, Variations on God Save the King, I (*Naxos* playlist Arts Key 04B Major and Minor [5] or keyword: 8.554372 [42]		
6. Beethoven, Variations on God Save the King, V (*Naxos* playlist Arts Key 04B Major and Minor [6] or keyword: 8.554372 [46]		
7. Beethoven, Variations on God Save the King, VII (*Naxos* playlist Arts Key 04B Major and Minor [7] or keyword: 8.554372 [48]		
8. Variations on Happy Birthday, Variation 8 (*Naxos* playlist Arts Key 04B Major and Minor [8] or keywords: Kremer Happy Birthday [11]		
9. Variations on Happy Birthday, Variation 9 (*Naxos* playlist Arts Key 04B Major and Minor [9] or keywords: Kremer Happy Birthday [12]		
10. Variations on Happy Birthday, Variation 11 (*Naxos* playlist Arts Key 04B Major and Minor [10] or keywords: Kremer Happy Birthday [13]		

CHAPTER 5
THE COLORS OF SOUND

"In music, instruments perform the function of the colors employed in painting."[1]

David Burliuk (1884–1967) *Orchestra* (1957), oil on panel, 40.5 x 51 cm (1 ft 4 in x 1 ft 8 in) Private Collection.

Color makes the arts come alive. The colors of sound and the colors of light provide a basis for the expressiveness of the arts. The sounds of music and the spoken words of storytelling, poetry, and acting bring the colors of the visual arts into auditory range. There are three basic properties of sound: dynamics, instrument pitch range, and timbre.

Dynamics (Soft/Loud)

Dynamics (volume) refers to the relative softness or loudness of a sound. The *strength* of a sound is measured in phons (perception of intensity by the ear) or decibels[2]

---
[1] Honoré de Balzac.
[2] A decibel is one-tenth of a Bel (named for Alexander Graham Bell).

abbreviated dB (measured by electronic devices). Decibel meters measure lower frequencies as being more intense than the human ear hears them. The ear is a sensitive and delicate instrument that can distinguish a great variety of dynamic levels. A gradual increase in loudness usually generates excitement, whereas a gradual decrease in loudness usually produces a sense of calmness. Changes in dynamics add variety and contrast.

The Italian terms for dynamics, their pronunciations, their English meanings, and their abbreviations are summarized below. Dynamics are closely related to *tempo* (rate of speed, see previous chapter). Be familiar with the Italian terms for dynamics in the following chart so that you can recognize them when you see them in music and correlate them with the Italian terms for *tempo*.

Tempo (slow<fast)		***Dynamics*** (soft<loud)		
Italian	English	English	Italian	Abbreviation
largo	very slow	very soft	*pianissimo (pē'ə-nĭs'-ə-mō)*	*pp*
adagio (ä -dä'zhō)	slow	soft	*piano*	*p*
andante (än-dän' tā)	moderately slow	moderately soft	*mezzo (mĕt'sō) piano*	*mp*
moderato (mŏd-ə-rä'tō)	moderately fast	moderately loud	*mezzo forte (mĕt'sō fôr'tā)*	*mf*
allegro	fast	loud	*forte (fôr'tā)*	*f*
presto	very fast	very loud	*fortissimo (fôr-tĭs'-ə-mō)*	*ff*
accelerando (ä-chĕl-ə-rän'dō)	gradually faster	gradually louder	*crescendo (crə-shĕn'dō)*	*cresc.*
ritardando	gradually slower	gradually softer	*decrescendo/diminuendo*	*decresc./dim.*
a (ä) tempo	back to the original pace			

The range of possible dynamics has increased in close correlation with the development of better and bigger instruments. For example, the piano (invented around 1700) was known as the *pianoforte* or "soft-loud" since it was capable of greater dynamic variation than previous keyboard instruments. With today's electronic amplification of the voice and other instruments such as the electric guitar, the possibilities of dynamic range go off the scale. The extremely high levels of sound made possible by today's technology pose a particular problem in our society. Many people suffer from noise-induced hearing loss caused by a variety of factors. A sample includes noise from arcade games, firecrackers, target shooting, speed boating, auto racing, lawnmowers, leaf blowers, chainsaws, stadium events, and amplified or continuously loud music (car stereos, dance/exercise clubs, and so on).

Listening to music with earphones set at more than 50% volume can cause irreversible hearing loss. A 2006 study produced the first-ever guidelines for safe listening levels using earphones with MP3 players. A quote from this study on the following page gives important information regarding the prevention of hearing loss.

% of Volume Control	Maximum listening time per day			
	Earbud	Isolator	Supra-Aural	iPod, stock earphones
10–50%	No limit	No limit	No limit	No limit
60%	No limit	14 hours	No limit	18 hours
70%	6 hours	3.4 hours	20 hours	4.6 hours
80%	1.5 hours	50 minutes	4.9 hours	1.2 hours
90%	22 minutes	12 minutes	1.2 hours	18 minutes
100%	5 minutes	3 minutes	18 minutes	5 minutes

Table 1. Maximum listening time per day using NIOSH damage-risk criteria. "Earbud" includes stock earphones and iPod In-ear earphones. "Isolator" includes Etymotic ER6i earphones and Shure E4c earphones. "Supra-Aural" includes Koss headphones that rest on top of the ear.

"The maximum listening times above represent the amount of time that a typical person could listen to their MP3 player every day without greatly increasing their risk of hearing loss. It is important to note, though, that not everyone shares the same risk of hearing loss. For some people who have "tougher" ears, these recommendations are overly conservative. For other people with more "tender" ears, these recommendations do not eliminate the risk of hearing loss. Today, however, we have no way of predicting who has "tough" ears and who has "tender" ears. Hearing loss occurs slowly and is often not noticed until it is quite extensive, so early prevention is the key."[1]

Because loud sounds can generate such a sense of excitement, these guidelines continue to be disregarded in a wide variety of venues including stadiums, theaters, and churches (where overpowering, amplified sound is often used without regard for differences in hearing sensitivity, especially that of younger children). Regrettably, the levels of sound prevalent in today's society have desensitized both performers and listeners to subtle differences in dynamics and have permanently damaged the hearing of many people. Hearing loss is irreversible, but much of it is preventable.

Instrument Pitch Range (Low/High)

Pitch (frequency) refers to the *lowness or highness* of a sound and is measured in cycles per second (cps) or Hertz (Hz).[2] We will explore pitch through three instruments of sound: piano (*pianoforte*), guitar (ukulele), and voice.

The Piano. The piano keyboard provides a visual aid for the pitch range of all instruments. As one moves to the right on the keyboard, the pitches get higher. There are 52 white keys and 36 black keys for a total of 88 keys. Notice that the bottom white key (at the very left) is named using the first letter of the alphabet (*A*). Each white key is named

---

[1] Cory D. F. Portnuff and Brian J. Fligor, *Sound Output Levels of the iPod and Other MP3 Players: Is There Potential Risk to Hearing?* Paper presented Thursday afternoon, October 19, 2006. NIHL in Children Conference, Cincinnati, OH, Summary at http://ucsu.colorado.edu/~portnuff/.
[2] Hertz (abbreviated Hz) is a unit of frequency equal to one cycle per second, named after the German physicist Heinrich Rudolf Hertz (1857–1894).

using the letters of the alphabet from *A–G*. When the eighth white key or **octave** (from Greek *okta,* meaning "eight") is reached, it begins with the same letter name. The octave sounds the same because each octave is exactly twice the frequency of the note that is eight white keys below it.[1] Notice also that the number designation[2] for each octave changes with each *C*. The first *C* on the piano is designated **C¹**, the second *C* is designated **C²**, and so on until the last *C* is reached, **C⁸** (with **C⁴** commonly known as "**Middle C**"). Thus, there are eight *C*'s on the keyboard, with each remaining pitch in that octave taking its designation from that *C*. The black keys (and some white keys) have two names, designated by sharps (#) and flats (♭).[3] The piano encompasses the range of fundamental frequencies for the voice and for almost all other instruments, so the range of tones produced in an orchestra is approximately the same as that of the piano.

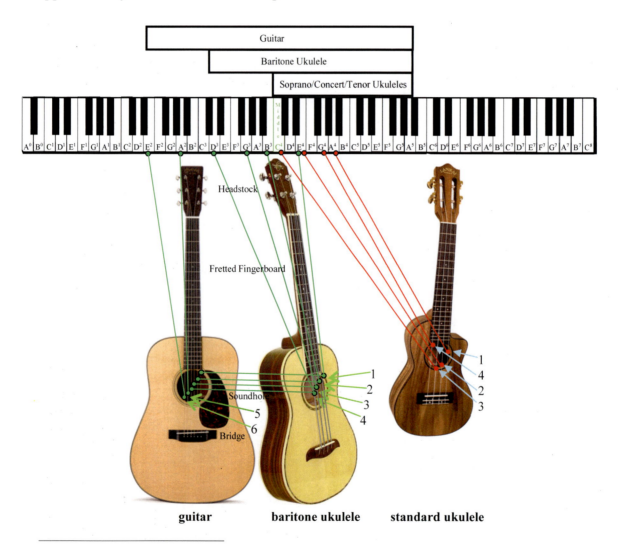

guitar   **baritone ukulele**   **standard ukulele**

---

[1] A^0 is 27.5 cycles per second; A^1 is 55 cycles per second; A^2 is 110 cycles per second; A^3 is 220 cycles per second; A^4 is 440 cycles per second; and so on.

[2] This system uses the recommendations of the International Acoustical Society.

[3] The first black key on the left side of the keyboard may be designated by either of the tones surrounding it (A^0 or B^0). If one goes higher (to the right), the very next note is called a sharp (#): thus, the first black key on the piano is sometimes designated A-sharp (A#). If one goes lower (to the left), the very next note is called a flat (♭): thus, the first black key on the piano is sometimes designated B-flat (B♭). The first black key on the piano may be called either A# or B♭ depending on the reference point.

The Guitar (Ukulele). The guitar is a tunable instrument that has six strings made of nylon or steel, usually tuned to G. The ukulele is an instrument in the guitar family that has four strings made of nylon, usually tuned to C. The player uses a finger of the left hand to press down a string to the left of a **fret** (ridge). This changes the length of the string in order to make different pitches. The right hand uses a **plectrum** (pick) or the fingers to pluck or strum the strings. [To approximate the sound of a plectrum, the nails on the back of the fingers may be used to strum downwards and the thumbnail to strum upwards.] Guitar strings are usually tuned to every other note of the G pentatonic scale (string 6=E^2, 5=A^2, 4=D^3, 3=G^3, 2=B^3, and 1=E^4). The soprano, concert, and tenor ukuleles are tuned to every other note of the C pentatonic scale with **re-entrant** (directed inward) tuning: (string 4=G^4 3=C^4 2=E^4 1=A^4).

The Voice. The voice is the most personal of all instruments, since our voices are part of our own bodies. Air supply, vibrator, and resonator are three components of this unique instrument used in music, poetry, story, and theatre. Air from the lungs makes the lower pair of vocal cords (folds or bands of mucous membrane in the throat) vibrate to produce a sound that is amplified by the throat, mouth, and nasal cavities. In turn, the vocal cords expand and contract in order to produce different pitches. The quality and range of the vocal instrument is determined by one's physical makeup.

Voice classifications (primarily Italian terms) from highest to lowest are as follows. Often voices are grouped in the broad general categories of soprano, alto, tenor, and bass (SATB). Using finer distinctions, boys and ladies may be grouped in one of three categories listed from highest to lowest: soprano, mezzo-soprano, or alto (also known as contralto). Men are generally grouped in one of three categories from highest to lowest: tenor, baritone, or bass. Notice that the guitar covers the range of all voices.

Men	Boys and Ladies
Tenor (B^2–G^4)	Soprano (C^4–A^5)
Baritone (G^2–E^4)	Mezzo-Soprano (A^3–F^5)
Bass (E^2–C^4)	Alto (Contralto) (F^3–D^5)

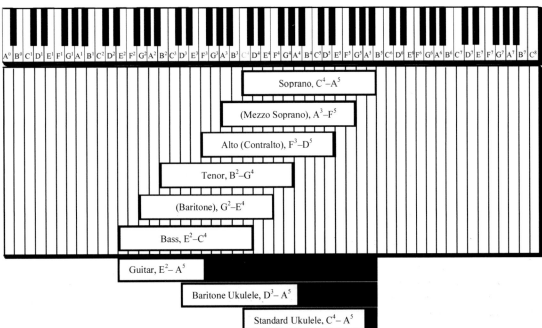

Boy's voices drop approximately one octave lower after puberty. Thus, a tenor (B^2–G^4) is approximately one octave lower than a soprano (C^4–A^5). A baritone (G^2–E^4) is approximately one octave lower than a mezzo soprano (A^3–F^5). A bass (E^2–C^4) is approximately one octave lower than a contralto (F^3–D^5), usually known as an alto. With proper training, the voice can reach two octaves or more. The majority of ladies' voices fall into the mezzo-soprano range, and the majority of men's voices fall into the baritone range.

Our voices are part of our humanity and part of our sexual identity. Boys have soprano, mezzo-soprano, and alto ranges. When boys reach puberty around age 14, the vocal folds begin to grow thicker and longer and the voice begins to sound deeper. Growth in the vocal folds makes it difficult to sing during that time. Men who have not learned to sing before the age of puberty will find that it may be easier to match pitch by using an instrument in their range (such as the guitar) rather than trying to imitate the higher range of women's voices. Many voices do not reach their full maturity until around the age of thirty. To hear the distinctive sound of boys' voices, listen to *La Nuit* and *Nous Sommes* (boys auditioning) from *Les Choristes*, a movie about the positive influence of music on boys' lives (*Naxos* playlist Arts Key 05A [1, 7] or keyword: 3020671532 [13, 21]).

From about 1550 to 1903, a musical custom existed that appears strange to contemporary minds. **Castrati** (singular, *castrato*) were male singers who were castrated before puberty in order to retain a soprano or alto range into adulthood. This made it possible to combine the lung power of an adult male with the vocal range and brilliance of an adult female. These *castrati* sang leading male roles and became international operatic stars. Three of the most famous carried the stage names of Senesino, Caffarelli, and Farinelli. The ban on women appearing on the stage contributed to this custom. The practice of admitting *castrati* to the Vatican's Sistine Chapel Choir also did little to discourage this custom and was banned in 1903 by Vatican authorities. Today, a few tenors (called countertenors) are able to train their voices in the alto and soprano range. Their singing suggests to us what the brilliance and power of the *castrati* must have been.

In Classical and Romantic operas, the role of a young man is sometimes played by a woman because of the lighter quality of a woman's voice. This is known as a **trouser role**. (Examples of trouser roles include Cherubino in *Le Nozze di Figaro* [*The Marriage of Figaro*] and Octavian in *Der Rosenkavalier* [*The Cavalier of the Rose*].)

A **register** is part of one's entire vocal range that consists of a particular quality of sound. In a classically trained voice, there are two and sometimes three recognized registers.[1] For purposes of beginning discussion, one may explore two registers: a lower, heavy register, and a higher, light register. The sudden shift from one register to another is called a **register break**.

---

[1] These three registers are sometimes labeled chest register, head register, and falsetto register for men, and chest register, middle register, and head register for women.

Methods of singing vary from style to style and culture to culture. Opera singers have trained their voices to cover wide ranges and to project to large numbers of people with no amplification. Popular and folk singers have much narrower ranges and rely on amplification to project their vocal styles to large audiences.

Timbre (Quality of Sound)

Timbre (mellow to piercing, legato to staccato, etc.) is the *characteristic quality* of a sound that distinguishes it from other sounds of the same pitch and dynamic level. Each instrument (including the voice) has a specific quality that distinguishes it from other instruments—bright, muddy, brilliant, mellow, rich, etc. The trumpet's brilliant sound is often expressive of military or royal themes, whereas the soothing sound of the flute is frequently expressive of calmness or serenity. A particular pitch played on a single instrument also varies in its own tone qualities depending on the way in which it is played, sung, or spoken. One's "tone of voice" may change from threatening to kind or frightened to confident. You may experiment with different vocal tone qualities by humming a pitch on "mm" and then opening your lips at the same volume level to say "ah"—you will get the word "Ma," the first word learned by infants, which has a surprising similarity of sound in all cultures. (If you do this twice, you will get the word "Ma-ma.")

Illustrations of Vocal Sound Colors

The Speaking Voice. The poem on the following page, *You Are Old, Father William* from *Alice in Wonderland* (1865) by Lewis Carroll (1832–1898), Romantic period, illustrates the use of sound color in the speaking voice. As you listen to the performance (*Naxos* playlist Arts Key 05A Vocal Sound Colors [1] or keyword: CDSDL294 [10]), notice how the dynamics, vocal pitch ranges, and timbres provide overall sound color.

The Singing Voice. Like the speaking voice, the singing voice can produce a wide variety of pitches, timbres, and dynamics. The a cappella album *Choral Songs on Shakespeare Texts* explores the sounds of men's and women's voices as compared with the album of boys' voices noted on the previous page. Selection 5 (and following) is especially recommended (*Naxos* playlist Arts Key 05A Vocal Sound Colors [3] or keyword: CDR90000-085 [5]). Again, notice how the dynamics, vocal pitch ranges, and timbres interact to provide overall sound color. For the sound of men's voices, listen to TZENA, TZENA (*Naxos* playlist Arts Key 05A Vocal Sound Colors [4] or keyword: EUCD1797 [13]).

"You are old, Father William," the young man said,   1
"And your hair has become very white;   2
And yet you incessantly stand on your head—   3
Do you think, at your age, it is right?"   4

"In my youth," Father William replied to his son,   5
"I feared it might injure the brain;   6
But now that I'm perfectly sure I have none,   7
Why, I do it again and again."   8

"You are old," said the youth, "As I mentioned before,   9
And have grown most uncommonly fat;   10
Yet you turned a back-somersault in at the door—   11
Pray, what is the reason of that?"   12

"In my youth," said the sage, as he shook his grey locks,   13
"I kept all my limbs very supple   14
By the use of this ointment—one shilling the box—   15
Allow me to sell you a couple?"   16

"You are old," said the youth, "And your jaws are too weak   17
For anything tougher than suet;   18
Yet you finished the goose, with the bones and the beak—   19
Pray, how did you manage to do it?"   20

"In my youth," said his father, "I took to the law,   21
And argued each case with my wife;   22
And the muscular strength which it gave to my jaw,   23
Has lasted the rest of my life."   24

"You are old," said the youth, "one would hardly suppose   25
That your eye was as steady as ever;   26
Yet you balanced an eel on the end of your nose—   27
What made you so awfully clever?"   28

"I have answered three questions, and that is enough,"   29
Said his father; "don't give yourself airs!   30
Do you think I can listen all day to such stuff?   31
Be off, or I'll kick you down stairs!"   32

Wind, Percussion, and Stringed Instruments

Today, instruments are traditionally divided into three primary categories: wind instruments, percussion instruments, and stringed instruments. Instruments have developed from ancient times into the modern instruments we know today. Psalm 150 lists the basic instruments of the ancient Hebrew orchestra, one of the earliest orchestras of which we have record. The ram's horn (shofar) is still in common use today for Jewish religious services.

> Hallelu Y<small>AH</small>!
> …
> Hallelu him with blast of ram's horn;
>   Hallelu him with harp and lyre!
> Hallelu him with hand drum and dance;
>   Hallelu him with strings and pipe!
> Hallelu him with sounding cymbals;
>   Hallelu him with shouting cymbals!
> Let everything breathing hallel Y<small>AH</small>!
>   Hallelu Y<small>AH</small>! [Translation, Allen Schantz]

Ram's Horn
[wind]

Hand Drum
[percussion]

Lyre
[stringed]

<u>Wind Instruments</u>. In wind instruments, the sound is produced by blowing air through an entry point to create a vibrating column of air. This initial sound is amplified by a resonating body of air within the instrument itself. The initial sound is produced 1) by blowing air across an open hole (e.g., whistling), 2) by blowing air through a vibrating reed or pair of reeds (e.g., a blade of grass between one's thumbs), or 3) by blowing air to buzz one's lips. The pipe organ combines the first two ways of producing sounds with its flue and reed pipes.

1. Oscillating air stream instruments (blowing air across an open hole)
    A. Flute (cylindrical tube open at both ends, a transverse flute)
    B. Piccolo (little flute, an octave higher than the transverse flute)
    C. Bottles
    D. Ocarina
    E. Whistle
    F. Panpipes (a set of small pipes held vertically and blown across the top, extant as early as -3500 and still used in South America, Africa, Oceania, and Romania)
    G. Recorder (an end-blown flute with a whistle-like mouthpiece)
    H. Pipe organ flue pipes

flute piccolo

2. Reed instruments
    A. Beating reed instruments (blowing air through a vibrating reed or reeds)
        1. Blade of grass
        2. Clarinet: single cane reed
        3. Oboe and bassoon: double cane reed
        4. Saxophone: single cane reed
    B. Free reed instruments
        1. Accordion, concertina, bandoneon
        2. Harmonica (mouth harp)
        3. Pipe organ reed pipes

clarinet oboe bassoon

3. Initial sound produced by buzzing lips rather than by air streams or reeds
    A. Shofar[1] (ram's horn), seashell, conch, etc.
    B. Trumpet
    C. French horn
    D. Trombone
    E. Tuba

trumpet French horn trombone tuba

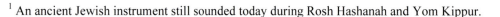
[1] An ancient Jewish instrument still sounded today during Rosh Hashanah and Yom Kippur.

Percussion Instruments. Percussion instruments are instruments in which the sound is produced 1) by a membrane stretched over a cylinder (a drum) or 2) by the body of the instrument itself. In the first type, the primary sound is produced by striking or rubbing the membrane. In the second type, the primary sound is produced by striking, shaking, rubbing, scraping, or bowing the instrument (such as when one plays a saw with a bow.)

1. Drums
    A. Drums with definite pitch (tunable)
        1. Timpani (kettledrums)
        2. Hand drums of all kinds that can be tuned—talking drum (Africa), tabla (India), and so on
    B. Drums with indefinite pitch
        1. Snare drum
        2. Bass drum
        3. Hand drums of all kinds that cannot be tuned
        4. Timbrel (an ancient instrument similar to a tambourine)
2. Vibrating bar instruments
    A. Celesta (played with a keyboard)
    B. Xylophone (played with a keyboard)
    C. Marimba (played with a keyboard)
    D. Vibraphone (played with a keyboard)
    E. Chimes
    F. Triangle
3. Vibrating plate instruments
    A. Cymbals (struck together)
    B. Gong
    C. Tam-Tam (gong used in a gamelan orchestra, struck with a felt-covered hammer)
    D. Bells (of all kinds)
    E. Carillon (bells in a tower, usually played from a keyboard)
    F. Shakers and rattles (shaken)
    G. Guiro (a hollow gourd with notches scraped by a stick, Latin American origin)
    H. Wood blocks (struck)
    I. Tambourine (combination of a hand drum and jingling discs on the rim)
    J. Saw (bowed)

timpani

celesta   xylophone   chimes   triangle

cymbals   gong   wood blocks   tambourine

Stringed Instruments. Stringed instruments are instruments in which the initial sound is produced by a vibrating string stretched across two points and amplified by a resonating chamber. The initial sound is produced by striking, plucking, or bowing the string (such as when one stretches a rubber band between two points and plucks it.) Stringed instruments include the piano, harp, guitar, ukulele, violin, viola, cello, and string bass.[1] Early stringed instruments include the lyre.

1. Usually bowed/sometimes plucked
   A. Violin—Strings are tuned G^3 D^4 A^4 E^5
   B. Viola—C^3 G^3 D^4 A^4
   C. Violoncello (Cello)—C^2 G^2 D^3 A^3
   D. Double bass—E^1 A^1 D^2 G^2
2. Usually plucked
   A. Guitar—Six strings made of nylon or steel
   B. Banjo
   C. Lute
   D. Mandolin
   E. Ukulele
   F. Harp
   G. Lyre
3. Usually Struck—percussion instruments as well as stringed instruments
   A. Piano
   B. Harpsichord
   C. Clavichord

violin   viola   violoncello   double bass   harp

The Symphony Orchestra

The **symphony orchestra** with its standard four sections (woodwinds, brass, percussion, and strings) came into being in the Classical Period (1750–1825) but did not

---

[1] In addition to their use in the orchestra, stringed instruments are often used in **chamber music** (music with one player to a part intended for performance in a room [chamber]). The most popular chamber music combination is a **string quartet**, which includes 1st violin, 2nd violin, viola, and cello. A **piano quintet** includes piano plus string quartet.

reach its full development until the end of the Romantic period (1900). The violin and other stringed instruments were perfected in the hands of Italian master craftsmen such as Antonio Stradavari (1644–1737). In the Baroque period (1600–1750), brass instruments played only a limited number of notes and used crooks (curved tubing) to change keys. Players also used differently tuned instruments (e.g., differently tuned clarinets) in order to change keys. Mozart used an *A* clarinet for his *Concerto in A for Clarinet and Orchestra*, K. 622 (October 1791, the year he died), which he wrote for clarinetist and friend Anton Stadler. With the invention of valves for brass instruments and full-key systems for woodwind instruments during the Romantic period (1825–1900), the symphony orchestra (with over 100 players) reached its contemporary form. The following chart shows symphony instruments in **score order** (as they appear in the musical score) and relates the range of these instruments to the piano keyboard (woodwind instruments at the top, followed by brass, percussion, and strings). [One of the best ways to learn the sound of the individual instruments of the orchestra and their corresponding ensembles is by listening to *Guide to the Orchestra* by Benjamin Britten (listening guide on the following page).]

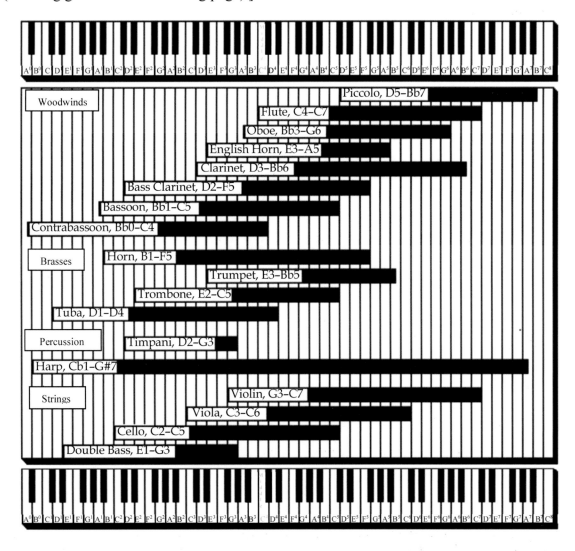

Guide to the Orchestra, Benjamin Britten
(*Naxos* playlist Arts Key 05B [2–7] or Britten Guide Pesek Orchestral [1–6]; *YouTube*: YouTube Symphony 2011 Britten Guide)

A. Theme six times

Naxos Playlist [Album[

Track 2 [1]
1. whole orchestra
2. woodwinds
3. brasses
4. strings
5. percussion
6. whole orchestra

B. Variations of this theme played 13 times

Track 3 [2]
1. piccolo, flutes
2. oboes
3. clarinets
4. bassoons

Track 4 [3]
5. violins
6. violas
7. cellos
8. basses

9. harp

Track 5 [4]
10. horns
11. trumpets
12. trombones/tuba

Track 6 [5]
13. percussion
    a. timpani, bass drum and cymbals
    b. timpani, tambourine, triangle, side (snare) drum and wood block
    c. timpani, xylophone
    d. timpani, castanets and gong
    e. timpani, whip
    f. timpani and entire percussion section

C. Fugue based on part of the theme

Track 7 [6]
1. piccolo
2. flutes
3. oboes
4. clarinets
5. bassoons
6. violins
7. violas
8. cellos
9. basses
10. harp
11. horns
12. trumpets
13. trombones, tuba
14. percussion
15. full orchestra
END

Typical Seating Arrangement for Symphony Orchestra

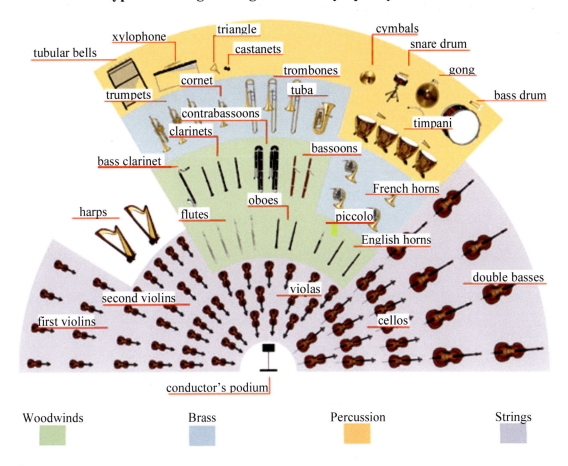

Typical Seating Arrangement for Concert Band

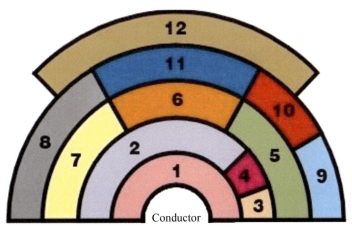

1. Flutes, Piccolo
2. Clarinets
3. Oboes
4. Bassoons
5. Saxophones
6. Trumpets
7. Cornets
8. Euphoniums
9. Horns
10. Trombones
11. Tubas
12. Percussion

The Concert Band

The **concert band** is "an orchestra with no strings attached." It deletes the contrabassoon and the strings (except for the double bass). It adds saxophones[1] to the woodwind section and adds additional instruments to the brass section such as the euphonium. A helpful example of music for the concert band (with differences in textures) is the patriotic song STARS AND STRIPES FOREVER (1896) with music and words (right hand side below) written by John Philip Sousa (1854–1932), the famous director of the United States Marine Band. (On a separate sheet, note the times for each section as you listen, *Naxos* playlist <u>Arts Key 05B Instrumental Sound Colors</u> [1] or keyword: <u>8.559013</u> [15]).

Interactive Guide for *Stars and Stripes Forever* (1896)

Instrumental Range/Timbre: Full concert band—2 piccolos, 8 flutes, 2 oboes, 22 clarinets, 2 alto clarinets, 2 bass clarinets, 2 bassoons, 4 alto saxes, 2 tenor saxes, 1 baritone sax, 1 bass sax, 12 cornets, 4 trumpets, 14 French horns, 2 baritones, 2 euphoniums, 16 trombones, 6 basses, 1 string bass, 1 timpani, 2 bass drums, and 4 small drums

Dynamics: *p* to *ff*/Rhythm: *Tempo di marcia* [March tempo] in Cut Time (2/2), Length 03:35
Melody: Major/Harmony: I, IV, V with some additional chords
Texture: Varies between homophonic and polyphonic with a little monophony
Form: IBBCCAInterA^{1}InterA^2 (see chapter 11)

Time	Dynamics	Instruments, Texture	Form	Lyrics
00:00	*ff*	full band Monophonic/Homophonic	I—Introduction	
	ff, p, f, p<f	Homophonic—3 layers 1-Melody B—piccolos, flutes, clarinets, cornets 2-Accompaniment: others except for basses 3-Basses	Melody B	
	ff, p, f, p<f	Homophonic—3 layers as before	Melody B repeated	
	p	Homophonic—3 layers 1-Melody C—woodwinds *p* 2-Accompaniment: others except for basses 3-Basses	Melody C	
	f	Homophonic—3 layers Melody C—repeated *f*, add cornets/trombones to woodwinds, otherwise as before	Melody C repeated	
	mf	Homophonic—3 layers 1- Melody A—choir, *mf*, substitutes for woodwinds 2-Accompaniment—other instruments 3-Basses	Melody A (refrain)	
	ff	Monophonic/Homophonic	Interlude, brasses	
	tune *p* countermelody *f*	Polyphonic—4 layers 1-Melody A repeated—clarinets, saxes, cornets, trumpets, *p* 2-Countermelody—piccolos *f* 3-Accompaniment—others 4-Basses	Tune A^1 (refrain) repeated	
	ff	Monophonic/Homophonic	Interlude, brasses	
	all *ff* *fff*	Polyphonic—5 layers 1-Melody A repeated—choir *ff* 2-Countermelody 1— piccolos *ff* 3-Countermelody 2—trombones *ff* 4-Accompiment—others 5-Basses	Tune A^2 (refrain) repeated again	

---

[1] The saxophone was invented by Adolphe Sax in 1841.

5—The Colors of Sound 65

STARS AND STRIPES FOREVER (excerpt), John Philip Sousa, 1896
The music for Tune A (refrain) is given below with the original words by Sousa.

The Jazz Band

A **jazz band** usually includes alto, tenor, and baritone saxophones (*bari sax*), trumpets, trombones, guitar, piano, double bass, and drum set.[1] Sometimes a player will *double* on another instrument such as flute or clarinet. A typical seating arrangement of the jazz band is shown below.

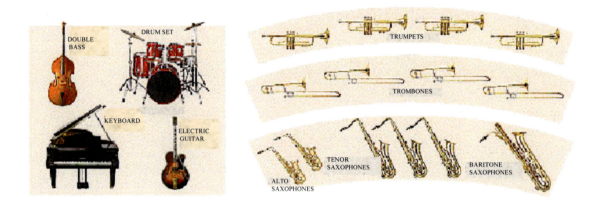

The Rock/Pop Band

The **rock/pop band** developed around the middle of the twentieth century and usually consists of 3–5 members, with 4 being the most common (Cream–3, Beatles–4, and Beach Boys–5). It always includes a rhythm section of drum set[1] and bass guitar—the rhythm section may also include rhythm guitar and keyboards. For melody it includes lead (melody) guitar and lead (melody) vocals. It may also include backing vocals (vocal harmony and/or countermelody). The best example of unusual timbres is the album *Pet Sounds* by the *Beach Boys*. The rock band depends on electronic amplification and manipulation to reach mass audiences.

---

[1] A drum set (sometimes called a drum kit or trap set) is a collection of drums and cymbals (and sometimes other percussion instruments) arranged for convenient playing by a single person. A typical drum set includes a snare drum, tom-tom drums, a bass drum, a crash cymbal, a ride cymbal, and a high-hat cymbal.

Actions for Practice and Delight

5/1. Learn to sing *Tzena, Tzena*, accompanied by bass and/or chords, on page C14. Listen to the following recordings illustrating various colors of sound produced by the human voice:

1) The sound of the speaking voice: *You Are Old, Father William* with words on page 56 of this chapter (*Naxos* playlist Arts Key 05A Vocal Sound Colors [1] or keyword: CDSDL294 [10]).
2) The sound of singing boys' voices: *La Nuit* from *Les Choristes* (*Naxos* playlist Arts Key 05A [2] or keyword: 3020671532 [13]).
3) The sounds of singing men's and women's voices: (*Naxos* playlist Arts Key 05A Vocal Sound Colors [3] or keyword: CDR90000-085 [5]).
4) The sound of men's voices with accompaniment: (*Naxos* playlist Arts Key 05A Vocal Sound Colors [4] or keyword: EUCD1797 [13]).

In writing discuss *in detail* the use of dynamics, vocal ranges, and timbres, for each selection separately. Which is your favorite selection, and why?

5/2. Learn to sing the chorus of *Stars and Stripes Forever* (page 65 of the text). Follow the listening guide on page 64 until you know each aspect thoroughly. On a separate sheet, note the times for each section as you listen, *Naxos* playlist Arts Key 05B Instrumental Sound Colors [1] or keyword: 8.559013 [15]).

5/3. Using the Listening Guide given in this chapter on page 62, view and listen to each section from *Guide to the Orchestra* (*Variations and Fugue on a Theme by Purcell*) by Benjamin Britten (*YouTube* keywords: YouTube Symphony 2011 Britten Guide, Naxos playlist: Arts Key 05B [2–7], or keywords: Britten Guide Pesek Orchestral [1–6] as many times as necessary until you can pick out each of the individual instruments and groups of instruments that you hear. Then, identify woodwinds, brasses, percussion, strings, full orchestra, and the individual instruments in any section without using the Listening Guide. Double-check your answers with the Listening Guide. Repeat this process until you are able to identify each instrument and group without fail. Write a paragraph summarizing your experience, and grade yourself on how well you are able to identify the instruments. Then, write a summary of the entire work discussing the uses of ranges, timbres, and dynamics. [Interactive resources for additional help in hearing and identifying instruments may be found on the Internet by using keywords Britten Guide Interactive Orchestra or the following sites if available: http://www.thirteen.org/publicarts/orchestra/ and <http://mhhe.com/socscience/music/kamien9e/part01/chapter02/youngpersonsguide/brittenguideinteractive.htm>.

5/4. Begin listening to the *YouTube* Symphony Grand Finale Concert (2 hours and 22 minutes) with 101 musicians from 33 different countries: *YouTube* keywords: YouTube Symphony 2011 Grand Finale. After listening to the introduction (2 minutes or so), sample as much or as little of the rest as you like. In writing, discuss your experience. How much of the video did you end up watching (list times spent and specific sections that you watched)? What puzzled you, and what did you like the most?

Chapter 6

Drawing the Line

"A drawing is simply a line going for a walk."—Paul Klee

Art (an image frozen in space) is the counterpart of sound through time. **Media** are the materials through which the artist works. Two-dimensional media include **D**rawing, **P**rintmaking, and **P**ainting. Three-dimensional media include **A**rchitecture, **S**culpture, and **A**pplied **D**esign.

Drawing is the art of presenting objects or forms on a surface primarily by the means of lines. A study (drawing or sketch) begins the process for the artist. It is the vital thread for all the visual arts. Two elements are required for drawing: an instrument and a prepared surface called a **ground**. The ground may be paper or a wall, for example. The instrument used to draw may be a pencil (graphite), charcoal, silverpoint, chalk, crayon (pigment in wax), pastel (pigment and glue), or a quill, pen or reed brush that applies ink. The architect Daniel Libeskind avers:

Avant-Garde (1900–1975) Pablo Picasso (1881–1973), *Portrait of Igor Stravinsky* (1920), graphite and charcoal on paper, 61 x 48 cm (2 ft. x 1 ft. 7 in.) Musée Picasso, Paris.

> Architecture is about drawing. Most people forget this, because we have computer simulations and sophisticated technologies, but the art of architecture is the ability to draw. But the lines are not just graphics. They represent a space that actually has to be built. You know, Michelangelo, when asked by his nephew what he should do to become an architect, said, '"Do nothing—just draw."[1]

---

[1] Daniel Libeskind in a conversation with Laura Caruso of the Denver Art Museum in *On & Off the Wall* (Denver Art Museum, July/August 2005), p. 4. Libeskind was the architect for the Jewish Museum Berlin, 1999-2001, the Food Theatre Cave in London, 2001, the Denver Art Museum, 2006, and the architect chosen for the reconstruction of the World Trade Center.

Printmaking is reproducing an image by mechanical and chemical means. It is closely related to drawing. A *woodcut* begins with an image drawn on a piece of wood. The artist then cuts away the areas not to be shown on the final print. The wood is then inked and the paper pressed against this wood block. *Intaglio* (from the Italian *intagliare,* "to incise") is the process of engraving (cutting lines with a steel tool called a burin) or etching (using a chemical process to incise lines) on the surface of metal. The engraved or etched lines are then filled with ink, and paper is pressed against the surface to transfer these inked lines as in the etching below. *Lithography* (Greek— λιθος + γραφη, stone writing) begins with a drawing on stone using a grease pencil or brush dipped in a greasy substance. The surface is covered with acid, which fixes the image. Then, the surface is dampened and inked with a roller. The paper is laid on the inked image and run through a press. *Silk screening* involves a process of making a stencil adhere to a screen made of silk, nylon, or similar material. When ink, paint, or dye is forced through the screen with a squeegee, the stencil does not allow the ink, paint, or dye to penetrate onto the surface underneath. Other areas of printmaking include photography, filmmaking, and computer graphics.

Renaissance (1450–1600) Albrecht Durer (1471–1528) *Small Horse* (1505), print of copper engraving, 16.5 x 10.8 cm (6½ x 4¼ in.) Private collection.

Painting is the art of applying color to a surface. Five elements are required for painting: pigment (dry coloring matter made up of minerals or plants), a binding element (to bind coloring matter together), a thinner, a ground, and an instrument for applying color, such as a brush. The ground may be paper, canvas, wood, a wall, and so on. In encaustic painting, pigment is combined with beeswax as a binder and thinned by heat. Sometimes this is applied to a wooden panel. In fresco, pigment is thinned with water and bound in moist, fresh plaster on a wall. In watercolor, the binder is gum resin, the thinner is water, and the ground is paper. In oil painting (such as the painting below), linseed oil is the binder, turpentine is the thinner, and canvas is the ground. In tempura, egg is the binder, and water is the thinner. In acrylic painting, synthetic polymer resin is the pigment. There is no thinner. Once it dries, that's it.[1]

Paul Cézanne (1839–1906) *Great Pine Tree Near Aix* (1890) oil on canvas, 72 × 91 cm (2 ft. 4¼ in. x 2ft. 11¾ in.) The State Hermitage Museum, St. Petersburg, Russia.

Architecture is the art of designing and erecting buildings. It includes all kinds of structures—from sod houses to cathedrals. Buildings *function* to provide physical, visual, and acoustical spaces for music and the other arts, including the visual arts (of which

---

[1] For much of this material, I am indebted to Dr. Roger Chandler.

architecture itself is a part). For example, Notre Dame Cathedral (rear view below) has served since the Middle Ages as a space for sculptures, stained glass windows, applied design of all kinds, paintings, a venue for all manner of concerts, a music school, the beginning of the university of Paris, the coronation of kings and queens, and on and on.

Maurice de Sully, Architect. *Notre Dame Cathedral* (1163–1250) [Rear View], Paris. Photograph © 2004 by Allen P. Schantz. All rights reserved.

Sculpture is the art or practice of shaping figures in the round or in relief (protruding out of a surface) as on the right and on the previous page. Sculpture may use carving or molding. Carving (stone, wood, plastic, and glass) uses a subtractive process (removing unwanted material). Molding (clay, metal, wax, and assemblage) uses an additive process (adding material from the inside out).

Charles Alphonse Achille Gumery (1827–1871) *L'Harmonie* [*Harmony*] (1868–69), gilded bronze, 7.5 m [24 ft. 7¼ in.] high, sculpture on upper left front of *Opera Garnier* [since 1985, *Palais Garnier*] (1857–1874), Paris. Charles Garnier, architect (1825–1898).

Applied design includes things like clothes, tables, chairs, stairs, books, and a variety of objects made of ceramics, metal, glass, wood, and other materials. Fashion design and interior design are both categories of applied design. Notice below the many objects of applied and interior design with the painting on the wall by William Turner.

Lobby of Hôtel Brittanique in the heart of Paris. Photograph © 2004 by Allen P. Schantz. All rights reserved.

The Aesthetic Raw Elements of Art

The raw elements of art may be roughly compared to the elements of music.

Music	*Art*
Melody—series of single pitches set to a rhythm (modal/major/minor)	**Line** (a continuous mark made on a surface)
Harmony—series of simultaneous pitches set to a rhythm (dissonant/consonant, I [i], IV [iv], V^7)	**Shape** (the characteristic surface outline of an object, may be 2-D or 3-D)
[Bass]—foundation of harmony from 1600 on	**[Perspective]**—the mathematical method for representing 3-D shapes in a 2-D space from 1425 on
Rhythm (Time)—pattern of sounds/silences in time	**Space** (positive—occupied by an image; negative—not occupied by an image)
Texture (Layers)—number, type, and relationship of layers	**Texture**—the surface characteristics associated with the sense of touch

Colors of Sound
  Volume [Dynamics] (soft<loud)
  Pitch Range (low<high)
  Timbre—quality of sound (mellow<piercing, etc.)
	Colors of Light
	  Value (black<white)
	  Hue Range (Palette)—range of color (red<violet)
	  Saturation (dull<vivid)

Form—the structure of a work with central theme (A), development (A^1, A^2, etc.), contrast (*B*, *C*, etc.), and dramatic shape (rising tension, climax, and release)	**Form**—the structure of a work with central theme (A), development (A^1, A^2, etc.), contrast (*B*, *C*, etc.), and dramatic shape (rising tension, climax [focal point], and release)

Line

A **line** is a continuous mark made on a surface. It is noticeably longer than it is wide. A basic quality of line is direction. It may be straight, or it may be curved. It may be vertical, horizontal, or diagonal. A straight line is the shortest distance between two points. In art, lines may be divided into outlines (general size and shape), contour lines (implying three-dimensions), implied lines (filled in by our minds), gestural lines (overall movement), and organizational lines (lines giving integration to a work). An open line is active. A closed line (such as an oval, a circle, a square) is passive. Line is the most personal shorthand of an artist. An artist's sketchbook is like his or her diary.

Various Examples of Lines

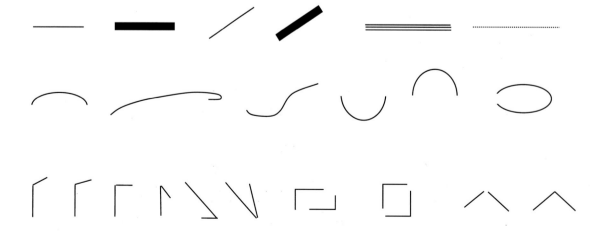

Shape

Shape is the characteristic surface outline of an object. It may be two-dimensional (enclosed by lines on a surface as in drawing, painting, printmaking, photography) or three-dimensional (sculpture, architecture, applied design). Regular geometric shapes have specific names such as triangles, squares, rectangles, circles, hexagons, and so on. Regular three-dimensional shapes also have specific names such as cubes, cones, boxes, spheres, and so on. Shapes may also have irregular and curvilinear contours.

Some Two-Dimensional Shapes

Rectangle   Triangle   Circle   Ellipse   Kidney

Perspective

Linear perspective is the mathematical method for representing three-dimensional shapes in a two-dimensional space. Filippo Brunelleschi (1377–1446), an Italian architect, is credited with inventing geometrical (linear) perspective. Based on the developing science of optics and experiments that he conducted in 1425, Brunelleschi developed specific mathematical ratios for the size of objects depending on their distance from the viewer. One-point perspective enabled painters to assume that the viewer is standing at a single, fixed spot and to create a vanishing point where parallel lines converge. In its simplest form, this occurs at the horizon on the viewer's eye level, but it can occur anywhere in a picture or even outside of it. Suppose that you are standing on railroad tracks. You look down at your feet and then gradually raise your eyes until the railroad tracks are lost from sight in the distance. This is called the **vanishing point** and occurs at the horizon or eye level. The height of the eyes (eye-level) is an important factor in how we see.

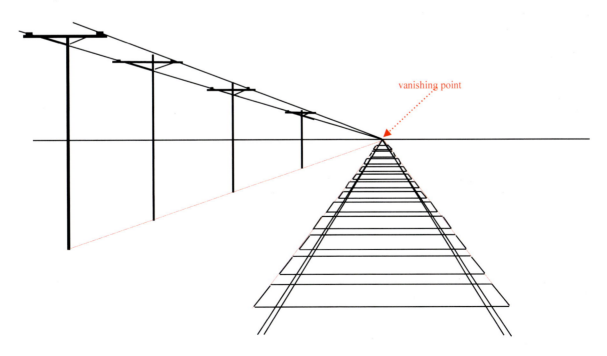

Perugino combines **atmospheric perspective**[1] (the illusion of distance through blurring and reducing the intensity of colors of objects farther away) with linear perspective in his 1482 painting *Consegna delle chiavi* [*Consignment of the Keys*] (see below). [Another famous example of the combination of atmospheric and linear perspective is da Vinci's *Mona Lisa*].

Pietro Perugino (1445–ca. 1523), *Consegna delle chiavi* [*Consignment of the Keys*] (1482), fresco, 348 x 570 cm (11 ft. 5½ in. x 18 ft. 8½ in.), Sistine Chapel, Vatican.

---

[1] An earlier technique from Roman tradition.

Drawing the Way the Eye Sees and Adding Additional Vanishing Points

The basic idea of perspective is to draw the way the eye sees. Always draw by looking at the scene and allow your pencil or brush to follow the scene itself rather than looking directly at the medium on which you are drawing. For example, look at your non-drawing hand and draw the outline of that hand without moving your eyes from that non-drawing hand. Additional vanishing points may be added when viewing a scene from the side. Two-point perspective is often used when viewing the corner of buildings. For a helpful illustration, view the following clip: http://www.youtube.com/watch?v=felys-u4nfk. To further explore the relationship of vision and art, visit the following website: http://psych.hanover.edu/krantz/art/index.html.

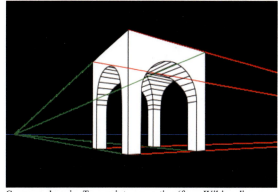

Common domain. Two-point perspective (from Wikimedia commons), newly drawn vector based on original png by Wolfram Gothe, GNU free documentation license.

Space (Positive and Negative)

Positive space is the space occupied by an image. **Negative space** is the space not occupied by an image. *Rubin's Vase*[1] shown on the right illustrates both positive (the vase) and negative space (the faces). Rhythm in music and space in art are closely connected. Usually, a work of art causes the eye to move toward a focal point or points in the composition. In music, rhythm is related to bodily movement. Art suggests frozen movement. In art, rhythm is related to the motion of the eye, which moves independently of the body as well as with it.

The frozen rhythm of the architecture of *Musée d'Orsay* [*Orsay Museum*, a converted train station in Paris] on the following page is intriguing. Notice how the glass panels in the roof and the repeated patterns in the walls draw one's eyes deep into the negative space of the building. What other aspects of the rhythm can you discover?

---

[1] Developed by Danish psychologist Edgar Rubin [1886–1951] as part of a set of optical illusions to illustrate figure-ground perception.

Musée d'Orsay (former train station), Paris, Photograph © 2004 by Allen P. Schantz. All rights reserved.

Texture

Texture refers to the surface characteristics associated with the sense of touch. Objects may be smooth or rough, hard or soft, stiff or pliable, and so on. Texture may be actual, or it may be implied, allowing our minds to fill in the details.

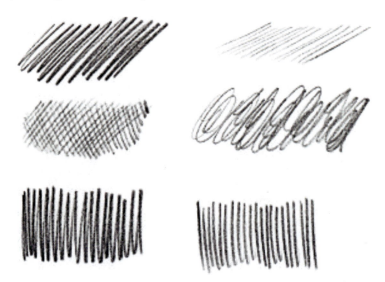

Common Domain. Illustration of textures from WikiHow: http://www.wikihow.com/Use-Pencil-to-Draw-Different-Textures

Actions for Practice and Delight

6/1. Learn the elements of art in comparison with the elements of music so that you can apply them when creating or viewing art. Also, learn the six categories of the visual arts (Drawing, Printmaking, Painting, Architecture, Sculpture, and Applied Design).

6/2. Find examples of each of the six categories of art (Drawing, Printmaking, Painting, Architecture, Sculpture, and Applied Design). For each example, list the name of the artist, the title of the work, the date(s) of its creation, materials used (e.g., oil on canvas), the size of the work, and the current location of the work. Examples in this book illustrate this process but may not be used as answers. (The Internet provides many resources that may be helpful in this process.)

6/3. Turn the drawing of Stravinsky (page 69) by Picasso upside down, and then copy it. Try to keep your eyes on the drawing itself without looking at your hand.

6/4. Review the materials on perspective on pages 75–77. Watch http://www.youtube.com/watch?v=felys-u4nfk or keywords: One and Two-Point Perspective Gude on *YouTube* to learn how to draw in one-point and two-point perspective. After watching this drawing on *YouTube*, practice it until you are able to draw it in perspective from memory. Submit your final copy drawn from memory, discuss your process, and grade yourself.

CHAPTER 7

THE COLORS OF LIGHT

In the best lighting conditions, the average human eye can distinguish up to 7,000,000 colors. Even the very best digital camera is not as sophisticated as the human eye. Visible light is a small part of the larger electromagnetic spectrum. Visible light can be broken up into its constituent colors by using a prism as in the rainbow (Genesis 9:13).[1]

The Electromagnetic Spectrum

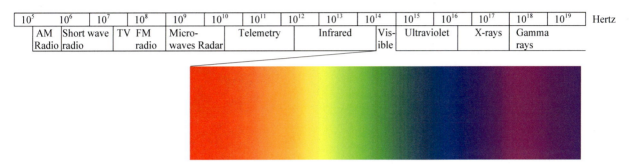

Color is that aspect of things caused by the differing qualities of the light emitted or reflected by them.[2] It may be divided into three parts: 1) value, 2) hue range, and 3) saturation. These may be compared with the colors of sound: 1) dynamics, 2) instrument pitch range, and 3) timbre.

Value (Shadow and Light, Black and White/Soft and Loud)

Comparable to dynamics in music, **value** is the relative blackness or whiteness of a two-dimensional image depending on the amount of light reflected from a surface. Black reflects no light at all and thus is dark, whereas white reflects all light. Gray reflects more light than black, but less than white. **Chiaroscuro** (Italian word meaning the contrast between *chiar*-light/*oscuro*-dark) is used extensively in the Baroque period, as illustrated by the painting on the right on the following page. Value can be isolated by just using black and white, as in a photocopy on the left on the following page. The black/white (*oscuro/chiar*) of reflected light has its aural counterpart in soft/loud (*piano/forte*). In order to explore this connection, it is helpful to explore a comparable work by Handel from the Baroque period exploiting the contrast between loud and soft (*Glory to God* from the *Messiah* [*Naxos* playlist <u>Arts Key 07 *Chiaroscuro* in Music</u> [1] or

---

[1] One way to memorize colors of the spectrum is by using the mnemonic device: ROY G. B[I]V (Red, Orange, Yellow, Green, Blue, [Indigo], Violet).

[2] Though some colors can be created by a single, pure wavelength, most colors are the result of a mixture of wavelengths. A French organization, the Commission International de L'Eclairage (CIE), worked in the first half of the 20th century developing a method for systematically measuring color in relation to the wavelengths they contain. This system became known as the **CIE color model** (or system).

keyword: 0077776378459 [16]). You may also wish to listen to Haydn's Classic period musical setting from *The Creation* of the representation of chaos and then of the words, "In the beginning God created the heaven and the earth. And the earth was without form and void. And **darkness** was upon the face of the deep. And the Spirit of God moved upon the face of the waters. And God said, "Let there be light." And there was ***LIGHT***!" [Genesis 1:1–3] (*Naxos* keyword: NPD85627-2 [1, 2]). Notice especially in the second part how Haydn combines an explosion in dynamics with a full-orbed **C** major chord fitting to brilliant light!

Baroque (1600–1750) Vermeer (1632–1675), *Meisje met de rode hoed* [*The Girl with the Red Hat*], ca. 1665 oil on panel, 22.8 x 18 cm (9 x 7 1/16 in.), National Gallery of Art, Washington.

Hue Range (Palette/Instrument Pitch Range)

Hue is synonymous with color in its pure sense, ranging from red to violet (roughly analogous to instrument pitch range in music). Green is one hue, whereas red is another. Each hue (or color) is a different frequency of light. Hues that have a common color are termed "analogous hues" and produce integrated unity or "color harmony" within a work of art. If only a single hue is used in a work, the work is *monochromatic*. If many contrasting hues are used, the work is *polychromatic*.

Primary Pigment Colors. In contrast to the additive colors of streaming light,[1] the colors of reflected light are subtractive (the colors reflected from a surface after the light

---

[1] Streaming light is light that passes *through* a medium such as glass, for example. White light can be recreated by adding three streaming colors together (red-orange, green and blue-violet, RGB for short). The colors seen on a computer screen are created by different mixtures of these three colors.

rays absorbed are subtracted). The **primary pigment colors for printing** are cyan, yellow, and magenta. In printing, it is possible to use only these three colors to mix almost all colors.[1] Theoretically, the **primary pigment colors for painting** are blue, yellow, and red as on the traditional color wheel. However, in practice, it is not possible to mix all colors from these three primary pigment colors or *any* three primary colors. (Thus, Munsell adds green and violet as primary colors in his five-color, three-dimensional tree).[2] For beginning artists, a recommended basic palette might consist of 10 or more colors (plus black and white), with other colors mixed from them. Throughout history, there have been many color wheels and systems, which are, for the most part, helpful for color harmony purposes. The traditional color wheel (the color spectrum put together in a circle) provides a starting point in exploring color systems.

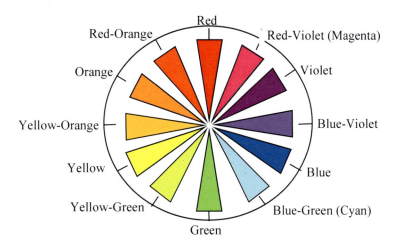

Traditional Color Wheel

Secondary, Complementary, and Intermediate Colors. **Secondary pigment colors** (in the traditional color wheel) are violet, green, and orange, which are in between two primary colors: violet is in between red and blue; green is in between blue and yellow; and orange is in between yellow and red. These colors are slightly less intense than the primary colors. The colors opposite each other are known as **complementary** colors: red and green (Christmas), blue and orange, yellow and violet (spring), and so on.[3] Complementary colors have the most contrast. When one stares at a complementary color for a long time, the color receptors of the eye may become fatigued and see only the

---

[1] Four-color printing uses the colors cyan, yellow, and magenta plus black (CYMK) and the white of paper to print thousands of the millions of streaming colors that can be seen on the computer screen. Even with this technology (used in this book), the colors on printed paper are slightly inaccurate. (The technology used for printing increasingly uses additional colors, e.g., yellow, cyan, light cyan, magenta, light magenta, black, blue, dark gray, and light gray in 9-color printing).

[2] Today, "the most widely adopted way of communicating about colors is the system developed by Albert Munsell and subsequently refined and recognized by the National Bureau of Standards, the Munsell Laboratory, and the Optical Society of America. It is the basis for standards used in the United States by various official color councils, by the Japanese Industrial Standard for Color, the British Standards Institution, and the German Standard Color System." [Zelanski, Paul and Mary Pat Fisher, *Color*, 4th ed. (Upper Saddle River, New Jersey: Prentice Hall Inc., 2003), pp. 72–73].

[3] In the Munsell system, the complementary colors are red-violet and green, red and blue-green, blue and orange (yellow-red), yellow and violet-blue, and yellow-green and violet.

complementary color after the original color has been removed. (This is called an *afterimage*.) When mixed together in the right proportion, complementary colors produce a neutral gray. **Intermediate colors** are colors in-between the primary and secondary colors: red-violet, blue-violet, and so on. Thus, the primary reflective colors anchor the three hues following each: *red*, red-violet (magenta), violet, blue-violet, *blue*, blue-green, green, yellow-green, *yellow*, yellow-orange, orange, red-orange, and back to red.

Warm and Cool Colors (Complementary Pairs). Colors are also divided into warm and cool categories. **Warm colors** include yellow, orange, red, and their intermediate colors. **Cool colors** include green, blue, violet, and their intermediate colors. Notice also that the colors below form complementary pairs: yellow (warm)/violet (cool), yellow-orange (warm)/blue-violet (cool), orange (warm)/blue (cool), and so on.

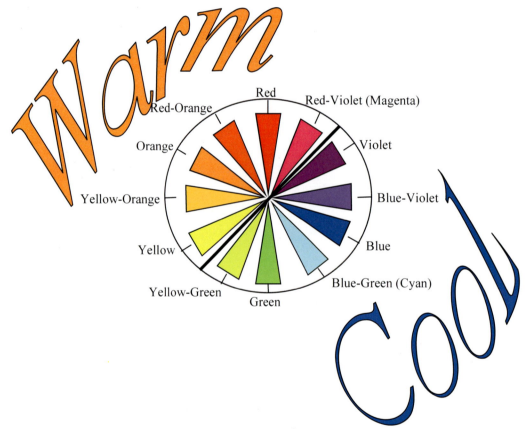

Color is the most emotional of all elements of the visual arts. The psychology of color is a fascinating topic. Red is sometimes correlated with anger ("seeing red"). Paint a bedroom in red, and it may engender arguments. Pink, on the other hand, is used in some insane asylums to calm people down. A fast food restaurant in mustard yellow encourages people to eat more. Too much yellow is disturbing and too much violet overwhelming.

Saturation (Dull to Vivid/Timbre: Mellow to Piercing)

Comparable to timbre in music, **saturation** is the dullness or vividness of a hue and can be changed by four methods: 1) adding white (tint), 2) adding black (shade), 3) adding gray (mixture of white and black), and 4) adding the complementary hue. Adding white to red makes it pink and thus less saturated. Adding gray to red makes it a duller red, and adding black makes it even duller and thus less intense. When green is added to red, it makes it grayish red or grayish green and thus duller.

The Interaction between Value, Hue Range (Palette), and Saturation

The interaction between value, hue range (palette), and saturation is shown on the left below using the hue red. When black or white is added to a hue, it alters the value (whiteness or blackness) of that hue but it does not change its hue. When one hue is added to another (for example, yellow added to blue), it changes both the value and the hue.

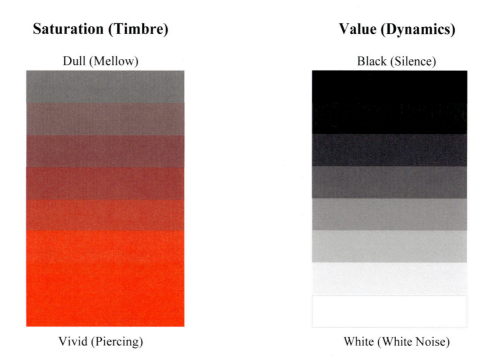

Putting the Colors of Sound and Light Together

Our ears and eyes are priceless gifts. With our ears we recognize dynamics, instrument pitch range, and timbre—the colors of sound. With our eyes we distinguish value, hue range (palette), and saturation—the colors of light. Eyes and ears go hand in hand and foot to foot as we explore Dance.

Actions for Practice and Delight

7/1. To explore the relationship between value or *chiaroscuro* [light and dark, Italian] in art and in music, learn *Angels We Have Heard on High* (page C6) to the tune GLORIA (page C7) with softer, darker echoes for the repeated phrase in each section. Then listen to the following selection: *Glory to God* from the *Messiah* (*Naxos* playlist Arts Key 07 *Chiaroscuro* in Music [1] or keyword: 0077776378459 [16]). In writing, compare the connection between music and light in the excerpt, especially the relationship between the *chiaroscuro* (light/dark) of the music (dynamics, pitch range, and timbre) and *chiaroscuro* (light/dark) of the painting on page 82 (value, hue range, and saturation).

7/2. For additional exploration of the relationship between value or *chiaroscuro* [light and dark, Italian] in art and in music, listen to the following selections: the first and second movements of Haydn's *Creation* (*Naxos* keyword: NPD85627-2 [1, 2]), with the second movement setting the following text from the beginning of the Bible: *"In the beginning God created the heaven and the earth. And the earth was without form, and void; and darkness was upon the face of the deep. And the Spirit of God moved upon the face of the waters. And God said, Let there be light: and there was light. And God saw the light, that it was good: and God divided the light from the darkness."* (Gen 1:1-4 KJV) At about two minutes, you will hear Haydn's connection between music and light. "And God said, 'Let there be light.' And there was **LIGHT!**" In writing, compare the connection between music and light in the excerpt, especially the relationship between the *chiaroscuro* of the music (dynamics, pitch range, and timbre) and *chiaroscuro* (value, hue range, and saturation) in art.

7/3. Learn the color wheel so that you can reproduce it without looking at the text. Be able to label primary, secondary, and complementary hues (colors). Be sure you understand the difference between value, hue range (palette), and saturation.

7/4. Try to copy *Paris Through the Window* on page 7 of your text by imitating the colors and blends of colors. Work especially on color blending. To get orange, begin with yellow and then add red. To get brown, begin with light blue, then add yellow, and finally add red.

CHAPTER 8

DANCING IN THE STREET

"Praise him with hand drum and dance."[1]

Pierre Auguste Renoir (1841–1919) Dance at Bougival (1883), oil on canvas, 182 x 98 cm (5 ft. 11⅝ in. x 2 ft. 7⅝ in.), Museum of Fine Arts Boston

Dance is a series of rhythmic and patterned steps and bodily movements (almost always performed to music). "Dance is music made visible."[2] It combines **body sculpting** (shaping oneself into different positions) in space with music in time. Repetition helps to form a lasting impression of one pose before changing to another. The steps and movements of the dancers parallel the rhythms of the music. The energy of the dance parallels the sound of the music. Dance steps also relate to the line of movement on the stage. Genres of dance include ballet, modern, jazz, hip-hop, and tap among many others.

Ballet forms the basis for all types of dancing and is a fundamental component in the training of any serious dancer in the western tradition. It includes set patterns of movement—five basic positions of feet, legs, arms, and body. These five positions can be varied ad infinitum to create other positions. The word *ballet* itself and terms for ballet are French, since ballet developed in France during the late Renaissance. King Louis XIV [1638–1715, reigned

---

[1] Psalm 150:4.
[2] George Balanchine.

1645–1715] was a ballet dancer himself and promoted the development of dance in France. Two well-known terms are *pas de deux* [dance for two] and *pas de trois* [dance for three]. Ballet is based on techniques that have been developed over centuries and often uses music and dance to tell stories. Ballet dancers have the ability to transport an audience to another world.

The Five Basic Positions

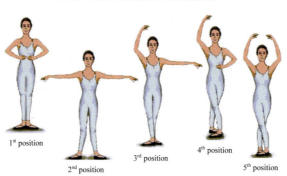

Modern Dance is a style of dance that blends classical, contemporary, and ethnic styles. It began as a rebellion against ballet, focusing on inner feelings, freedom of movement, and improvisation rather than on adherence to rigid rules. Dancers usually dance barefoot and wear costumes related to the dance theme.

Jazz is a free style of dance, relying on improvisation and originality (including music that is improvised while the dancer is dancing). It has a unique rhythm and flow, using accents in head, hands, hips, and feet. It uses both French and English to describe choreography. Dancers usually wear jazz shoes or boots and costumes related to the theme of the dance.

Hip-Hop is an even different style of dance that also emphasizes improvisation and personal interpretation. It includes various moves such as **breaking** (rapid acrobatic moves in which different parts of the body touch the ground), **popping** (quick tensing and releasing of muscles), **locking** (freezing of joints to maintain a particular position), and **krumping** (clown dancing).

Tap Dance is a style of dance in which dancers concentrate on rhythm and footwork. Dancers use **tap shoes** (equipped with metal taps on the bottom) to create drum like patterns with their feet. Tap dance, an American dance form, developed from English, Irish, and African roots.

The Raw Elements of Dance

The elements of dance[1] may be compared with the elements of music and art. The elements of rhythm in music and dance are essentially the same, although dance mimics the rhythmic patterns of sound and silence with patterns of motion and rest. Insofar as its relationship to art, dance may be thought of as sculpture in motion.

Music	*Art*	*Dance*
Melody	Line	**B**ody Shape—the form created by the body's position in space
Harmony	Shape	**E**nergy—the force of an action (weight, tension, flow)
[Bass]	[Perspective]	**A**ction—any movement that the dancer makes (axial—in one place and locomotor—from one place to another)
Rhythm (Time)	Space	**R**hythm (Time)—pattern of motion/rest through time and **S**pace (positive and negative)
Texture	Texture	
Colors of Sound Dynamics (Volume) Instrument Pitch Range Timbre	Colors of Light Value Hue Range Saturation	Colors of Sound and Colors of Light
FORM	FORM	FORM

Body Shape

Body Shape is the form created by the body's position in space. The five basic ballet positions are the essence of body-shape design. The body is sometimes relatively still and sometimes in motion as when the dancer moves in place or travels through space. Dancers may emphasize specific parts of their bodies in a dance phrase or their whole bodies. They may concentrate on head, shoulder, back, arm, leg, foot, hand, and torso, etc., on joint action such as neck, wrist, elbow, knee, hip etc., or on total body awareness and movement. Sculpting shapes include straight, bent/angular/crooked, twisted, curved, symmetrical, asymmetrical, etc. Another way to describe the body in dance is to consider the body systems—muscles, bones, organs, breath, balance, reflexes. A dancer's training includes working on posture, balance, flexibility, strength, and coordination.

Energy

Energy is the force of an action. It includes weight, tension, and flow. **Weight** may be weak<strong, light<heavy, or gentle<powerful. **Tension** may be tight<loose (bound flow<free flow). **Flow** may be legato (smooth, with light flowing ease)<staccato (sharp, explosive, percussive).

---

[1] The elements of dance may be learned by using the following acronym: **BEARS F**orm.

Action

Action is any movement that the dancer makes. **Axial movement** occurs in one place, and **locomotor movement** occurs from one place to another through space. Axial movement includes things such as bending, bouncing, freezing, pushing, sinking, slashing, stretching, and twisting, etc. Locomotor movement includes such things as walking, running, galloping, jumping, hopping, leaping, skipping, or sliding, etc. Axial and locomotor movement are often combined. For example, a dancer might run, stretch, freeze, sink, explode, and spin into a walk.

Rhythm (Time)

Rhythm in dance is the pattern of motion and rest through time and space. It is closely tied to rhythm in music, and includes beat, meter, and *tempo*. It may also be unmetered following rhapsodic rhythms of wind, water, breath, etc. Many of the terms of dance are the terms of music. For example an *adagio* (slow in music) means a dance to slow music, and an *allegro* (fast in music) means a dance to fast music. There are multitudes of dance rhythms, a number of which are listed in the second footnote below in alphabetical order.[1]

Space

Positive Space is the area occupied by the dancer's body. **Negative Space** is the area around the dancer. Space includes level, size (range of motion), direction, and pathways. <u>Level</u> is the vertical distance from the floor. Movement takes place on one of three levels: high, middle or low. <u>Size</u> (range of motion) is the magnitude of a body shape or movement. It ranges from large to small, wide to narrow. <u>Direction</u> is the way a dancer faces or moves. It may be forward, backward, sideways, upward, downward, toward, away, out, in, etc. Focus and gaze may be toward or away or constantly changing. <u>Pathways</u> are patterns on the floor (straight, curved, zigzag, etc.) or through the air (straight, angular, twisting, etc.). As noted earlier, they can be made with locomotor or non-locomotor movements, separately or in combination.

---

[1] The *ballo, basse dance, cachuca, cakewalk, Cancan, country dance, fandango, fox-trot, mazurka pavane, pas de deux* (dance for two), *polka, quadrille, square dance, tango,* and *waltz* are just a few of the plethora of dances and corresponding rhythms around the world.

The *Nutcracker*

Perhaps the most well-known ballet is the *Nutcracker* with music by Tchaikovsky, performed during the Christmas season in cities all over the world. It is based on a children's book by Alexandre Dumas père[1] [father, i.e., Sr.] (see right), which is in turn based on a darker story by E. T. A. Hoffman.[2] (Thus, the historical sequence is German story, French Story, Dance Story.) The Nutcracker Ballet is based on the story of a young girl (7½ years old in the French story on the right) who dreams that a Nutcracker becomes a Prince who fights a fierce Mouse King. The story of the ballet begins when young

Marie (sometimes named Clara in the ballet) receives a Nutcracker doll (a large wooden soldier doll whose mouth opens and closes to crack nuts) from her godfather for Christmas. In a jealous rage, Marie's brother Fritz grabs the Nutcracker and breaks it. Marie's godfather (Mr. Drosselmeyer) repairs it. After everyone goes to bed, Marie comes back out to see if the Nutcracker is all right. Holding the Nutcracker, she goes to sleep under the Christmas tree and dreams that a wicked Mouse King leads mice and rats in a pitched battle against the Nutcracker who comes to life to lead wooden soldiers. The Nutcracker and his soldiers are no match for the Mouse King and his rats. In desperation, Marie takes off her slipper, hurls it at the mouse king, scoring a direct hit and killing him instantly. The mice drag their lifeless leader's body away. In the ballet version, the Nutcracker then turns into a handsome Prince who takes Marie through an enchanted wonderland beginning with the Land of Snow. In the Land of Sweets, they are greeted by the Sugar Plum Fairy and rewarded for their bravery with the following dances: Spanish, Arabian, Russian, Chinese, Reed Flutes, and Waltz of the Flowers. The dream ends with the Sugar Plum Fairy and the Prince dancing a beautiful *pas de deux*. Marie awakens to find herself under the Christmas tree with the Nutcracker doll in her arms.

---

[1] *Histoire d'un casse-noisette* [*Story of a Nutcracker*] (approximately 33,500 words) by Alexandre Dumas père [father] (1802-1870), the author of *Le Compte de Monte Cristo* [*The Count of Monte Cristo*] and *Les Trois Mousquetaires* [*The Three Musketeers*]. Text is available at http://www.gutenberg.org/etext/5104. For original format go to http://gallica.bnf.fr/.

[2] *Nussknacker und Mausekönig* [*Nutcracker and Mouse King*] (approximately 20,750 words), 1816 by E.T.A. Hoffman (1776–1822). Downloadable at http://gutenberg.spiegel.de/etahoff/nussknac/nussknak.htm.

The program for the *Nutcracker* ballet is given below in English and then in the two languages paralleling those in which it was originally written. If possible, watch a live performance during the Christmas season. As an alternative, take advantage of the many performances available on DVD or *YouTube*. You will find it easy to follow the story by referring to the written program below.

English	**French**	**German**
Overture	Ouverture	Ouvertüre
Act 1	**Acte 1**	**1. Akt**
Christmas Eve	La veille de Noël	Heiliger Abend
March	Marche	Marsch
Drosselmeyer and the Distribution of Presents	Drosselmeyer et la distribution des jouets	Drosselmeyer und Bescherung
The Dancing Puppets	Les marionettes dansantes	Die tanzenden Puppen
The presentation of the Nutcracker	La presentation de Casse-Noisette	Der Nussknacker
Grandfather Dance	Danse Grand-père	Grossvatertanz
Night	Nuit	Nacht
The King of the Mice—the Battle	Le Roi des souris—La bataille	Der Mäusekönig—Die Schlact
The Transformation of the Nutcracker	La transformation de Casse-Noisette	Die Verwandlung des Nussknackers
A Pine Forest in Winter—Waltz of the Snowflakes	Une forêt de sapins en hiver—Valse de flacons de niege	Ein Tannenwald im Winter—Schneeflockenwalzer
Act 2	**Acte 2**	**2. Akt**
Journey to the Enchanted Realm	Voyage au pays enchanté	Reise in das Zauberreich
The Arrival of Marie and the Prince	L'arrivée de Marie et du Prince	Auftritt von Marie und dem Prinzen
Entertainment I Spanish Dance II Arabian Dance III Chinese Dance IV Russian Dance (Trepak) V Dance of the Reed Flutes (*pas de trois*)	**Divertissment** Danse espagnole Danse arabe Danse chinoise Danse russe Danse des mirlitons	**Unterhaltung** Spanischer Tanz Arabischer Tanz Chinesischer Tanz Russischer Tanz Tanz der Rohrflöten
Waltz of the Flowers	Valse des fleurs	Blumenwalzer
Grand *pas de deux* I *Pas de deux* (Sugar Plum Fairy and the Prince) II Tarantella (solo: the Prince) III Dance of the Sugar Plum Fairy IV Coda (*Pas de deux*)	Danse de la Fée Dragée	Tanz der Zuckerfee
Final Waltz and Apotheosis (deification)	Valse finale et Apothéose	Schlusswalzer und Apotheose

Actions for Practice and Delight

8/1. Learn the raw elements of dance and their definitions so that you know them thoroughly in comparison to the raw elements of music. Review *TZENA* on page C14 (and watch it on *YouTube* keywords: Tzena Weavers), and learn to sing *I Danced in the Morning* [SIMPLE GIFTS] on page C15.

8/2. Watch and listen to the following three dance scenes, each in a different style: 1) Gregory Hines and Mikhail Baryshnikov from the movie *White Nights*, 2) Gene Kelly from the movie *American in Paris*, and 3) Evie Johnson in Stravinsky's ballet *Petrouchka*. To access these on *YouTube*, type in the following keywords: 1) Tap Dance Shop White Nights Hines 1985; 2) segwon kelly rhythm; 3) Petroucha Northwest) or paste the following three clips into your browser: 1) http://youtu.be/wAW42KQi3X4; 2) http://youtu.be/4zLjF9hlH2k; 3) http://youtu.be/uFlXULEk32s). In writing, compare the correlation of the music to the dancing for each piece separately. Which one is your favorite, and why?

8/3. Watch the following clip from the *Nutcracker* Ballet, which includes four dances from the *Entertainment* portion in Act 2 (see page 92): Spanish Dance, Arabian Dance, Chinese Dance, and Russian Dance. Use the following keywords on *YouTube* Mariinsky theatre ballet nutcracker (begin at 51:00 and end at 58:00) or paste the following into your browser: http://youtu.be/pO1tGHD6zr8?t=51m0s through 58:00 (on *YouTube*). In writing, compare each dance separately using each of the elements of dance. Which dance is your favorite, and why?

CHAPTER 9

YOU'RE A POET AND DON'T KNOW IT

But your feet show it!
They're Longfellows.

"Prose = words in their best order.
Poetry = the best words in their best order."[1]

Poetry is word pictures and word sounds packed in flowing lines. Can you determine the words to the following poem (and song) by viewing the three lines of images below?

 and

 and

---
[1] Samuel Taylor Coleridge.

The poem pictured on the previous page combines vivid images with the sound of music (see footnote[1]), and introduces the two primary streams of English poetry: 1) fine-art poetry (intended for aesthetic contemplation), and 2) folk song-poetry (intended for community singing). Consider the word pictures and sounds of the following animal poems by reading them aloud several times, thinking about them, and then listening to them.

[Ancient Hebrew]—song-poem used as fine-art poetry
Psalm 104: 10–12, 14, 16–20, 24, KJB, 1611
(Playlist Arts Key 09 [2] or Psalm 104 Monaco [43])

[10] He sendeth the springs into the valleys,
    which run among the hills.
[11] They give drink to every beast of the field:
    the wild asses quench their thirst.
[12] By them shall the fowls of the heaven have their habitation,
    which sing among the branches.
...
[14] He causeth the grass to grow for the cattle,
    and herb for the service of man:
        that he may bring forth food out of the earth;
...
[16] The trees of the LORD are full *of sap*;
    the cedars of Lebanon, which he hath planted;
[17] Where the birds make their nests:
    as for the stork, the fir trees *are* her house.
[18] The high hills *are* a refuge for the wild goats;
    and the rocks for the conies.
[19] He appointed the moon for seasons:
    the sun knoweth his going down.
[20] He makest darkness, and it is night:
    wherein all the beasts of the forest do creep *forth*.
...
[24] O LORD, how manifold are thy works!
    in wisdom hast thou made them all:
    the earth is full of thy riches.

[Renaissance 1450–1600]
The Proud Horse, excerpt from *Venus and Adonis*
William Shakespeare (1564–1616)
(Playlist Arts Key 09 [3] or Proud Horse Monaco [17])

Imperiously he leaps, he neighs, he bounds,
And now his woven girths he breaks asunder;
The bearing earth with his hard hoof he wounds,
Whose hollow womb resounds like heaven's thunder;
    The iron bit he crusheth 'tween his teeth,
    Controlling what he was controlled with.

His ears up-prick'd; his braided hanging mane
Upon his compass'd crest now stand on end;
His nostrils drink the air, and forth again,
As from a furnace, vapours doth he send:
    His eye, which scornfully glisters like fire,
    Shows his hot courage and his high desire.

…

Round-hoof'd, short-jointed, fetlocks shag and long,
Broad breast, full eye, small head, and nostril wide,
High crest, short ears, straight legs and passing strong,
Thin mane, thick tail, broad buttock, tender hide:
    Look, what a horse should have he did not lack,
    Save a proud rider on so proud a back.

---

[1] Raindrops on roses and whiskers on kittens,
    Bright copper kettles and warm woolen mittens,
Brown paper packages tied up with strings,
    These are a few of my favorite things.
(*My Favorite Things* by Oscar Hammerstein II, Williamson Music, ©1959, from *The Sound of Music*).
Playlist Arts Key 09 [1] or Favorite Things Casserole [5]

[Baroque: ca. 1600–1660 in poetry] **The Elephant**
XXXIX. from *Metempsycosis* (published in 1633)
John Donne (1572–1631)

Nature's great masterpiece, an elephant
(The only harmless great thing), the giant
Of beasts, who thought none had to make him wise,
But to be just and thankful, loth to offend
(Yet nature hath given him no knees to bend)
Himself he up-props, on himself relies,
And, foe to none, suspects no enemies,
Still sleeping stood; vex'd not his fantasy
Black dreams; like an unbent bow carelessly
His sinewy proboscis did remissly lie.

[Neo-Classical: ca. 1660–1800 in poetry]
Alexander Pope (1688–1774)

Epigram Engraved on the Collar of a Dog Which I Gave to His Royal Highness

I am his Highness' dog at Kew;
Pray tell me, sir, whose dog are you?

Excerpt from **Sound and Sense** (1711)

True ease in writing comes from art, not chance,
  As those move easiest who have learned to dance.
'Tis not enough no harshness gives offense,
  The sound must seem an echo to the sense.
…

Epitaph on Sir Isaac Newton
(Died March 21, 1727)

NATURE and Nature's Laws lay hid in Night:
  God said, "Let Newton be!" and all was light.

[Romantic: 1800–1900 in poetry]
The Eagle (1851) (Fragment)
Alfred Lord Tennyson (1809–1892)
(Playlist Arts Key 09 [4] or Eagle Monaco [13])

He clasps the crag with crooked hands;
Close to the sun in lonely lands,
Ringed with the azure world, he stands.
The wrinkled sea beneath him crawls;
He watches from his mountain walls,
And like a thunderbolt he falls.

Avant-Garde (1900–1975)
excerpt from ***The Rum Tum Tugger*** (1930s)
T. S. Eliot (1888–1965)
…
…

  The Rum Tum Tugger is a curious beast:
His disobliging ways are a matter of habit.
If you offer him fish then he always wants a feast;
When there isn't any fish then he won't eat rabbit,
If you offer him cream then he sniffs and sneers,
For he only likes what he finds for himself;
So you'll catch him in it right up to the ears,
If you put it away on the larder shelf.
The Rum Tum Tugger is artful and knowing,
The Rum Tum Tugger doesn't care for a cuddle;
But he'll leap on your lap in the middle of your sewing,
For there's nothing he enjoys like a horrible muddle.
Yes the Rum Tum Tugger is a Curious Cat—
  And there isn't any need for me to spout it:
    For he will do
      As he do do
        And there's no doing anything about it!

The Raw Elements of Poetry

The elements of poetry may be roughly compared to the elements of music as shown below. Poetry is intended to be spoken aloud with careful attention to the sounds and meaning of the words.

Music—organized sound	*Poetry*—packed word sounds and pictures
Melody—series of single pitches set to a rhythm (pentatonic/modal/major/minor)	**Line**
Harmony—series of simultaneous pitches set to a rhythm (dissonant/consonant, I [i], IV [iv], V^7)	**Packed Word Pictures** (image, metaphor, simile, symbol, pun, IMSSP)
[Bass]—lowest note of the harmony	**Packed Word Sounds** (head-rhyme [alliteration], mid-rhyme [assonance], end-rhyme, whole-rhyme [onomatopoeia], HMEW)
Rhythm (Time)—pattern of sounds/silences in time: <u>Beat</u>—steady pulse; <u>Meter</u>—organization of the beat (even/odd); and *Tempo*—speed of the beat (slow>fast)	**Rhythm (Time)**—pattern of sounds/silences in time: <u>Syllable</u>—a single uninterrupted sound; <u>Meter</u>—1) the organization of syllables into groups (even or odd) of *stressed* and unstressed syllables and 2) the number of units per line; and *Tempo*—speed of speech
Texture—number, type, and relationship of layers (monophonic homophonic, or polyphonic)	

Colors of Sound
  Dynamics (soft<loud)
  Instrument Pitch Range (low<high)
  Timbre—quality of sound (mellow<piercing, legato<staccato, etc.)
	Colors of Sound
	  Dynamics (soft<loud)
	  Voice Pitch Range (low<high)
	  Timbre—quality of sound (mellow<piercing, legato<staccato, etc.)

Form—structure of a work with central theme (A), development, (A^1, A^2, etc.), contrast (B, C, etc.), and dramatic shape (rising tension, climax, and release)	**Form**—structure of a work with central theme [image] (A), development, (A^1, A^2, etc.), contrast (B, C, etc.), and dramatic shape (rising tension, climax, and release)

Line

The **line** is the basic unit in poetry, whereas in prose it is the sentence. In a work of poetry, the length is determined by the total number of lines. In turn, lines are grouped into **stanzas**, usually of 4 lines each. (Often, in popular terminology, a stanza is called a *verse*, but technically a verse is just one line of a poem.)

From Blank to Blank— by Emily Dickinson (1830–1886)	Lines
From Blank to Blank—	1
A Threadless Way	2
I pushed Mechanic feet—	3
To stop—or perish—or advance—	4
Alike indifferent—	5
If end I gained	6
It ends beyond	7
Indefinite disclosed—	8
I shut my eyes—and groped as well	9
'Twas lighter—to be Blind—	10

Sometimes shorter poems are combined to make a longer work. T. S. Eliot's *Old Possum's Book of Practical Cats* is a poem cycle with 14 poems in the cycle. Each of these, however, is a separate poem. One of the longest poems in English is John Milton's *Paradise Lost*. It has over 10,000 lines divided into 12 chapters (called books). It is almost 25 times the size of Eliot's *The Waste Land*, which has 5 movements (parts) and 403 lines.

Packed Word Pictures

Poetry also uses **packed word pictures** (vivid figures of speech that use words in distinctive ways) to paint with words. Poetry achieves intense concentration in very little space without using the connectives of prose. [A prose version of *My Favorite Things* might begin as follows: "After a gentle rain, I noticed the roses in my garden glistening with raindrops. As I went out to view them more closely, I spied milk on the whiskers of the kittens who had come onto the porch to get out of the rain and…"] Poetry removes the connectives, and juxtaposes the images: "*Raindrops on roses and whiskers on kittens*." By its very nature, poetry is a meditative and reflective form. A figure of speech requires time to understand and let the figure sink in. There are five basic types of packed word pictures: 1) image, 2) metaphor, 3) simile, 4) symbol, and 5) pun (paronomasia) [IMSSP].

An **image** is a word or phrase that names a concrete item or action (raindrops on roses, whiskers on kittens, bright copper kettles, warm woolen mittens, brown paper packages). A **metaphor** is a comparison that designates one thing by using another: ("Juliet is the sun") or ("The Lord *is* my shepherd"). A **simile** may be thought of as a metaphor that uses *like* or *as*: "My love is like a red, red rose," or "His eyes are like a flame of fire." A **symbol** is a word picture that represents something else ("a metaphor *that's not all there*") as when one part of a metaphor is used independently, keeping the same significance: "Shrew" (referring to a woman with a scolding temperament) or "heart" referring to love. The devices above all share the principle of comparison.

Paronomasia or **pun** (play on words) designates two different things by using the same word or similar sounding words: "We must *hang* together, or assuredly we shall all *hang* separately," said Benjamin Franklin at the signing of the Declaration of Independence. In the pun below, the word "springs" could mean the season or gushing water.

> Girls in white dresses with blue satin sashes
>   Snowflakes that fall on my nose and eyelashes
> Silver white winters that melt into springs
>   These are a few of my favorite things

Other common figures of speech used in literature include **apostrophe** (addressing someone who is absent as though they were present: "O Danny Boy"), **hyperbole** (exaggeration for the sake of effect: "My mother told me a million times never to exaggerate," cf. Matthew 18:21–35—100 talents of silver versus 100 pennies), and **personification** (giving inanimate objects or abstractions human qualities or human form: "Father time sat shivering on the road"). Additional figures of speech are listed in the footnote below.[1] Be careful not to be intimidated by these technical terms. What is important is to picture packed word images (whatever their designations), and to word-paint some of your own.

Packed Word Sounds (Rhyme in General)

Like music, poetry uses sounds for their own sake. **Rhyme in general** may be defined as the correspondence of sounds with each other. It is divided into four categories: 1) head rhyme (alliteration), 2) mid rhyme (assonance), 3) end rhyme (what is usually thought of when rhyme is mentioned), and 4) whole rhyme (onomatopoeia).

Head rhyme (alliteration) is the correspondence of the same first sound in consecutive words or on stressed syllables ("raindrops on roses," "copper kettles," "warm woolen," "paper packages") as illustrated below by *My Favorite Things* and Petruchio's first meeting with Kate in *Taming of the Shrew*.

Raindrops on roses and whiskers on kittens,
   Bright copper kettles and warm woolen mittens,
Brown paper packages tied up with strings,
   These are a few of my favorite things.

You lie, in faith, for you are called plain Kate,
And bonny Kate, and sometimes Kate the cursed,
But Kate, the prettiest Kate in Christendom,
Kate of Kate Hall, my super-dainty Kate—
For dainties are all Kates—and therefore, Kate,
Take this of me, Kate of my Consolation:

Mid rhyme (assonance) is the correspondence of the internal sounds of words as in the following examples from *My Favorite Things*.

Raindrops on roses and whiskers on kittens,
   Bright copper kettles and warm woolen mittens,
Brown paper packages tied up with strings,
   These are a few of my favorite things.

Girls in white dresses with blue satin sashes,
   Snowflakes that fall on my nose and eyelashes,

End rhyme is the correspondence of the terminal sounds of words as illustrated below. It is important to understand that some poetry (blank verse, for example) does not have end rhyme, but all poetry has sound rhymes of some kind.

   Raindrops on roses and whiskers on kittens,
      Bright copper kettles and warm woolen mittens,
   Brown paper packages tied up with strings,
      These are a few of my favorite things.

Whole rhyme (onomatopoeia) is a figure of speech in which entire words rhyme with the sound they denote (such as *buzz, crackling, crunching, ding-dong, meow, murmur,* and *ping*) or used and adapted to suggest a sound (such as *snow crackling* and *crunching*). Sound and sense reinforce each other.

---

[1] The following devices are also quite common: *acrostic, allegory, allusion, climax, irony, metonymy, paradox,* and *synecdoche*.

Poetic Rhythm

Poetic Rhythm and Syllable. **Poetic rhythm** itself is a pattern of sounds and silences through time. Instead of the beat, poetry uses the **syllable** (one or more letters representing a unit of spoken language consisting of a single uninterrupted sound).

Poetic Meter. English (in contrast to some other languages) has accents that seem to group themselves into a natural pattern of *stressed* and unstressed syllables: I *tried* to *catch* a *cab* the *oth*-er *day*. **Poetic meter** is 1) the organization of syllables into groups (even or odd) of *stressed* and unstressed syllables, and 2) the number of syllables per line. A **poetic foot** is a grouping consisting of two or three syllables. There are three prevalent types of metrical feet—two even (iambic, trochaic) and one odd (dactylic).[1] These types of poetic meter are illustrated below. *Stressed* syllables are shown in *italics*.[2]

Even (two-syllable group)		Odd (three-syllable group)
Iamb (*iambic*) (begins on unaccented syllable)	*Trochee* (*trochaic*) (begins on accented syllable)	*Dactyl* (*dactylic*) (begins on accented syllable)
weak-*strong* com-*pare*	*strong*-weak *joy*-ful	*strong*-weak-weak *pack*-a-ges
Shall I com-*pare* thee *to* a *sum*-mer's *day*? Iambic (10 syllables) [sometimes called iambic pentameter since there are 5 iambic feet]	*Joy*-ful, *joy*-ful *we* a-*dore* thee, Trochaic (8 syllables)	*Rain*-drops on *ros*-es and *whis*-kers on *kit*-tens, ... *Brown* pa-per *pack*-a-ges *tied* up with *strings*, Dactylic (11 and 10 syllables respectively)

There are three prevalent subdivisions of iambic meter: Common (Ballad) Meter, Long Meter, and Iambic Pentameter. They are distinguished by the number of syllables per line in each stanza (8.6.8.6; 8.8.8.8; and 10.10.10.10 respectively). Iambic pentameter is most often used for fine-art poetry, and common and long meter for folk song-poetry, although there is some crossover. [For example, most of the poetry of Emily Dickinson is written in common (ballad) meter.]

Common Meter [Iambic 8.6.8.6]	**Long Meter [Iambic 8.8.8.8]**	**10.10.10.10 [Iambic Pentameter]**
A-*maz*-ing *grace*! (how *sweet* the *sound*) That *sav'd* a *wretch* like *me*! I *once* was *lost*, but *now* am *found*, Was *blind*, but *now* I *see*.	All *peo*-ple *that* on *earth* do *dwell*, Sing *to* the *Lord* with *cheer*-ful *voice*; Him *serve* with *joy*, his *praise* forth *tell*, Come *ye* be-*fore* him *and* re-*joice*.	Shall *I* com-*pare* thee *to* a *sum*-mer's *day*? Thou *art* more *love*-ly *and* more *tem*-per-*ate*. Rough *winds* do *shake* the *dar*-ling *buds* of *May*, And *sum*-mer's *lease* hath *all* too *short* a *date*.

---

[1] Amphibrachic and anapestic meters are also odd but not as prevalent as dactylic.
[2] Sometimes poets will elide [slur over] syllables in order to maintain the metrical foot [o'er for over]. On the other hand, sometimes poets will *add* syllables in order to maintain the metrical foot [fixèd for fixed]. At other times, poets will mix meters but maintain the same number of accented syllables even though the number of unaccented syllables will change. Other poems are not entirely regular due to rhetorical or syntactic demands.

Trochaic and dactylic meter may have any number of syllables. One possibility for each is shown below. Notice that the second has the same number of syllables as iambic pentameter, but is different because the syllables are divided into three parts rather than two.

8.7.8.7 [Trochaic]	10.10.10.10 [Dactylic]

Joy-ful, *joy*-ful *we* a-*dore* thee,
   God of *glo*-ry *Lord* of *love*;
Hearts un-*fold* like *flowers* be-*fore* thee,
   o-pening *to* the *sun* a-*bove*.
	Be thou my *vi*-sion, O *Lord* of my *heart*;
	Naught be all *else* to me *save* that thou *art*—
	Thou my best *thought*, by *day* or by *night*,
	Wak-ing or *sleep*-ing, thy *pres*-ence my *light*.

A Metrical Index for Setting Poetry to Music and Vice Versa

A metrical index in a songbook (or hymnbook) gives the number of syllables in each line of a tune in order to find tunes that will fit a particular poetic text (or vice versa). It specifies the number of syllables per line rather than the poetic foot and the number of feet. A metrical index usually begins with common meter and long meter (see below for the beginning of a metrical index) and then lists meters in the ascending order of the number of syllables in each line. Any tune on the left in the same category may be used to set any poem on the right and vice versa, so that different poems may be sung to the same tune, and different tunes may set the same poems.

METRICAL INDEX of TUNES

C.M. (Common Meter: 8.6.8.6 iambic) [Ballad Meter]
ANTIOCH -- C3 [*Joy to the World* (Psalm 98)]
GILLIGAN'S ISLAND --- C3 [*Just Sit Right Back and You'll Hear a Tale*]
NEW BRITAIN --- C3 [*Amazing Grace*]

L.M. (Long Meter: 8.8.8.8 iambic)
OLD HUNDREDTH --- C5 [*All People That on Earth Do Dwell* (Psalm 100)]
IN CHRIST ALONE --- C5 [*In Christ Alone*]

7.7.7.7 [Trochaic]
AH, VOUS DIRAIS-JE MAMAN --------------------------------- C7 [*Hallelujah, Praise the Lord* (Psalm 150)]
GLORIA -- C7 [*Angels We Have Heard on High* (Luke 2:8–20)]

8.7.8.7 [Trochaic]
AUSTRIAN HYMN --- C9 [*Glorious Things of Thee Are Spoken*]
ODE TO JOY --- C8 [*Joyful, Joyful, We Adore Thee*]

10.10.10.10…[Iambic]
LONDONDERRY AIR -- C11 [*O Danny Boy*]
FINLANDIA --- C11 [*Be Still, My Soul*]

10.10.10.10 [Dactylic]
MY FAVORITE THINGS --- C12 [*Raindrops on Roses*]
SLANE -- C12 [*Be Thou My Vision*]

Poetic Colors of Sound

Poetic colors of sound (including dynamics, voice pitch range, and timbre) were treated in Chapter 5. Recall the poem *You Are Old, Father William* (page 56). Poetry is intended to be spoken aloud with careful attention to colors of sound as they reflect the images portrayed.

Form in Poetry

Form (discussed later in the text) is the structure of a work with central theme (a), development (a^1, a^2), contrast (b), and dramatic shape (rising tension, climax, and release). In poetry, the theme refers to the central image. In Shakespeare's Sonnet 18, the central image is the comparison between "thee" [you] and "a summer's day." "Thee" [you] is the *a* theme, whereas "a summer's day" is the contrasting *b* theme. Line 2 begins the development of this idea. The climax in a sonnet is known as the **volta** (turning point in a sonnet that is indicated by such words as "But", "Yet," or "And yet" occurring at the beginning of the 9th or 13th lines. [Notice the *volta* ("And then,") in the 9th line of Vivaldi's sonnet for *Spring* on page 134.] A listening guide plus an outline of the form for Shakespeare's Sonnet 18 is provided below.

Guide for Shakespeare's Sonnet 18—*Shall I Compare Thee to a Summer's Day*

Line—14 lines in a Sonnet, grouped 4, 4, 4, and 2
Packed word pictures—You, summer's day, darling buds of May, summer's lease, date, hot eye of heaven, gold complexion, fair, nature's changing course, eternal summer, shade of death, eternal lined, breathing men, seeing eyes, long-living poem, life-giving poem
Packed word sounds—*abab* rhyme for first three stanzas; *cc* for last couplet.
Rhythm/Meter—iambic pentameter throughout
Colors of Sound—reading aloud should portray the meanings and images to the listener

Form	Sonnet 18 (between 1592 and 1609) Shakespeare (Playlist Arts Key 09 [6] or Sonnet 18 Antiqua [15])
central image—*a* (thee) compared to *b* (summer's day) a^1—development b^1 rising tension	Shall I compare thee to a summer's day? Thou art more lovely and more temperate. Rough winds do shake the darling buds of May, And summer's lease hath all too short a date.
b^2 b^3	Sometime too hot the eye of heaven shines, And often is his gold complexion dimmed; And every fair from fair sometime declines, By chance or nature's changing course untrimmed;
volta-a^2 climax a^3	But thy eternal summer shall not fade Nor lose possession of that fair thou ow'st; Nor shall death brag thou wander'st in his shade, When in eternal lines to time thou grow'st:
release a^4	So long as men can breathe, or eyes can see, So long lives this, and this gives life to thee.

The meaning of this poem interacts with its form. Shakespeare begins by comparing his subject to a summer's day, which pales in comparison with his subject. The flowers of May will fade and the beautiful summer will end all too soon. The *volta* begins with the turning point "But thy eternal summer shall not fade…" and culminates with the words "Nor shall death brag thou wander'st in his shade, When in eternal lines to time thou grow'st." The reason that Shakespeare's subject will never see death is that Shakespeare has immortalized his subject in the "eternal lines" of this poem. The subject will live in his poem as long as people "can breathe" or their "eyes can see," as evidenced by the fact that we, five centuries later, are still reading this poem and considering the beauty of its subject!

The Translated Song Poetry of the Bible

In learning about poetry, it is helpful to understand the extraordinary influence of the translated poetry of the Bible on English language and literature, beginning with the Renaissance to the present day (see Insight 10-1 in the following chapter). Approximately one-third of the Bible is poetry. In translated poetry, the word sounds of the original language are lost. However, instead of regular meter and end rhyme, biblical poetry uses parallelism (sometimes referred to as "thought rhyme") in which a second line parallels the first. Psalm 23 provides a helpful example of this parallelism (see divisions of lines) as well as the packed word pictures of poetry. In this lyric poem by David, the shepherd king, the main word picture is simply two words together without any connectives (*adonai—roi*: the Lord—my shepherd). Other vivid word pictures include sheep, green pastures, still waters, paths of righteousness, valley of the shadow of death, rod, staff, table, anointing oil, overflowing cup, and house of the Lord.

Psalm 23

The Lord *is* my shepherd;
    I shall not want.
He maketh me to lie down in green pastures:
    He leadeth me beside the still waters.
He restoreth my soul:
    He leadeth me in the paths of righteousness for his name's sake.

Yea, though I walk through the valley of the shadow of death,
    I will fear no evil:
For thou *art* with me;
    Thy rod and thy staff they comfort me.
Thou preparest a table before me
    In the presence of mine enemies:
Thou anointest my head with oil;
    My cup runneth over.

Surely goodness and mercy shall follow me
    All the days of my life:
And I will dwell in the house of the Lord
    Forever.

The direct English translations of the biblical poetry influenced English poetry by their parallelism and word pictures, but were not suitable for singing. The Psalms were therefore metricized and rhymed in **Psalters** (translated Psalms set to meter and rhyme), which provided the linchpin for hymnody in both England and America. Like the direct translations, these Psalters retained the original word pictures and form of the Psalms. [The history of American music education is tied to Psalm singing: 1640—Publication of the Bay Psalm Book (first full length product of a printing press in America); 1721—*A Practical Introduction to the Singing of Psalm Tunes* by William Tufts; 1832—Lowell Mason becomes the first music teacher in the Boston Public Schools under the direction of Horace Mann.]

The Lord's My Shepherd, I'll Not Want Francis Rous, 1650, Scottish Psalter	*My Shepherd Will Supply My Need* (1719) Isaac Watts (1674–1748)	*The King of Love My Shepherd Is* (1868) Henry W. Baker (1821–1877)	*The LORD, My Shepherd, Rules My Life* Christopher M. Idol, 1977, © 1982. Hope Publishing Co. All rights reserved. Used by permission.
The Lord's my Shepherd; I'll not want. He makes me down to lie In pastures green; He leadeth me The quiet waters by.	My Shepherd will supply my need: The LORD God is His Name; In pastures fresh He makes me feed, Beside the living stream.	The King of love my shepherd is, Whose goodness faileth never; I nothing lack if I am his And he is mine forever.	The LORD, my shepherd, rules my life and gives me all I need; he leads me by refreshing streams; in pastures green I feed.
My soul He doth restore again; And me to walk doth make Within the paths of righteousness, E'en for His own name's sake.	He brings my wandering spirit back When I forsake His ways, And leads me, for His mercy's sake, In paths of truth and grace.	Where streams of living water flow, My ransomed soul he leadeth And, where the verdant pastures grow, With food celestial feedeth.	The LORD revives my failing strength, he makes my joy complete; and in right paths, for his name's sake, he guides my faltering feet.
Yea, though I walk through death's dark vale, Yet will I fear no ill; For Thou art with me, and Thy rod And staff me comfort still.	When I walk through the shades of death, Thy presence is my stay; A word of Thy supporting breath Drives all my fears away.	In death's dark vale I fear no ill With thee, dear Lord, beside me, Thy rod and staff my comfort still, Thy cross before to guide me.	Though in a valley dark as death, no evil makes me fear; your shepherd's staff protects my way, for you are with me there.
My table Thou hast furnished In presence of my foes; My head Thou dost with oil anoint, And my cup overflows.	Thy hand, in sight of all my foes, Doth still my table spread; My cup with blessings overflows, Thine oil anoints my head.	Thou spreadst a table in my sight; Thine unction grace bestoweth; And, oh, what transport of delight From thy pure chalice floweth!	While all my enemies look on, you spread a royal feast; you fill my cup, anoint my head, and treat me as your guest.
Goodness and mercy all my life Shall surely follow me; And in God's house forevermore My dwelling place shall be.	The sure provisions of my God Attend me all my days; O may Thy house be my abode, And all my work be praise! There would I find a settled rest, While others go and come; No more a stranger, nor a guest, But like a child at home.	Perverse and foolish oft I strayed, But yet in love he sought me And gently on his shoulder laid And home, rejoicing, brought me. And so through all the length of days Thy goodness faileth never. Good Shepherd, may I sing thy praise Within thy house forever.	Your goodness and your gracious love pursue me all my days; your house, O LORD, shall be my home— your name, my endless praise.

Enjoying Poetry

Poetry is intended to be heard and read aloud. The elements of poetry are intended to provide a helpful guide. Be careful not to catch *paralysis by analysis*:

The purpose of analysis—
Enjoyment, not paralysis!

Back off if you find yourself analyzing more than enjoying. It is also important to experience poetry independently from music (even if intended to be combined with music). Excellent poetry can stand on its own. After reading aloud (and hearing) the following familiar poems, see if you can pick out the packed word pictures, the packed word sounds, the meter, and the form. [The underlined portions show syllables elided when pronounced. They should be counted as one syllable.] Most of all, enjoy!

Sonnet 116 (between 1592 and 1609)
Let Me Not to the Marriage of True Minds?
William Shakespeare
(Playlist Arts Key 09 [7] or Sonnet 116 Antiqua [13])

Let me not to the marriage of true minds
Admit impediments. Love is not love
Which alters when it alteration finds,
Or bends with the remover to remove:
O no; it is an ever-fixéd mark,
That looks on tempests, and is never shaken;
It is the star to every wandering bark,
Whose worth's unknown, although his height be taken.
Love's not time's fool, though rosy lips and cheeks
Within his bending sickle's compass come;
Love alters not with his brief hours and weeks,
But bears it out even to the edge of doom.

  If this be error and upon me proved,
  I never writ, nor no man ever loved.

The Road Not Taken (1916) Robert Frost

Two roads diverged in a yellow wood,
And sorry I could not travel both
And be one traveler, long I stood
And looked down one as far as I could.
To where it bent in the undergrowth,

Then took the other, just as fair,
And having perhaps the better claim,
Because it was grassy and wanted wear,
Though as for that, the passing there
Had worn them really about the same,

And both that morning equally lay
In leaves no step had trodden black.
Oh, I kept the first for another day!
Yet knowing how way leads on to way
I doubted if I should ever come back.

I shall be telling this with a sigh
Somewhere ages and ages hence:
Two roads diverged in a wood, and I—
I took the one less traveled by,
And that has made all the difference.

Actions for Practice and Delight

9/1. Learn the elements of poetry and their definitions in comparison with the elements of music and their definitions. Learn the nine types of word pictures and word sounds and their definitions (i.e., **I**mage, **M**etaphor, **S**imile, **S**ymbol, and **P**un; **H**ead rhyme [alliteration], **M**id rhyme [assonance], **E**nd rhyme, and **W**hole rhyme (onomatopoeia);) [IMSSP and HMEW]. Listen to the music and poetry on Playlist <u>Arts Key 09 Poetry and Music</u>. In writing, describe your experience and list your favorites.

9/2. Read the six poems at the beginning of this chapter aloud a number of times and let them percolate in your mind. In writing, describe the differences between them and answer the following questions. How does reading these poems aloud help you to understand them? Which one is your favorite, and why? Then, choose your favorite poem from this chapter and practice performing it aloud paying attention to vocal sound color. If you wish, you may alternate lines with a friend. Practice your choice as if you were entering a poetry slam, and be prepared to perform your choice aloud either by yourself or with someone else. [You may wish to memorize your choice.] (As part of this exercise, listen to the recordings of poems and music in <u>Arts Key 09 Poetry and Music</u>.)

9/3. Be sure to know the following three meters and the corresponding song-poems from APPENDIX C: **trochaic** (8.7.8.7 trochaic): *Joyful, Joyful We Adore Thee* (page C8); **iambic pentameter** (10.10.10.10 iambic): *Shall I Compare Thee to a Summer's Day?* (page C10 and C11); and **dactylic** (10.10.10.10 dactylic): *Be Thou My Vision* and/or *My Favorite Things* (page C12). Then, using APPENDIX C, find your favorite song-poem. Practice reading the poem aloud. In writing, explain why it can stand on its own without music. [You may wish to memorize your choice.] Then, find the best tune for that poem. In writing, explain why you chose this tune. (A few of these song-poems are available on recordings in Playlist <u>Arts Key 09 Poetry and Music</u>.)

9/4. Practice reading aloud Shakespeare's Sonnet 116, *Let Me Not to the Marriage of True Minds* and Frost's, *The Road Not Taken* on the previous page. [You may wish to memorize one or both of these poems.] Then, using the elements of poetry, write out a guide for one of these poems as illustrated in the guide on page 103. Using your analysis, continue to practice reading your choice aloud. Submit your written guide, and discuss how your analysis has helped you in learning and reading the poem you have chosen.

9/5. Write a poem. Begin by thinking up (aloud) as many word sounds and word pictures as you can. Keep doing this until a main picture (theme) emerges. Then, work aloud on packing word sounds and pictures relating to the main picture together in different orders. See if you can begin with the main picture, develop your ideas, come to a climax, and attain release. Add rhythm and meter. Write out and turn in your poem, and keep a hard copy for yourself. Then practice it as if you were entering a poetry slam, and be prepared to perform it aloud (or to have someone else perform it), paying attention to dynamics, voice range, and timbre.

Chapter 10
Putting Some English on the Dramatic Story

"Come, come, we are friends, let's have a dance ere we are married, that we may lighten our own hearts and our wives' heels.... Therefore, play music.... Strike up, pipers."[1]

Final scene from Shakespeare's *Much Ado About Nothing* (ca. 1598), directed by Kenneth Branagh, 1993

Many people think of the late Renaissance in England as the time of Shakespeare (1564–1616), poetry, and love. Renaissance is French for "rebirth." The Renaissance in the west (ca. 1450–1600) saw a rebirth of human creativity, adventure, and exploration. (In 1492, Columbus sailed the ocean blue.) Renaissance humanism focused on human life and its accomplishments. Leonardo da Vinci (1452–1519), the model of the *Renaissance man*, was a painter, sculptor, architect, engineer, scientist, and musician. The arts and languages of ancient Hebrew, Greek, and Roman [Latin] cultures provided the resources for a revitalized European world. The Reformation (1517) and subsequent translation of the Bible into vernacular languages spurred the development of widespread literacy and songs based on the Psalms that were sung by common people in their own languages all over Europe. The Bible was translated from Hebrew (Old Testament) and Greek (New Testament) into German by Martin Luther and into English by William Tyndale (not completed when he was burned at the stake), a development that had a formative and lasting influence on both German and English. Subsequently, Shakespeare and the King James Version (using much of Tyndale's work) provided the bedrock for the English language and literature that persists to this day (see following special insight).

---

[1] William Shakespeare, *Much Ado About Nothing*, Act 5, Scene 4, lines 116–118, 120, 127.

Special Insight 10-1 (Page 1 of 2)
The Key to the Aesthetic Development of English: The Two Williams

The key to the aesthetic development of English is found in the works of two Williams, who influenced the English language to an extent never before or since: William Tyndale (ca. 1492–1536) and William Shakespeare (1564–1616). Their contributions during the Renaissance (1450–1600), helped form the English language.

The First William. The translation of the Bible into English by the first William (burned at the stake 28 years before the second William was born) had a lasting impact on English literature that continues to the present day. The linguist and scholar William Tyndale (ca. 1494–1536) began to translate the Bible (roughly 2/3 story and 1/3 poetry) from its original languages into English in 1522. Because the religious authorities in England wanted to allow only the existing Latin translation of the Bible, he was forced to flee for his life. He was able to complete the translation of the entire New Testament, the Torah (first five books of the Bible), Joshua, Judges, Ruth, 1st and 2nd Samuel, 1st and 2nd Kings, 1st and 2nd Chronicles, and the book of Jonah before he was found, extradited to England, and burned at the stake in 1536. (It was illegal to print the Bible in English in England until after his death.) William Tyndale accurately represented the immediacy and poetic parataxis[1] of the Bible by translating the text into English word for word (a feat that helped to distinguish the developing English language from other languages such as Latin). His fresh and direct translation of Greek and Hebrew prose and poetry (left hand column) helped to mold English idioms. In translating the Bible, he used already existing English words in new ways and coined new words and phrases (right hand column) in order to convey the precise sense of the original Hebrew and Greek texts in English.

In the beginning God created heaven and earth. The earth was void and empty and darkness was upon the deep and the Spirit of God moved upon the water. Then God said: Let there be light and there was light.

(Genesis 1:1–3, translated by William Tyndale)

A few examples of his coined words used today

- "*let there be light*" (Genesis 1:3)
- "*my brother's keeper*" (Genesis 4:9)
- "*beautiful*" (Genesis 29:17, et al.)
- "*passover*" (Exodus 12:12–14, et al.)
- "*scapegoat*" (Leviticus 16:8, 10, 26)
- "*peacemakers*" (Matthew 5:9)
- "*the salt of the earth*" (Matthew 5:12)

Tyndale's "unsurpassed ability was to work as a translator with the sounds and rhythms as well as the senses of English to create unforgettable words, phrases, paragraphs and chapters… He has reached more people than even Shakespeare."[2] His translation work was incorporated into almost every subsequent English translation including the Great Bible (Coverdale) in 1539, the Geneva Bible in 1560, the Bishop's Bible in 1568, and the King James Bible in 1611 (over three-fourths of the portions that Tyndale translated)[3], and continues to influence Bible revision and translation to this day. Tyndale's translation provided the spark that ignited the roaring fire of English literature in the 16th century.

---

[1] Side by side placement of phrases or clauses in sequence connected by *and* or with no connectives at all: "In the beginning God created heaven and earth. The earth was void and empty, *and* darkness [*was*] upon the deep, *and* the Spirit of God moved upon the water. Then God said: *and* there was light" (Genesis 1:1–4). "Raindrops on roses *and* whiskers on kittens; bright copper kettles *and* warm woolen mittens" provides yet another example of parataxis.

[2] David Daniell, *William Tyndale: A Biography* (New Haven & London: Yale University Press, 1994), p. 2.

[3] "Based on 18 sampled passages from those portions of the Bible that Tyndale translated, we conclude that for the New Testament Tyndale' contribution is about 84 per cent of the text, while in the Old Testament about 76 per cent of his words have been retained" from Jon Nielson and Royal Skousen, "How Much of the King James Bible Is William Tyndale's? An Estimation Based on Sampling," in *Reformation* 3 (1998): 49-74.

Special Insight 10-1—*The Key to the Aesthetic Development of English* (Page 2 of 2)

<u>The Second William</u>. The poetry and plays of William Shakespeare (1564–1616) added the fuel that turned the roaring fire of English literature into an inferno. There is evidence Shakespeare was familiar with the work of Tyndale (either in Tyndale's original translations or in his translations incorporated into the Geneva Bible). For example, he takes King Henry VI's words ("For blessèd are the peacemakers on earth"[1]) directly from Tyndale's translation (using one of Tyndale's coined words): "Blessed are the peacemakers: for they shalbe called the chyldren of God" (original spelling).[2] With hundreds of references and a number of direct quotes from the Bible, Shakespeare's forty plays average forty references each.[3] Shakespeare expanded the six thousand different words of the English Bible to almost four times as many. His one hundred fifty-four sonnets were the culmination of a tradition originating in the late Middle Ages with the Italian Francesco Petrarch (1304–1374). Regarded as the greatest English author ever, Shakespeare continues to set the standard for English today.[4]

<u>In Their Own Words</u>. To understand Tyndale and Shakespeare, it is helpful to be familiar with the following words that are still, on occasion, used today (for example, in the movie *O Brother, Where Art Thou*).[5] The use of *Thou*, *Thee*, *Thy*, and *Thine* parallels the use of *I*, *Me*, *My*, and *Mine*.

The Two Williams' Words and Ours (First Person)	The Two Williams' Words (and Ours) (Second Person)	Part of Speech
I	*Thou* (You)	Singular Subject
Me	*Thee* (You)	Singular Object
My	*Thy* (Your)	Singular Possessive
Mine	*Thine* (Yours)	Singular Possessive Object
We	*Ye* (You)	Plural Subject

Verbs for the third person singular use <u>th</u> or <u>eth</u> in place of our current <u>s</u> or <u>es</u>. In turn, the second person singular *thou* uses an <u>st</u> or <u>est</u> instead of the third person singular <u>th</u> or <u>eth</u>. Representative examples are given below.

Our Words and (*the Two Bills' Words*)		Parts of Speech
You have (*Thou* ha*st*)	Second person	You lead (*Thou* lead*est*)
He has (He ha*th*)	Third Person	He leads (He lead*eth*)

In certain irregular instances, verbs for the second person singular *thou* simply add a *t* while the third person singular remains the same as our usage today.

Our Words and (*the Two Bills' Words*)		
You are (*Thou* art)	You were (*Thou* wast)	You will/shall (*Thou wilt/shalt*)
He is	He was	He will/shall

---

[1] *King Henry VI*, Part II, Act 2, Scene 1, line 34 (in perfect iambic pentameter).
[2] Tyndale's translation of Matthew 5:9.
[3] See Naheeb Shaheen, *Biblical References in Shakespeare's Plays* (Newark, Delaware: University of Delaware Press, 1999).
[4] Reams of references regarding Shakespeare make additional commentary superfluous here.
[5] *O Brother, Where Are You* just lacks the same ring as *O Brother, Where Art Thou* (released in 2000).

Bringing the Stories of the Bible to Life for the English Reader

It was William Tyndale (ca. 1484–1536) who brought the stories of the Bible to life for the English reader, shortly after Columbus sailed the ocean blue in 1492. [Well-known stories from the Bible include *The Creation of the World*, *Noah and the Flood*, *Abraham and Isaac*, *Joseph and His Brothers*, *Moses and the Exodus*, *Samson and Delilah*, and *David and Goliath*. The list goes on and on. For a helpful overview of the Bible as literature see *The Bible as Literature* at *http://bibleasliterature.wordpress.com*.] Tyndale's translation captures the beauty and shape of the original Hebrew, molding the developing English language and subsequent literature and culture to the present day.

The Raw Elements of Story

The biblical folk story of *Samson and Delilah*, as translated into English by William Tyndale, illustrates the elements of story. A story is an organized account of events in time, whereas music is organized sound in time. For purposes of comparison, the raw elements of music and story are shown below.

Music—organized sound in time	*Story*—organized account of events in time
Melody—series of single pitches set to a rhythm (pentatonic/modal/major/minor)	**Characters**—what people are like, their psychological make-up and motivation
Harmony—series of simultaneous pitches set to a rhythm (dissonant/consonant, I [i], IV [iv], V^7)	**Word Choice**—word usage and vocabulary
[Bass]—the lowest note of a chord	**Setting**—<u>cultural</u>: pattern of behaviors and values in the society; <u>historical</u>: when (hour, day, time, year, and context of activities); and <u>physical</u>: specific location and its conditions.
Rhythm—pattern of sounds/silences in time: <u>Beat</u>—steady pulse; <u>Meter</u>—organization of the beat (even/odd); and <u>Tempo</u>—speed of the beat (slow>fast)	**Rhythm**—pattern of sounds/silences in time: no steady beat; unmetered (except for poetry); and <u>Tempo</u>—speed (slow>fast)
Texture—number, type, and relationship of layers	
Colors of Sound Dynamics (soft<loud) Instrument Pitch Range (low<high) Timbre—quality of sound (mellow<piercing, etc.)	**Colors of Sound** Dynamics (soft<loud) Voice Pitch Range (low<high) Timbre—quality of sound (mellow<piercing, etc.)
FORM—Central theme (A), development (A^1, A^2), contrast (B, C), and dramatic shape.	**FORM**—Central theme (A), development (A^1, A^2), contrast (B, C), and dramatic shape.

Characters show what people are like, their psychological make-up and motivation. Characters have major roles and minor roles. Interest and variety lie in how the people in the story react to specific situations. Characters may be introduced by direct description either by themselves or someone else, by the response of other characters, by their own words and thoughts, and/or by their actions. In a short story (500–10,000 words that can be read in one sitting), characters are usually introduced by dialogue and action rather than by comment and description. [*Samson and Delilah* is a short story of approximately 1,000 words.] Every story has a central character or **protagonist** (hero). There may be more than one protagonist, although in classical Greek literature there could only be one. There may also be an **antagonist** (villain), who is the opposite of the protagonist. [In the story of *Samson and Delilah*, Samson is the protagonist and Delilah and the Philistines are the antagonists.)

Word choice refers to word usage and vocabulary in a story. Prose opens up and unpacks the packed word pictures of poetry. It adds connectives, subordinate clauses, and narrative sequences. In addition, prose narrative often includes poetry. A story may even be told completely in poetry as in an epic poem.

Setting includes physical, historical, and cultural aspects of a story. The cultural setting is the pattern of behaviors and values in the society (family relationships, political climate, gender roles, etc.). The historical setting is the hour, day, time, year, and context of the activities that make up the mood for that period. The physical setting is the specific location (a room, a house, a street, etc.) and its conditions (objects, geography, and climate).

The **rhythm** of a story may be defined as the pattern of sounds and silences in time. Prose stories have no regular beat or meter, although they do have *tempo* or pace. Poetic stories have regular meter.

A story is intended to be told aloud with careful attention to the **colors of sound** and meaning of the words including dynamics, voice pitch range, and timbre as noted in Chapter 5. In pre-literate societies, stories were passed along from generation to generation by oral tradition.

Form (thought, plot) is the structure of a work with central theme (**A**), development (A^1, A^2, etc.), contrast (*B*, *C*, etc.), and dramatic shape (*rising tension, climax,* and *release*). In story and theatre, form is synonymous with **thought** and **plot**, which refers to overall design. [The central theme is equivalent to *Aristotle's Thought/Theme/Ideas* and the remainder to Aristotle's *Plot*]. The beginning **theme(s)** section states the theme(s), and provides background information for what is to come. The **development** (complication) section introduces a conflict and **contrast** that frustrates the expected course of events. It builds tension and leads to a **climax**. The final section, the **release** (sometimes called the *dénouement*, Old French for "untangling"), provides the resolution of the plot after the climax of the development section. Sometimes there is a **prologue** (an introduction) and an **epilogue** (an afterword telling what happened afterward). Other aspects of the plot include **foreshadowing** (an advance hint of something that is about to happen, preparing for something to come), **discovery** (the revelation of unexpected information), and **reversal** in which fortune turns to disaster or vice versa.

Samson and Delilah

Samson and Delilah [*Dalilah*] is an ancient folk story found in Judges (the seventh book in the Bible), found on the following pages with Tyndale's translation on the left and his words with current meanings on the right. A helpful approach is to read the story aloud in both the 1534 and the updated versions, paying careful attention to sound colors (volume, pitch range, and timbre) and the word choice of each character and the narrator.

Judges 16—William Tyndale Translation (1534)	**Tyndale's words updated into current language**
And after that he loved a woman, upon the river of Sorek, called Dalilah unto whom came the Lords of the Philistines, and said unto her: Flatter with him and see wherein his great strength lieth, and by what means we may have power over him, that we may bind him, to bring him under, and we will give every man eleven hundred silverlings. And Dalilah said to Samson. Oh, tell me where thy great strength lieth, and if thou were bound wherewith men might constrain thee.	And after that he loved a woman, *in the valley* of Sorek, called Dalilah *to* whom came the Lords of the Philistines, and said *to* her, "Flatter him and see *where* his great strength *lies*, and by what means we may have power over him, that we may bind him, to bring him under, and we will give every man eleven hundred *pieces of silver*." And Dalilah said to Samson, "Oh, tell me where *your* great strength *lies*, and if *you* were bound *how* men might *restrain you*."
And Samson said unto her: If men bound me with seven green withies that were never dried, I should be weak and as another man. And then the Lords of the Philistines brought her seven withies that were yet green and never dried and she bound him therewith. Notwithstanding she had men lying in wait with her in the chamber. And she said unto him, the Philistines be upon thee Samson. And he brake the cords as a string of tow breaketh, when it feeleth fire. And so his strength was not known.	And Samson said *to* her, "If men bound me with seven *fresh bowstrings* that were never dried, I should be weak and as another man." And then the Lords of the Philistines brought her seven *fresh bowstrings* that were never dried and she bound him *with them. Now* she had men lying in *ambush in an inner room*. And she said *to* him, "The Philistines *are* upon *you* Samson." And he *broke* the *bowstrings* as a *thread of flax breaks*, when it *touches* fire. And so *the secret of* his strength was not known.
Then said Dalilah to Samson: See thou hast mocked me and told me lies. Now yet tell me I pray thee, wherewith thou mightest be bound. And he said: If I were bound with new ropes that never were occupied, then should I be weak, and as another man. And Dalilah took new ropes and bound him therewith, and said unto him, the Philistines be upon thee Samson. And there were layers of wait in the chamber, and he brake them from off his arms, as they had been but a thread.	Then said Dalilah to Samson, "See, *you have* mocked me and told me lies. Now tell me *please, how you might* be bound." And he said, "If I were bound with new ropes that never were *used*, then should I be weak, and as another man." And Dalilah took new ropes and bound him with *them*, and said *to* him, "The Philistines *are* upon *you* Samson." And there were *men lying in ambush in an inner room*, and he *broke the ropes* off his arms, *like* a thread.
And Dalilah said unto Samson, hitherto thou hast beguiled me and told me lies: I pray thee yet tell me wherewith men may bind thee. And he said unto her: If thou plaitedest the seven locks of my head with an hair lace and fasten them with a nail. And she said unto him, the Philistines be upon thee Samson. And he awaked out of his sleep, and plucked and went away with the nail that was in the plaiting and with the hair lace.	And Dalilah said *to* Samson, "*Up to now you have deceived* me and told me lies: *please* tell me *how* men may bind *you*." And he said *to* her, "If *you weave* the seven locks of my *hair into the fabric on the loom* and *tighten* them with a *pin*." And she said *to* him, "The Philistines *are* upon *you* Samson." And *he awoke* out of his sleep, and *pulled* and went away with the *pin* that was in the loom and with the *fabric*.
Then she said unto him: How canst thou say that thou lovest me, when thine heart is not with me: for thou hast mocked me this three times, and hast not told wherein thy great strength lieth. And as she lay upon him with her words continually vexing of him, his soul was encumbered even unto the death. And he told her all his heart, and said unto her: there never came razor nor shears upon mine head, for I have been an abstainer to God even from my mothers womb. If mine hair were cut off, my strength would go from me, and I should wax and be like all other men.	Then she said *to* him, "How *can you* say that *you love* me, when *your* heart is not with me: for *you have* mocked me *these* three times, and *have* not told *where your* great strength *lies*." And as she *pressed* him *daily* with her words *and urged him*, his soul was *annoyed* to death. And he told her all his heart, and said *to* her, "*A razor has never come on my* head, for I have been *a Nazarite* to God even from my mother's womb. If *my* hair *was* cut off, my strength would go from me, and I should *become weak* and be like all other men."

10—Putting Some English on the Dramatic Story

And when Dalilah saw that he had told her all his heart, she sent for the Philistines saying, come up yet this once, for he hath showed me all his heart. Then the Lords of the Philistines came and brought the money in their hands. And she made him sleep upon her lap, and sent for a man, and cut off the seven locks of his head and began to vex him. But his strength was gone from him. And she said the Philistines be upon thee Samson. And he awoke out of his sleep and thought to go out as at other times before and shake himself, and knew not that the Lord was departed from him. But the Philistines took him and put out his eyes, and brought him down to Gaza, and bound him with fetters. And he was made to grind in the prison house, how be it the hair of his head began to grow again after that he was shorn.

Then the Lords of the Philistines gathered them together, for to offer a solemn offering unto Dagon their God, and to rejoice: for they said, our God hath delivered Samson our enemy into our hands. And when the people saw him, they praised their God: for they said our God hath delivered into our hands our enemy, that destroyed our country and slew many of us. And when their hearts were merry, they said: send for Samson and let him play before us. And they fetched Samson out of the prison house, and he played before them, and they set him between the pillars. And Samson said unto the lad that led him by the hand: set me that I may touch the pillars that the house stands upon, and that I may lean to them. And the house was full of men and women. And there was all the lords of the Philistines. And there were upon the roof a three thousand men and women, that beheld how Samson played.

And Samson called unto the Lord, and said: my Lord [God] think upon me, and strengthen me, at this time only O' God, that I may be avenged of the Philistines for my two eyes. And Samson caught the two middle pillars on which the house stood and on which it was borne up, the one in his right hand, and the other in his left, and said: my soul die with the Philistines, and bowed them with might. And the house fell upon the lords and upon all the people that were therein. And so the dead which he slew at his death, were more than they which he slew in his life. And then his brethren and all the house of his father; came down and took him up, and brought him and buried him between Zaraah and Esthaol, in the burying place of Manoah his father. And he judged Israel twenty years.

Taken from William Tyndale's translation in the Matthew Bible.

And when Dalilah saw that he had told her all his heart, she sent for the Philistines saying, "Come up *once more*, for he hath showed me all his heart." Then the Lords of the Philistines came and brought the money in their hands. And she made him sleep *on* her lap, and sent for a man, and cut off the seven locks of his head and began to *torment* him. But his strength was gone from him. And she said, "the Philistines *are* upon *you* Samson." And he awoke out of his sleep and thought, "*I will* go out as at other times *and shake myself free*," and *did not know* that the Lord *had* departed from him. But the Philistines took him and *gouged* out his eyes, and brought him down to Gaza, and bound him with *chains*. And he *ground at the mill* in the prison house; *however*, the hair of his head began to grow again after *it was shaved off*.

Then the Lords of the Philistines gathered together to offer a *great sacrifice to* Dagon their God, and to rejoice: for they said, "Our God *has* delivered Samson our enemy into our hands." And when the people saw him, they praised their God: for they said, "Our God *has* delivered *our enemy into our hands, who* destroyed our country and *killed* many of us." And when their hearts were merry, they said, "Send for Samson and let him *entertain* us." And they *called* Samson out of the prison house, and he *entertained* them, and they set him between the pillars. And Samson said *to* the *boy who* led him by the hand, "*Let me feel* the pillars that the house *rests on, so that I can* lean *on* them." And the house was full of men and women. And there *were* all the lords of the Philistines. And there were upon the roof three thousand men and women *looking on while* Samson *entertained them*.

And Samson called *to* the Lord, and said, "My Lord *God* think *about* me, and strengthen me, at this time only, O God, *so that* I may be avenged of the Philistines for my two eyes." And Samson *grasped* the two middle pillars on which the house stood and on which it *rested*, the one in his right hand, and the other in his left, and said, "*Let me* die with the Philistines," and *bent* them with *all his* might. And the house fell upon the lords and upon all the people that were *in it*. And so the dead *whom* he *killed* at his death were more than *those whom* he *killed* in his life. And then his *brothers* and all the house of his father; came down and took him up, and brought him and buried him between Zaraah and Esthaol, in the *tomb* of Manoah his father. And he judged Israel twenty years.

Guide to *Samson and Delilah*

Characters—Samson, the tragic hero; Delilah (*Dalilah*), the villainess; Lords of the Philistines, villains

Word Choice—First full English translation of the Bible from original languages with the coined words of William Tyndale

Setting—<u>cultural</u>: the values of the Hebrews (Samson) are set against the values of their enemies (the Philistines); <u>historical</u>: ca. 1050 B.C.; <u>physical</u>: valley of Sorek near Gaza in Philistia

Colors of Sound—change according to specific characters and narrator

Form: See below

Form	Dramatic Shape	Setting	Story
A B C	Themes	Valley of Sorek, Delilah's house	Samson (A) falls in love with Delilah (B) who is a Philistine The Philistine lords (C) ask Delilah to discover the secret of Samson's strength
B^1 A^1	rising tension release		Delilah's first request Samson's reply: green bowstrings Samson breaks bowstrings
B^2 A^2	rising tension release		Delilah's second request Samson's reply: new ropes Samson breaks new ropes
B^3 A^3	Tension release		Delilah's third request Samson's reply: hair woven into the fabric of the loom Samson breaks loom and extracts his hair
B^4 A^4	rising tension release		Delilah's fourth request Samson's reply: shave off my hair Samson cannot break free
A^5		Philistia—Prison-house	Samson's eyes gouged out and grinding at the mill in the prison-house
C^1 A^6	rising tension ultimate climax	Temple of Dagon	Philistines mock Samson Samson bends pillars of the house, and the roof falls in
A^7	release	Manoah's tomb between Zaraah and Esthaol	Samson is buried and remembered

As another example of story, you may wish to read the longer story of *Joseph and His Brothers* in Genesis, chapters 37, 39–45. Appendix B (page B1) contains a reading guide, and page B2 contains food for thought.

Story and the Other Arts

There is a close relationship between story and the other arts. Many times stories are told in poetry, and this poetry is often set to music. Examples include the folk song *Samson and Delilah* as popularized by *The Grateful Dead* and others, and the popular song *Run, Samson, Run* by Neil Sedaka. The opera *Samson and Delilah* contains the famous dance, *Bacchanale*. Many artists have painted scenes from *Samson and Delilah*, including the *The Blinding of Samson* by Rembrandt.

Rembrandt van Rijn (1606–1669) *The Blinding of Samson* (1636) oil on canvas, 236 x 302 cm, Städelsches Kunstinstitut, Frankfurt.

The Raw Elements of Theatre

There is an even closer relationship between story and theatre. Any story may be made into a play by adding ***Artistic*** Setting and **Action** in place of narrative connections.

Story—organized account of events in time	*Theatre*—story acted out through time and space
Characters—what people are like, their psychological make-up and motivation	Characters—what people are like, their psychological make-up and motivation [*Aristotle's characters*]
Word Choice—word usage and vocabulary	Word Choice—word usage and vocabulary [*Aristotle's characters/language*]
Setting—cultural: pattern of behaviors and values in the society; historical: when (hour, day, time, year, and context of activities); and physical: specific location and its conditions.	***Artistic*** Setting (lights/sets/costumes/props) [*Aristotle's Spectacle*]
Rhythm—pattern of sounds/silences in time: no steady beat; unmetered (except for poetry); and *Tempo*—speed (slow>fast)	Rhythm—poetry or prose [*Aristotle's music*] and Space—positive or negative

Colors of Sound
    Dynamics (soft<loud)
    Voice Pitch Range (low<high)
    Timbre—quality of sound (mellow<piercing, etc.)
	Colors of Sound and Colors of Light +
	Body Shape
	Energy
	Action

FORM	FORM

Artistic Setting in a play includes: 1) relationship between actors and audience, 2) scene design, 3) lighting design, 4) costume design, and 5) props (properties). The *relationship between actors and audience* may be changed by the theatre design: arena, thrust, or proscenium. In an arena theatre (theatre in the round), the audience surrounds the actors on all sides. In a thrust (three-quarter) theatre, the audience surrounds the stage on three sides. In a proscenium theatre, the audience sits on one side and views the action through a frame. *Scene design* uses the elements of art to create an environment appropriate to the play. [A **scene** is a stage setting where a particular event occurs.] *Lighting design* includes setting the mood for the play, illuminating the times and places of the action (night, day, inside, outside), spotlighting major characters and settings, and highlighting tempo and dynamics of the action. *Costume design* also underscores the times and places of the action, emphasizes important characters and their characteristics, and points out the relationships between them. *Props* (divided into *hand props* and *set props*) underline the character of the characters and the mood of the play.

Action in a play includes the movement of the actors, blocking the action, and choreography of fight scenes and dances. The playwright may give sparse or extensive directions as to the movement of a play.

The story of *Samson and Delilah* illustrates how a story may be turned into a play. We might begin by using the dialogue given, and changing narrative connections into sets and actions. Try writing the *Samson and Delilah* story as a play, as illustrated below. Then cast the actors using people you know, design the scenes, design the costumes, describe the props, and describe the lighting.

THE PERSONS OF THE PLAY

SAMSON, muscular he-man, Hebrew
DELILAH, feminine charmer, Philistine
LORDS OF THE PHILISTINES, politicians
PHILISTINE CROWD, raucous spectators

ACT 1, SCENE 1
[*Delilah in a secret room with the Philistines*]
Lords of the Philistines (to Delilah): Flatter him and see *where* his great strength *lies*, and by what means we may have power over him, that we may bind him, to bring him under, and we will give every man eleven hundred *pieces of silver*.
[*Delilah in her living room, stroking Samson's hair*]
Delilah: Oh, tell me where *your* great strength *lies*, and if *you* were bound *how* men might *restrain you*.
Samson: If men bound me with seven *fresh bowstrings* that were never dried, I should be weak and as another man.
[*Delilah binds Samson with fresh bowstrings.*]
Delilah: "The Philistines *are* upon *you* Samson."
[*Samson snaps the fresh bowstrings like a thread.*]
Delilah: "See, *you have* mocked me and told me lies. Now tell me *please, how you might* be bound."
Samson: If I were bound with new ropes that never were *used*, then should I be weak, and as another man.
[*Delilah binds Samson with new ropes.*]
Delilah: "The Philistines *are* upon *you* Samson."
[*Samson snaps the new ropes like a thread.*]
etc.

Much Ado About Nothing

Much Ado About Nothing, written by William Shakespeare in 1598–1599, serves as our primary example of play. This fine-art story has a different purpose than the folk story of *Samson and Delilah*. Rather than being primarily about family relationships (after all, it is *about nothing*), it is about the aesthetic enjoyment of *how* the story *about nothing* is told. It revels in the *witty use* of words, the *stilted use* of words, and the *misuse* of similar sounding words with humorous results (**malapropism**). Look for aesthetic wit, *putting English on*[1] English (Beatrice and Benedick), *putting no English* on English (Claudio), and *putting reverse English on* English (Dogberry, the constable).

An enjoyable way to get into this play is to watch the highly-acclaimed 1993 movie of this play (directed by Kenneth Branagh), available through *iTunes* and *Netflix*. Shakespeare's play presents comedy about two sets of romances, one between Beatrice (Emma Thompson) and Benedick (Kenneth Branagh), and the other between Hero (a pun since she is a heroine, Kate Beckinsale) and Claudio (Robert Sean Leonard). There is a villain, Don John (Keanu Reeves), a hilarious bumbling constable (Michael Keaton), and a Prince, Don Pedro (Denzel Washington).[2]

A brief introduction follows. There are five **acts** (major divisions of the play) with two scenes in Act 1 and two in Act 2, five scenes in Act 3, two scenes in Act 4, and four scenes in act 5. The play begins with Beatrice (a confirmed bachelorette) and Benedick (a confirmed bachelor) sparring intensely, matching wit for wit. Then, Claudio falls in love with Hero (the heroine). Don Pedro (the Prince) agrees to ask Hero to marry Claudio. Hero agrees, and Don John secretly hatches a plot to foil the marriage by accusing Hero of infidelity. Meanwhile, Don Pedro, Claudio, and Hero conspire to set a lover's trap for Beatrice and Benedick. Later, Dogberry (the Constable) and his men discover Don John's plot. The details and the rest of the story are left for you to discover on your own.

Before watching the play in its entirety, it may be helpful to read and understand several of the sections in Shakespearian English and their translation and to watch the corresponding clips on *YouTube* where available. Shakespeare's original words are in the left hand column with a translation into more current language on the right by the author of this text. Beatrice (Emma Thompson) begins with a derogatory pun for Benedick, calling him *Mr. Uppercut*.

---

[1] To "*put English on*" means literally to put spin on the ball when you hit it, or figuratively to stylize something with great panache.
[2] As a matter of interest, Michael Keaton played Batman in *Batman* and *Batman Returns*, and Kenneth Branagh, Emma Thompson, and Imelda Stanton were *Harry Potter* professors in one or more of the movies, *Chamber of Secrets*, *Prisoner of Azkaban*, and *Order of the Phoenix*: Gilderoy Lockhart, Sybil Trelawney, and Dolores Umbridge respectively.

Clip 1: Act 1, Scene 1, excerpts from lines 29–90. (The script below follows the Branagh movie, 3:45–5:20.)

[Shakespeare's words]	[Contemporary translation by Allen Paul Schantz]
Beatrice: *Is Signior Montanto returned from the wars or no?* ***Messenger***: *I know none of that name, lady.* ***Hero***: *My cousin means Signior Benedick of Padua.* ***Messenger***: *He's returned and as pleasant as ever he was.* ***Beatrice***: *I pray you, how many hath he killed and eaten in these wars? But how many hath he killed? For indeed I promised to eat all of his killing.* ***Messenger***: *He hath done good service and a good soldier too, lady.* ***Beatrice***: *And a good soldier to a lady. But what is he to a lord?* ***Messenger***: *A lord to a lord. A man to a man, stuffed with all honorable virtues.* ***Beatrice***: *It is so, indeed. He is no less than a stuffed man.* ***Leonato***: *You must not, sir, mistake my niece. There is a kind of merry war betwixt Signior Benedick and her. They never meet but there's a skirmish of wit between them.* ***Beatrice***: *Who is his companion now? He hath every month a new sworn brother.* ***Messenger***: *He is most in the company of the right noble Claudio.* ***Beatrice***: *O, lord! He will hang upon him like a disease. He is sooner caught than the pestilence, and the taker runs presently mad. God help the noble Claudio! If he have caught the Benedick it will cost him a thousand pound ere he be cured.* ***Messenger***: *I will keep friends with you, lady.* ***Beatrice***: *Do, good friend.* ***Leonato***: *You will never run mad, niece.* ***Beatrice***: *No, not till a hot January.* ***Messenger***: *Don Pedro is approaching!*	**Beatrice**: Please tell me, has Mr. *Uppercut* returned from battle or not? **Messenger**: I don't know anyone by that name, lady. **Hero**: My cousin means Mr. Benedick from Padua. **Messenger**: Yes, he's returned, and he is as pleasant as ever. **Beatrice**: Please tell me, how many men has he killed and eaten in this battle? I promised him I would eat anyone he killed. **Messenger**: He has served well, and he's a good soldier too, lady. **Beatrice**: So he's a good soldier *to a lady*. So what is he to a lord? **Messenger**: He's lord's lord and a man's man, stuffed with all good virtues. **Beatrice**: You're so right. He is a *stuffy* man. **Leonato**: (aside) Please don't take my niece the wrong way. There is kind of a battle between Mr. Benedick and her. Every time they meet, they go at it to see who can outwit the other. **Beatrice**: Who is his companion now? Every month he has a new best friend. **Messenger**: His new best friend is the right noble Claudio. **Beatrice**: O, lord! He will infect him like a disease. He is more infectious than the plague, and whoever is infected will go mad. God help the noble Claudio. If he's *caught the Benedick*, it will cost him lots of money before he can be cured. **Messenger**: I'll be sure to stay on your good side, lady. **Beatrice**: Do that, good friend. **Leonato**: You will never *catch the Benedick* and go mad, niece. **Beatrice**: No, not till hell freezes over. **Messenger**: Don Pedro is coming!

Clip 2: Act 1, Scene 1, excerpts from lines 98–139 (9:50–11:26) [*YouTube* keywords: Much Ado Scene 1 Branagh Eluria8].

[*Benedick arrives with Don Pedro and both join the conversation.*] **Don Pedro**: I think this is your daughter. **Leonato**: Her mother hath many times told me so. **Benedick**: Were you in doubt, sir, that you asked her? **Leonato**: Signor Benedick, no. **Benedick**: If Signior Leonato be her father she would not have his head on her shoulders for all Messina. **Beatrice**: I wonder that you will still be talking, Signior Benedick. Nobody marks you. **Benedick**: What, my dear Lady Disdain! Are you yet living? **Beatrice**: Is it possible disdain should die while she hath such meet food to feed it as Signior Benedick? Courtesy itself must convert to disdain if you come in her presence. **Benedick**: Then is courtesy a turncoat. But it is certain I am loved of all ladies, only you excepted and I would I could find in my heart that I had not a hard heart, for truly I love none. **Beatrice**: A dear happiness to women. They would else be troubled with a pernicious suitor. I thank God and my cold blood, I am of your humor for that. I had rather hear my dog bark at a crow than a man swear he loves me. **Benedick**: God keep your ladyship still in that mind so some gentleman or other shall 'scape a predestinate scratched face. **Beatrice**: Scratching could not make it worse, an 'twere such a face as yours were. **Benedick**: Well, you are a rare parrot-teacher. **Beatrice**: A bird of my tongue is better than a beast of yours. **Benedick**: I would my horse had the speed of your tongue! But keep your way, in God's name I have done. **Beatrice**: You always end with a jade's trick. I know you of old.	[*Benedick arrives with Don Pedro and both join the conversation.*] **Don Pedro**: I think this is your daughter. **Leonato**: Her mother has many times told me so. **Benedick**: Were you so much in doubt, sir, that you had to ask her? **Leonato**: Mr. Benedick, no. **Benedick**: Even if Mr. Leonato is her father she wouldn't want to have his head on her shoulders. **Beatrice**: I wonder why you are still talking, Mr. Benedick. Nobody's listening to you. **Benedick**: Well, hello, dear *Lady Disdain*. Aren't you dead yet? **Beatrice**: How could *Lady Disdain* die as long as she can feed on you, Mr. Benedick? Even *Lady Courtesy* becomes *Lady Disdain* when you're around. **Benedick**: Then *Lady Courtesy* is a traitor. But it is certain that all ladies love me except for you, and it's too bad for them that I'm so hard-hearted—I don't love anyone. **Beatrice**: Women should be very happy they don't have a destructive suitor like you. I thank God and my cold blood, that like you, I don't want romance. I would rather hear my dog bark at a crow than hear a man swear he loves me. **Benedick**: God keep your ladyship in that frame of mind, so some poor gentleman can escape having his face scratched up. **Beatrice**: Scratching couldn't make it worse, even if he had a face as ugly as yours **Benedick**: Same to you, rare parrot-teacher! **Beatrice**: Better to be a talking parrot than your horse's mouth. **Benedick**: If only my horse had the speed of your tongue. But have your way—I'm done with you. **Beatrice**: You always end with a vicious horse's trick. You never change.

Clip 3: Benedick and Claudio, Act 1, Scene 1, excerpts from lines 154–185 [12:22–13:52]

[*Exit all but Benedick and Claudio*] ***Claudio***: *Benedick, didst thou note the daughter of Signior Leonato?* ***Benedick***: *I noted her not, but I looked on her.* ***Claudio***: *Is she not a modest young lady?* ***Benedick***: *Do you question me for my simple true judgment or would you have me speak after my custom, a professed tyrant to their sex?* ***Claudio***: *No. I pray thee speak in sober judgment.* ***Benedick***: *Why, i'faith me thinks she's too low for a high praise, too brown for a fair praise, and too little for a great praise. This commendation I can afford her, that were she other, she were unhandsome and being no other but as she is, I do not like her.* ***Claudio***: *Thou thinkest I am in sport. I pray thee tell me truly how thou likest her.* ***Benedick***: *Would you buy her, that you enquire after her?* ***Claudio***: *Can the world buy such a jewel?* ***Benedick***: *Yea, and a case to put it into. But speak you this with a sad brow?* ***Claudio***: *In mine eyes, she is the sweetest lady that ever I looked on.* ***Benedick***: *I can see yet without spectacles and I see no such matter. There's her cousin, an' she were not possessed with a fury exceeds her as much in beauty as the first of May doth the last of December. But I hope you have no intent to turn husband. Have you?* ***Claudio***: *I would scarce trust myself though I had sworn the contrary if Hero would be my wife.*	[*Exit all but Benedick and Claudio*] **Claudio**: Benedick, did you notice the daughter of Signior Leonato? **Benedick**: I didn't *notice* her, but I did see her. **Claudio**: Isn't she a nice young lady? **Benedick**: Do you want my simple true opinion or would you rather have me speak in my usual way, critical of all women? **Claudio**: No. Please give me your serious opinion. **Benedick**: Well, in my opinion, I think she's too short for high praise, too dark for bright praise, and too small for great praise. I can only commend her in this way: if she was anything else than the way she is, she'd be ugly, but since she's the way she is, I don't like her. **Claudio**: You think I'm kidding you. Please, tell me what you really think of her. **Benedick**: Are you intending to buy her? Is that why you're asking about her? **Claudio**: Can all the money in the world buy such a jewel? **Benedick**: Yes, and a jewel case to put it into. But, are you really serious? **Claudio**: In my eyes, she is the sweetest woman that I've ever seen. **Benedick**: I can still see without glasses and I can't see what you're talking about. There's her cousin (Beatrice) who, if she didn't have such a temper, would be so much more beautiful than her (Hero) that it would be like comparing first of May to the last of December. But I hope you're not thinking about getting married. Are you? **Claudio**: I wouldn't trust myself to keep any promises to the contrary if Hero would consider being my wife.

Clip 4: Act III—Scene 5 (excerpts from lines 1–57) [Branagh movie, 59:40 to 1:01:40]

Leonato: What would you with me, neighbors? *Verges: Marry, sir, our watch tonight, excepting your Worship's presence, hath ta'en a couple of as arrant knaves as any in Messina.* *Dogberry: A good old man, sir; he will be talking: as they say, when the age is in, the wit is out: Well said, i' faith, neighbor Verges: well, God's a good man; an' two men ride of a horse, one must ride behind. All men are not alike; alas, good neighbor!* *Leonato: Indeed, neighbor, he comes too short of you.* *Dogberry: Gifts that God gives.* *Leonato: Neighbors, you are tedious.* *Dogberry: It pleases your worship to say so, but we are the poor duke's officers; but truly, for mine own part, if I were as tedious as a king, I could find it in my heart to bestow it all on your worship.* *Leonato: All thy tediousness on me, ah? I would fain know what you have to say.* *Dogberry: Our watch, sir, have indeed comprehended two auspicious persons, and we would this morning have them examined before your worship.* *Leonato: Take their examination yourself and bring it me: I am now in great haste, as it may appear unto you. Drink some wine ere you go: fare you well.* *Dogberry: We are now to examination these men. Meet me at the jail.*	**Leonato**: What would you like from me, friends? **Verges**: Please, sir, our watch tonight—*excepting* [*respecting*] your presence, sir—has captured a couple of the worst criminals as you can find in Messina. **Dogberry**: Verges is a good old man, sir; he's always blabbering: as they say, when age comes, the wit goes: You did well, honestly, Verges. Well, God's a fair man; if two men ride on the same horse, one must ride behind. All men are not created equal; am I right, my friend? **Leonato**: Indeed, friend, he isn't nearly as smart as you are. **Dogberry**: It's God who has gifted me with wit. **Leonato**: Friends, you are *tedious* [*boring*]. **Dogberry**: Thank you so much for saying that, sir, but we are just poor duke's officers; but really, on my own, if I were as *tedious* [*wealthy*] as a king, I would find it in my heart to give it all to you, sir. **Leonato**: (*playing along*) So you'd give me all your tediousness?—I'd like to hear your news. **Dogberry**: Our watch, sir, as you know, has *comprehended* [*apprehended*] two *auspicious* [*suspicious*] persons, and we'd like you, sir, to question them this morning. **Leonato**: Question them yourself and let me know the results. I am now in a great hurry, as you can see. Drink some wine before you go: farewell. **Dogberry**: We will now go to *examination* [*examine*] these men. Meet me at the jail.

The Story of Musical Theatre

Musical theatre provides the perfect illustration of a "total artwork" [***gesamtkunstwerk***[1]], which fuses all the arts together: music, art, dance, poetry, story, and play. When a play is set to music, it becomes an *opera* (Latin for "works") or a *musical*. An **opera** is a multi-act play that is sung throughout, using singing (some of which is speech-like) as a substitute for dialogue. A **musical** is similar to an opera, but

---

[1] German term first coined by Richard Wagner meaning "total artwork," *gesamt*=total + *kunst*=art + *werk* = work.

has a greater focus on spoken dialogue (in place of the speech-like singing) and has only two acts. In an opera, the orchestra is from 40–100 instruments, whereas in a musical the orchestra is smaller (10–20 instruments). Opera singers develop a different vocal timbre since they must learn to project their voices in order to be heard over a large orchestra. In an opera, singers rarely use a microphone, whereas in a musical singers usually perform *with* one. In an opera, the focus is on the music itself rather than on the story. In a musical, there are often parts that can be performed by non-singers or dancers. Someone who can act, dance, *and* sing is called a "triple threat."

Any story or play can be transformed into a work for musical theatre. *Dalilah* [alternate spelling] is a character in *Samson*, an **oratorio** (like an opera, but without staging, costumes, or action) by George Frederick Handel (1743). The *Story of Samson and Delilah* has been made into an opera in three acts by Camille Saint-Saëns (1877). *Beatrice and Benedick* (based on *Much Ado About Nothing*) is an opera by Hector Berlioz (1890).

Common Genres in Story, Theatre, and Musical Theatre

Common genres in story, theatre, and musical theatre include: 1) epic, 2) comedy, 3) tragedy, 4) tragicomedy, and 5) melodrama. An **epic** is an extended literary or dramatic work celebrating heroic feats, for example, the biblical story of *David*.

A **comedy** is a literary or dramatic work that is lighthearted and often satirical or humorous in tone, although it sometimes treats a serious subject. It has what is usually considered a happy ending. The biblical story of *Joseph and His Brothers*, Shakespeare's *Much Ado About Nothing*, *Comedy of Errors*, *Midsummer Night's Dream*, *As You Like It*, *Merchant of Venice*, *Taming of the Shrew*, and *Twelfth Night* are examples of comedies. The *Nutcracker* ballet is also an example of comedy.

A **tragedy** is a literary or dramatic work in which the main character(s) is/are brought to ruin by a tragic flaw, a moral weakness, or an inability to cope with unfavorable circumstances. The biblical stories of *Samson and Delilah* and Shakespeare's *Romeo and Juliet*, *Julius Caesar*, *Hamlet*, *Othello*, *King Lear*, and *Macbeth* are examples of tragedies. The musical *West Side Story* is also an example of tragedy.

A **tragicomedy** is a literary or dramatic work that combines elements of tragedy and comedy. It is a serious play that ends without catastrophe. Shakespeare's *Measure for Measure* and *All's Well That Ends Well* are examples of tragicomedies.

A **melodrama** is a dramatic work characterized by exaggerated emotions, stereotypical characters, and interpersonal conflicts. It literally means "song drama" and is accompanied by background music, similar to the music played along with silent films. It typically has a hero, a heroine, a villain, and a villainess. This is a genre that became popular in the nineteenth century.

Actions for Practice and Delight

10/1. Read aloud the story of *Samson and Delilah* on pages 114 and 115 of this text. After reading the story in its entirety, study the guide on page 116, and be sure that you understand and are able to trace the main themes without using the guide. Then, from memory, write the entire story in your own words (and, if you wish, retell it to someone else). Below the story you have written in your own words, write about your experience.

10/2. Finish writing the *Samson and Delilah* story as a play, as illustrated on page 118. Then cast the actors using people you know, draw the scenes, draw the costumes, describe the props, and describe the lighting.

10/3. Read aloud the clips from *Much Ado About Nothing* as found on pages 120, 121, 122, and 123 of the text, paying careful attention to characters, vocabulary, and sound colors. (Some clips are available on *YouTube*.) Comment on your experience. What are the themes in each of these clips? Were you able to follow the story, the words, and actions? Include any word images that especially struck you. (Especially explore the differences in the use of language between Beatrice/Benedick [witty], Claudio [stilted], and Dogberry [humorous misuse].)

10/4. Watch the entire Branagh 1993 movie (*available on iTunes, Netflix, YouTube,* etc.). Comment on your entire experience. Then, write a reading and a viewing guide for your favorite scene using the model provided for the story of *Samson and Delilah* on page 116 of this chapter.

10/5. Read aloud the story of *Joseph and His Brothers* in Genesis, chapters 37, 39–45. After reading the story in its entirety, study the guide in Appendix B on page B1, and be sure that you understand and are able to trace the main themes without using the guide. Then, from memory, write the entire story in your own words (and, if you wish, retell it to someone else). Below the story you have written in your own words, write about your experience. End your writing by commenting on the food for thought on page B2.

CHAPTER 11
CREATING FORM

"The arts are nothing without form."[1]

Vincent van Gogh (1853–1890) *Nuit étoilée à Saint Remy* [*Starry Night at St. Remy*] (1889), oil on canvas, 73 x 92 cm. (28¾ x 36½ in.) Museum of Modern Art, New York.

Dramatic Shape

Have you ever discovered an idea that you enjoy so much that you revisit it over and over again? An understanding of form will help you participate even more in this process. One of the important aspects of form is **dramatic shape** (psychological contour of tension, climax [focus], and release). In art, the tension increases as the eye moves toward the focal point [the starry sky in the painting above], focuses, and then gradually releases to move to the other parts of the work. In music, dance, poetry, story, and theatre, the ebb and flow of tension, climax, and release occurs throughout a work but most commonly with a contour of the greatest tension building near the end of a work leading to the ultimate climax and release (as in many hour-long television dramas). An excellent

---

[1] Gustave Flaubert, *Letter to Madame Louise Colet*, October 23, 1846: "Dans les arts, il n'est rien sans la forme."

example of dramatic shape is the Beatles' song *A Day in the Life*, with its buildup of tension (42 seconds) and subsequent release toward the middle of the song (01:58–2:40) and then again with the thrilling build of tension toward the very end (43 seconds) with subsequent climax, and gradual release through a long decrescendo of 28 seconds until the very end at 05:30 (*Naxos* playlist <u>Arts Key 11A Dramatic Shape and Variation Form</u> [1]).

Form in Art and Music

Form is the structure of a work with central theme (**A**), development (**A**^{1}, **A**^{2}, etc.), contrast (*B*, *C*, etc.), and dramatic shape (*rising tension*, *climax* [*focus*], and *release*). In the painting on the previous page, the title announces the theme of the night sky (**A**) with its development of the eleven stars (**a**^{1}–**a**^{11}) alternating with the swirls in the sky (*b*^{1}, *b*^{2}, etc.). The circular motion of the stars and the swirls of the night sky develop the idea and produce rising tension leading to the focal point of the moon against the sun (**a**^{12}). The peaceful village below (theme *B*) provides release. The cypress tree (*C*), mirrored by the steeple of the church, points back toward the starry sky beginning the cycle again. Notice also the differences among the circular flowing rhythm of the sky, the ordered regularity of the rhythm of the hills, trees and houses, and the singular rhythm of the church and the tree pointing back toward the sky. Form gives structure to the discussion of a work. As the eye moves around the painting, the form might be viewed as **A B C A B C A**.

In music, the basic unit of form is a **phrase** (a musical thought ending with a pause, usually 4 *bars* in length) with its own miniature dramatic shape (tension, climax, ending). Phrases combine to make tunes (often four *phrases* in length or 16 bars) as illustrated by the tune below. Each phrase of a tune may be labeled with a small letter to show the relationship between phrases, in this case **a a**^{1} *b* **a**^{2}, a prevalent outline used by hundreds of familiar tunes including I GOT RHYTHM and ODE TO JOY.

Variation Form

The entire four-phrase tune on the previous page may be used as a big **A** in a larger composition. **Variation form** occurs when an entire tune or theme is stated (**A**) and then reiterated again and again, developed each time with a different variation (A^1, A^2, A^3, etc.), with rising tension, climax and release. For example, the tune for *Amazing Grace* [known as NEW BRITAIN] is used as the theme for variations by Frank Ticheli in his arrangement for Wind Symphony (*Naxos* keywords: Ticheli Vol. 1 Amazing Grace [6]).

Variation form is present throughout all types and styles of music[1] and in all the arts. The American composer Aaron Copland (1900–1990) uses the folk hymn tune SIMPLE GIFTS as the basis for variations in the last section of his *Appalachian Spring Suite*. Begun in 1942 as a $500 commission, the original music underlies a legendary dance composition titled *Appalachian Spring* by the American dancer and choreographer Martha Graham (1894–1991). In 1945, a year after its first performance, Copland's score (for a small intimate ensemble of 13 instruments) received the Pulitzer Prize as the best musical work in that year. In that same year, Aaron Copland arranged the music into a shorter concert version (approximately 25 minutes as opposed to the original 35-minute ballet score) as the *Appalachian Spring Suite* for full orchestra. The section that we will follow occurs toward the end of the full orchestral version. Before listening to this excerpt, you may wish to sing, play, and/or listen to the tune on the following page until it is thoroughly familiar (*Naxos* keywords: Simple Gifts Willard White Concert [11]). Then, listen for the beginning of each different variation of the tune in the full orchestral version and for the release provided by the long coda at the end (Keywords: Bay Appalachian [1, 24]). You will be able to identify each variation by listening for the distinctive timbre of the instrument(s) playing the tune, highlighted in the listening outline on the page following the tune. Also, listen for patterns of tension leading to the climax. On a separate sheet, outline the dramatic shape and describe the mood for each variation.

---

[1] Other well-known examples of tunes that have been used for variation include AH, VOUS DIRAI-JE MAMAN (ABC SONG) and AMERICA (recall Chapter 3 for both), and AUSTRIAN HYMN from Haydn's String Quartet, Op. 76, No.3, II (now the music for the German national anthem and for several hymns). The second movements of many sonatas, concertos, symphonies, and chamber works are in variation form, for example, the well-known second movement of Haydn's Symphony No. 94 in G Major (*Surprise*). Rather than melodies, bass lines and chord progressions have also been extensively used as the basis for variation form such as the ever familiar Pachelbel *Canon in D* and the omnipresent blues progressions the world over, for example, *Crossroads* as set by Robert Johnson (two versions) and Eric Clapton (two different versions with *Cream* and *Blind Faith*). Hundreds of other examples could be listed.

SIMPLE GIFTS[1]

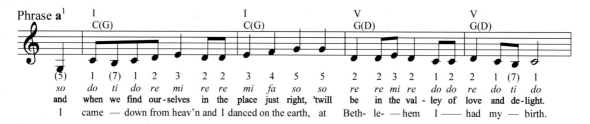

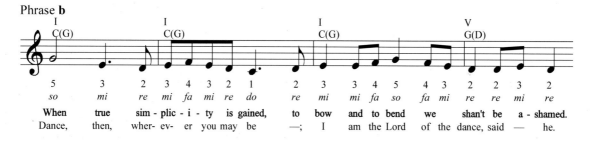

---

[1] Other words that have been set to this tune include the following excerpt from a poem (1963) by Sydney Carter:
I danced in the morning when the world was begun, and I danced in the moon and the stars and the sun.
I came down from heaven and I danced on the earth, at Bethlehem I had my birth.
Dance, then, wherever you may be; I am the Lord of the dance said he.
I'll lead you all wherever you may be, and I'll lead you all in the dance, said he.

Guide for Variations on SIMPLE GIFTS from *Appalachian Spring*

Melody in A♭, G♭, D, and C Major
Harmony: Uses mainly I, IV, and V chords
Rhythm: 2/4 meter, variations in *tempo*
Texture: Varied, see below
Dynamics: *pp–ff*
Instrument Pitch Range and Timbre: Full orchestra including timpani, triangle, glockenspiel, harp, and piano
Form: Variation (A, A^1, A^2, A^3, A^4 [only second half of the tune], A^5, and extended coda)
KEY: Listen for the different colors of the instruments playing the tune to identify each variation.

Time	Form	Instrumental Pitch Range/Timbre, Dynamics, Rhythm, Melody, Harmony	Texture	Mood
Excerpt 00:00	A (Theme)	A Theme, Tune: clarinet(s) Background rhythm/harmony: flute and harp (percussive overtones), later joined by piccolo. An added triangle note introduces the tune's second half. (Tempo: 72 beats per minute)	homophonic	
00:31	A^1	A^1 Tune: oboe and bassoon, joined by the clarinets in the second half Background rhythm/harmony: muted trumpets. Again, an added triangle note, joined by flutes and French horns, introduces the tune's second half (Tempo: a trifle faster, 80 beats per minute)	homophonic	

00:58
 	
 01:10
 01:13
	A^2 rising tension	A^2 Tune (twice as slow): violas and trombones
		    1st countermelody: horns and 1st violins mimic the tune
		    2nd countermelody: cellos and basses enter with short countermelody
		 Background rhythm/harmony: glockenspiel*, harp, piano, woodwinds, horns
		 *(a percussion instrument with metal bars usually played from a piano-like keyboard)
			homophonic
			
			 polyphonic	

01:34	*interlude*	Strings and woodwinds provide a 6-bar interlude using tune fragments.	polyphonic	
01:44	A^3	A^3 Tune (fast again): trumpets, joined in the second half by oboes and clarinets Countermelody: swirling strings at times Background rhythm/harmony: trombones, joined later by French horns	polyphonic	
02:08	A^4	A^4 Tune (second half only, indicated by A): solo clarinet (slower) Background rhythm/harmony: woodwinds; slow, steady rhythm in cellos/basses	homophonic	
02:22	A^5 climax	A^5 Tune (slowly and broadly): flutes, clarinets, trombones, 1st violins, and violas Background rhythm/harmony (slow, steady): full orchestra	homophonic	
00:00–02:51	Coda Release	Extended section	homophonic	

Alternating Form

In contrast to variation form, which uses the same idea or progression over and over again, **alternating form** begins with a theme but then departs from it and comes back to it one or more times. The contrasting sections are named sequentially using different letters of the alphabet (*B*, *C*, etc.). In alternating form, the general principle is that the primary idea or progression (labeled **A**) returns after different material is presented. In music, there are several types of standard alternating form: 1) three-part (**ABA**); 2) five-part rondo (**ABACA**); and 3) seven-part rondo (**ABACABA**/**ABACADA**). Three-part form includes the tune for ODE TO JOY on page 35 (in small **a a^1 b a^1** form, as are hundreds of songs) and the Beatles' *A Day in the Life* (large **A A^1 A^2 B A^2** form). In the Baroque period, *ritornello* form substitutes for the five- and seven-part rondo forms of the Classical and Romantic periods.[1]

Ritornello Form

Ritornello form is a special type of alternating form in which the *ritornello* (Italian for "refrain") returns frequently but usually not as the complete theme, although it is stated completely at the beginning. The *ritornello* (called **A**), played by all instruments, alternates with contrasting material sandwiched in between it: **A**, *B*, **A**, *C*, **A**, *D*, **A**, *E*, **A**, etc. **A** indicates that only the second half of the refrain is played. A familiar example of *ritornello* form may be found in the first movement of Antonio Vivaldi's (1675–1741) *La primavera* [*Spring*] (1725), in which a refrain (**A**) alternates with violin solos indicating thunder and lightning, bird songs, and brooks. The full refrain (**A**) or *ritornello* is given on the following page. Before you listen, it will be helpful to sing or play this refrain on the keyboard or ukulele/guitar, concentrating especially on the second phrase. Then, learn the second phrase in minor (**A**^{2}, see the fifth box from the bottom on the following page), so that you can recognize these phrases when you listen to the music.

This selection is based on a sonnet written by Antonio Vivaldi to go along with his music. The first two stanzas of the sonnet correlate with this first movement (see full sonnet on page 134). Above the music, Vivaldi wrote excerpts from the words of the poem to indicate the connection between the poetry and the music. Listen to the music as you follow the interactive guide on the next page. On a separate sheet, list the minutes and seconds when each section of the music enters (thus, the blank left hand column). Listen especially for the repeated refrain (second half only after the first statement).

Guide for the First Movement (*Allegro*) of *La primavera* [*Spring*] (1725)
(*Naxos* Playlist Arts Key 11B Four Seasons [1] or keywords: Vivaldi 4 Seasons Spring Tafelmusik Santo [1])

Melody: Theme in E major; later in C# minor, then back to E major (transposed to C and Cm on the following page for ease in reading)
Harmony: 4 parts; I and V chords only in major and then i in minor
[Bass]: Steady beat of quarter notes (sometimes 8th notes) underneath theme
Rhythm: See above, 4/4 meter; Allegro,
Texture: homophonic for theme; polyphonic birdsongs
Dynamics: Terraced *f p f p* for beginning
Instrument Pitch Range: String orchestra (solo violin, 1st violins, 2nd violins, violas, cellos, double basses), harpsichord
Timbre: String Orchestra
Form: Alternating (see following page)

---

[1] Well-known examples of three-part form include *Dance of the Reed Pipes* from the *Nutcracker* ballet by Tchaikovsky, the third movement of Mozart's *Eine kleine Nachtmusik*, *Ev'ry Valley* (the third section of Handel's *Messiah*), and the jazz piece *Take Five* by Paul Desmond. Five- and seven-part rondo form is present in final movements of many sonatas, concertos, symphonies, and chamber works.

11—Creating Form

Time	Texture	Form	
00:00	Homo-phonic	**A** (Theme, Refrain)	*Giunt'é la primavera* [Spring has come] Repeat *p* Repeat *p*
	Poly-phonic	**B** contrast	Song of the Birds
	Homo-phonic	**A**¹ (development)	Refrain, Second Phrase *Once* in Major—with full string orchestra
	Homo-phonic	**C** contrast	Murmuring Brooks
	Homo-phonic	**A**¹	Second phrase of refrain with full string orchestra
	Homo-phonic	**D** (rising tension)	Thunder and Lightning
	Homo-phonic	**A**² (climax)	Refrain, Second Phrase *Once* in *Minor*—with full string orchestra
	Poly-phonic	**B**¹ (release)	*Indi tacendo questi, gl' Augeletti, Tornan' di nuovo allor Canto d' Ucelli* [When these have quieted down, the little birds return to their enchanting song.]—Violin solo in minor against contrapuntal material in two additional violins imitates bird songs with ground rhythm of long held notes
	Homo-phonic	**A**³	Variation (not exact) of first phrase of refrain with full string orchestra
	Homo-phonic	**B**²	[Song of the birds continues]—Violin solo in major against ground rhythm in bass and keyboard
	Homo-phonic	**A**⁴	Refrain, Second Phrase *Twice* in Major—by full orchestra Repeat entire phrase *p* to end

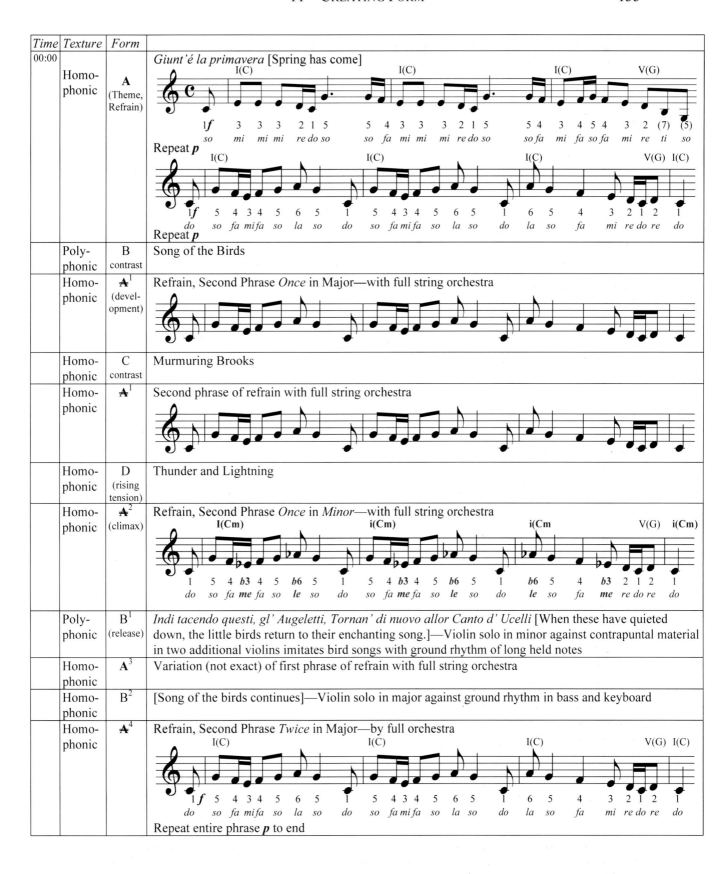

The Form of the Whole Concerto

The composition on the previous page is the first piece in a series of three separate pieces put together in a longer work titled *La primavera* [*Spring*]. Each of these individual pieces is known as a **movement** (i.e., a single piece that can stand alone, with a beginning and an end). These movements (pieces) come together to form a category (or **genre**), usually named for the particular instrument or groups of instruments that they use. The composite-work *La primavera* [*Spring*] fits into the category of the **concerto**, which is a multi-movement work for orchestra plus solo instrument(s), usually consisting of three movements (fast, slow, and fast). In *La primavera*, the orchestra is a string orchestra, and the solo instrument is a violin. The second and the third movements go along with the 3rd and 4th stanzas of the sonnet respectively (see below).

La primavera [*Spring*]

Movement 1—*Allegro*
Giunt' è la primavera e festosetti
la salutan gl'augei[1] con lieto canto,
e i fonti allo spirar de'zeffiretti
con dolce mormorio scorrono intanto.

Vegnon' coprendo l'aer di nero amanto,
e lampi, e tuoni ad annuntiarla eletti.
Indi tacendo questi, gl'augeleti;
tornan' di nuove allor canoro incanto:

Movement 2—*Largo e pianissimo sempre*
E quindi sul fiorito ameno prato,
Al caro mormorio di fronde e piante,
Dorme'l caprar col fido can'a lato.

Movement 3—*Allegro* (*Danza pastorale*)
Di pastoral zampogna al suon festante
danzan ninfe e pastor nel tetto amato
di primavera all'apparir brillante.

Concerto in E Major

Spring has come, and joyfully,
The birds greet it with happy song.
And the streams, fanned by gentle breezes,
Flow along with a sweet murmur.

Covering the sky with a black cloak,
Thunder and lightning come to announce the season.
When these have quieted down, the little birds
Return to their enchanting song.

And then, on a pleasant meadow covered with flowers,
Lulled by the soft murmuring of leaves and branches,
The goatherd sleeps, his faithful dog at his side.

To the festive sounds of country bagpipes,
Nymphs and shepherds dance in their beloved fields,
When spring appears in all its brilliance.[2]

Notice above that the first movement is labeled *allegro* [cheerful, fast], whereas the second movement is labeled *largo e pianissimo sempre* [slow and very soft always]. In contrast to the first movement, it is in minor. The third movement (like the first) is in alternating *ritornello* form with an *allegro* tempo. It is a *danza pastorale* [shepherds' dance] with a triple division of the beat. Listen to the whole concerto as you contemplate the poetry (*Naxos* Playlist <u>Arts Key 11B Four Seasons</u> [1–3] or keywords: <u>Vivaldi 4 Seasons Spring Tafelmusik Santo</u> [1–3]). What are the similarities in mood and association that you hear between the poetry and the music?

---

[1] The Italian word *augei* is a shortened form of *augelli*, which in turn is an ancient, poetic version of the word *ucelli* (today *uccelli*) meaning birds (singular is *uccello*). This word *augei* appears frequently in poetry including Dante's *Purgatorio* (*Purgatory*), Canto XXIV, verse 64: "*come li augi che vernan lungo 'l Nilo.*"
[2] Translated by Allen Schantz.

Guide for *Spring*, Movement 2
Melody: C# minor
Harmony: i, iv, V, and VI chords
Bass: Steady background rhythm throughout 2nd half of 1st beat plus 2nd beat
Rhythm: As above, uses 32nd notes in melody, ¾ meter, *Largo*
Texture: homophonic throughout
Dynamics: *pp* (very soft) throughout
Instrument Pitch Range: solo violin, 1st violins, 2nd violins, viola playing bass notes
Timbre: Higher part of string orchestra, no harpsichord
Form: steady, fittingness-intensity, peaceful, tender/expansive melody for solo violin, rocking figure in violins suggest rustling of leaves, violas imitate the barking of the goatherd's faithful dog

Guide for *Spring*, Movement 3
Melody: E major and C# Minor
Harmony: I, i, IV, iv, V
Bass: Steady, long-held notes
Rhythm: 12/8 meter, *Allegro*, Lively Dance
Texture: mostly homophonic (listen for drone bass in full orchestra refrain sections), some polyphony
Dynamics: Terraced, *fp* like 1st movement
Instrument Pitch Range: Solo violin, string orchestra (Vln. I, Vln. 2, Cello, Bass, Harpsichord)
Timbre: Muted strings
Form: Alternating—**A** (major) B **A¹** (minor) C (major) D **A²** (major/minor) E (minor) **A³** (major)

A (refrain) lively melody in major full orchestra	0:00	*Danza Pastorale* — Di pastoral zampogna al suon festante Danzan Ninfe e Pastor nel tetto amato Di primavera all'appariri brillante — Allegro
B solo violin over cello/harpsichord	0:28	
A¹ (refrain)	0:49	in C# minor, full orchestra
C	1:17	in E major, solo violin joined by another violin
D solo violin accompanied by 1st and 2nd violins	1:48	Violin solo / Violin I (Tutti, *p*) / Violin II (*p*)
A² (refrain)	2:08	in E major, then C# minor, full orchestra
E	2:39	In C# minor, solo violin with drone in cellos and basses
A³ (refrain)	3:02	In E major, full orchestra

The Whole Set of Four Concertos (*Four Seasons*)

To complement his concerto *La primavera* [*Spring*], Vivaldi wrote additional concertos, each depicting one of the other four seasons. His *Le quattro stagioni* [*The Four Seasons*] depicts each of the seasons as a separate concerto: *La primavera* [*Spring*], *L'estate* [*Summer*], *L'autunno* [*Autumn*], and *L'inverno* [*Winter*]. Each concerto (including the first, previously discussed) has three movements (fast—slow—fast), and is approximately 10 minutes long (depending on the performance). Vivaldi correlates each concerto with a sonnet that he has written by including key phrases of the corresponding sonnet in the musical score. At this point, you will want to listen to the remaining three concertos of Vivaldi's *Four Seasons* (*Naxos* Playlist <u>Arts Key 11B Four Seasons</u> [4–6, 7–9, 10–12] or keywords: <u>Vivaldi 4 Seasons Summer Tafelmusik Santo</u> [4–6], <u>Vivaldi 4 Seasons Autumn Tafelmusik Santo</u> [7–9], and <u>Vivaldi 4 Seasons Winter Tafelmusik Santo</u> [10–12]) before returning to the first concerto that begins the entire cycle. You will be rewarded and refreshed by the wonderful variety that is present in each concerto. Can you correlate the music and the poetry?

La primavera [*Spring*]	*L'estate* [*Summer*]	*L'autunno* [*Autumn*]	*L'inverno* [*Winter*]
Allegro	*Allegro non molto* [not much]	*Allegro*	*Allegro non molto*
Largo	*Adagio e* [and] *piano/Presto e forte*	*Adagio molto* [much]	*Adagio*
Allegro	*Presto*	*Allegro*	*Allegro*

L'estate [*Summer*]   **Concerto in G Minor**

Movement 1—Allegro non molto
Sotto dura Staggion dal Sole accesa
Langue L'huom, langue 'l gregge, ed arde il Pino;
Scioglie il Cucco la Voce, e tosto intesa
Canta la Tortorella e'l gardelino.

Beneath the blazing sun's relentless heat
men and flocks are sweltering, pines are scorched.
We hear the cuckoo's voice; then sweet songs of the
turtle dove and finch are heard.

Zeffiro dolce Spira, mà contesa
Muove Borea improviso al Suo vicino;
E piange il Pastorel, perche Sospesa
Teme fiera borasca, e'l Suo destino;

Soft breezes stir the air....but threatening north
wind sweeps them suddenly aside.
The shepherd trembles, fearful of violent storm and
what may lie ahead.

Movement 2—Adagio e piano-Presto e forte
Toglie alle membra lasse il Suo riposo
Il timore de'Lampi, e tuoni fieri
E de mosche, e mossoni il Stuol furioso!

His limbs are now awakened from their repose by
fear of lightning's flash and thunder's roar, as gnats
and flies buzz furiously around.

Movement 3—Presto
Ah che pur troppo I Suoi timor Son veri
Tuona e fulmina il ciel e grandinoso
Tronca il capo alle Spiche e a'grani alteri.

Alas, his worst fears were justified, as the heavens
roar and great hailstones beat down upon the
proudly standing corn.[1]

---

[1] Translator unknown. Translation available in multiple program notes and sources on the internet including http://www.baroquemusic.org/vivaldiseasons.html.

L'autunno [Autumn]

Concerto in F Major

Movement 1—Allegro
Celebra il Vilanel con balli e Canti
Del felice raccolto il bel piacere
E del liquor de Bacco accesi tanti
Finiscono col Sonno il lor godere

The peasant celebrates, with song and dance,
the harvest safely gathered in.
The cup of Bacchus flows freely,
and many find their relief in deep slumber.

Movement 2—Adagio molto
Fà ch' ogn' uno tralasci e balli e canti
L' aria che temperata dà piacere,
E la Staggion ch' invita tanti e tanti
D' un dolcissimo Sonno al bel godere.

The singing and the dancing die away
as cooling breezes fan the pleasant air,
inviting all to sleep
without a care.

Movement 3—Allegro
I cacciator alla nov' alba à caccia
Con corni, Schioppi, e canni escono fuore
Fugge la belua, e Seguono la traccia;

The hunters emerge at dawn,
ready for the chase,
with horns and dogs and cries.

Già Sbigottita, e lassa al gran rumore
De' Schioppi e canni, ferita minaccia
Languida di fuggir, mà oppressa muore.

Their quarry flees while they give chase.
Terrified and wounded, the prey struggles on,
but, harried, dies.[1]

L'inverno [Winter]

Winter—Concerto in F Minor

Movement 1—Allegro non molto
Aggiacciato tremar trà neri algenti
Al Severo Spirar d' orrido Vento,
Correr battendo i piedi ogni momento;
E pel Soverchio gel batter i denti;

Shivering, frozen mid the frosty snow
in biting, stinging winds;
running to and fro to stamp one's icy feet,
teeth chattering in the bitter chill.

Movement 2—Largo
Passar al foco i di quieti e contenti
Mentre la pioggia fuor bagna ben cento
Movement 3—Allegro
Caminar Sopra 'l giaccio, e à passo lento
Per timor di cader gersene intenti;

To rest contentedly beside the hearth,
while those outside are drenched by pouring rain.

We tread the icy path slowly and cautiously,
for fear of tripping and falling.

Gir forte Sdruzziolar, cader à terra
Di nuove ir Sopra 'l giaccio e correr forte
Sin ch' il giaccio si rompe, e si disserra;

Then turn abruptly, slip, crash on the ground
and, rising, hasten on across the ice
lest it cracks up.

Sentir uscir dalle ferrate porte
Sirocco Borea, e tutti i Venti in guerra
Quest' é 'l verno, mà tal, che gioja apporte

We feel the chill north winds course through the home
despite the locked and bolted doors…
this is winter, which nonetheless brings its own delights.[1]

---

[1] Translator unknown. Translation available in multiple program notes and sources on the internet including http://www.baroquemusic.org/vivaldiseasons.html.

Form in Dance

Dance follows the basic forms and patterns of music. Dancers may choose standard moves and shapes (such as the 5 ballet positions), they may vary moves they have learned from others, or they may make up their own original moves. Comparable to composition in music, **choreography** is the art of creating and arranging the sequence of movements, steps, and patterns in dance. A *coda* (concluding section in music) is the third and final part of the classical *pas de deux* of ballet. A **narrative** is a choreographic structure that follows a specific story line to convey specific information through a dance. In a narrative dance, mime is substituted for spoken dialogue of a play.

Pointed Toward Aesthetic Excellence

We have come full circle around the raw elements of **M**usic, **A**rt, **D**ance, **P**oetry, **S**tory, and **T**heatre (and Music Theatre) culminating in form which ties them all together. Our trek through the elements has prepared us for the next step. We are now pointed toward aesthetic excellence and its relationship to other modes of living.

Actions for Practice and Delight

11/1. Memorize the definitions for dramatic shape on page 127 and for form on page 128. Then, listen to an instrumental version of *A Day in the Life* by the Beatles (*Naxos* playlist Arts Key 11A Dramatic Shape and Variation Form [1] or keyword: CDC012 [20]). Draw a line outlining the dramatic shape (with explanation). In writing, discuss the effectiveness of this song in building and releasing tension.

11/2. Learn to sing the tune SIMPLE GIFTS on page 130, and (if you wish) accompany it with chords. Review the interactive outline on page 131. Then, sitting (or lying) in a quiet place with your eyes closed (you may wish to use headphones), listen to Aaron Copland's variations on SIMPLE GIFTS (*Naxos* playlist Arts Key 11A Dramatic Shape and Variation Form [2, 3] or keywords: Copland *Appalachian Spring* Ainsworth [1, 24]). Do this several times in spaced intervals over the course of two or more days [minimum three times]. After each complete hearing, record your experience in writing and how you progress on the following questions. Hint: Listen for the instrument(s) playing the melody. Using the interactive outline, test yourself by seeing if you can identify whether a section is A, A^1, A^2, A^3, A^4, or A^5 by finding random points in the selection.

1) How soon are you able to hear each time the tune repeats and when it is only partly there? [*Count and list the number of times you hear the tune repeat each time you listen.*]
2) Which new elements of the music are you able to hear each time you listen? What aspects (if any) have you discovered that are not in the listening outline?
3) Which variation is your favorite, and why?
4) Conclude your written comments by discussing how you might improve your listening experience.

11/3. Using *do-re-mi* syllables and dynamics, learn to sing the tune for the *ritornello* [refrain] of the first movement in Vivaldi's *La primavera* [*Spring*] on page 133, and (if you wish) to accompany it with chords. Learn the second phrase in minor as in the fifth box from the bottom. [Remember that *mi* and *ti* are pronounced "mee" and "tee" and that *re, me,* and *le* are pronounced "ray," "may" and "lay."] Then, listen to the first movement (*Naxos* playlist Arts Key 11B The Four Seasons [1] or keyword: SMCD5194 [1]). Using the listening outline on page 133, test yourself by seeing if you can identify whether a section is thunder/lightning, birds, brooks, or part of the *ritornello* [refrain] in major or minor by finding random points in the selection. Then, read the entire Italian poem for Spring (on page 134) and then listen to all three movements of the concerto as you follow the guides on pages 133 and 135 (*Naxos* playlist Arts Key 11B The Four Seasons [1, 2, 3] or keywords: Vivaldi 4 Seasons Spring Tafelmusik Santo [1–3]). In writing, discuss how movements 1, 2, and 3 illustrate the poem. Be prepared to identify any section of movement 1, the first part of movement 2, or the first part of movement 3 when they are played at random.

11/4. Listen to all four concertos—*Spring, Summer, Autumn,* and *Winter* (*Naxos* Playlist Arts Key 11B The Four Seasons [1–3, 4–6, 7–9, 10–12] or keywords: Vivaldi

Spring Tafelmusik Santo [1–3], Vivaldi Summer Tafelmusik Santo [4–6], Vivaldi Autumn Tafelmusik Santo [7–9], and Vivaldi Winter Tafelmusik Santo [10–12]) of *The Four Seasons* as you follow Vivaldi's poetry for that season in this chapter (pages 134, 136, 137). You may prefer listening to all four concertos in one sitting (about 40 minutes for all 12 tracks), or you may prefer to listen to one concerto at a time. In a paragraph for each season, discuss what is distinctive about Vivaldi's portrayal of each season (in his use of the elements of music) and how the music illustrates the poetry. Then, discuss your entire listening experience.

Chapter 12

The Goal: Aesthetic Excellence

"If you foolishly ignore beauty, you will soon find yourself without it. Your life will be impoverished. But if you invest in beauty, it will remain with you all the days of your life." Frank Lloyd Wright

Have you ever experienced a starlit night? You dare not move your eyes from the heavens lest you miss the incredible stars. All your senses capture the gorgeous night as you wrap yourself in it. What if you could paint its vivid colors or catch its image in a poem? You could capture beauty, allowing you to hold and share the moment forever.

Vincent Van Gogh (1853–1890) La nuit étoilée sur le Rhône [The Starry Night over the Rhone] (1888), oil on canvas, 72.5 x 92 cm (28.5 x 36.2 in.) Musée d'Orsay, Paris.

To review, **aesthetic** means "the structural and perceptual principles for clarifying and confirming critical statements about works of art." The word aesthetic is derived from the Greek word *aisthētikos*—sense perception, which in turn comes from the Greek word *aisthanesthai*—to perceive. What makes something aesthetically pleasing ("beautiful")? What gives a work in the arts aesthetic excellence? The aesthetic elements of the arts (see page 27) are the necessary but not the sufficient condition for aesthetic excellence. The idea of **imagination** ("the act or power of forming a mental image of something not present to the senses or never before wholly perceived in reality"[1]) introduces us to aesthetic excellence.

---

[1] Merriam-Webster Dictionary.

The Idea of Imag*e*ination

God creates out of nothing (*ex nihilo*), but we create out of something (*ex material*) that has already been created. Imag*e*ination begins with imitation (Aristotle's *mimesis*, Greek for *imitation*), moving ultimately to abstraction. In music, for example, we may imitate the sound of a bird, a cricket, or a thunderstorm. In art, we may image a tree, a person, or the night sky (as in the previous painting). Throughout history, those who become expert at imag*e*ining what they perceive are regarded as artists and in turn are imitated. Students imitate them, and those students who are gifted soon develop their own style by varying and rearranging what their teachers have done and originating ideas of their own. In turn, these artists teach their disciples to imitate them and the people who taught them, in an ever widening cycle and circle of abstraction. Some artists produce works that are heard or seen for only a short time, but then drop off the edge of history. Other artists surpass their teachers and produce works that survive history and make the final cut. These works become *masterworks* or *classics* and in turn become the basis for future imag*e*ination.

What are the aspects of these works that help them survive the cutting board of human history? The thoughtful reflection of many people from many ages and cultures including artists, arts historians, aesthetic philosophers, and critics (of all kinds including our own careful reflection based on our experience in previous chapters) seems to indicate at least three ingredients for aesthetic excellence that surface again and again in these *masterworks*: unity, diversity, and fittingness-intensity,[1] mediated through the aesthetic elements of each art.

Unity

The first aspect of aesthetic excellence is unity. **Unity**[2] may be defined as how coherently a work is integrated in each of its elements: is it unified in its character to a significant degree? Terms and descriptions such as balance, symmetry/asymmetry, proportion, harmony, order, repetition, imitation, sequence, and variation often refer to the unity of a work. When critics speak of a work as "well-organized," "formally perfect" or "full of inner logic in structure and style," they are speaking of its being unified to a significant degree. In its form, for example, does it have a central theme or idea (a) that ties the parts together? Is this central theme repeated (a) and varied (a^1, a^2, etc.) throughout the work?

---

[1] In his seminal work, *Aesthetics: Problems in the Philosophy of Criticism* (New York: Harcourt, Brace and Company, 1958), pp. 462–464, Monroe Beardsley calls these values *unity*, *complexity*, and *intensity*. The aesthetic philosopher Nicholas Wolterstorff develops these ideas as *unity*, *internal richness*, and *fittingness-intensity—Art in Action* (Grand Rapids: Eerdmans, 1980), pp. 163–168.
[2] Leonard B. Meyer calls this "grammatical simplicity" [*Grammatical Simplicity and Relational Richness: The Trio of Mozart's G Minor Symphony*, pp. 693–759 in *Critical Inquiry*, Summer, 1976].

Diversity

The second aspect of aesthetic excellence is *diversity*.[1] **Diversity**[2] may be defined as how deeply a work possesses rich variety and contrast in each of its elements: Is it internally rich, varied, and/or complex? Does it have a diversity of significantly differentiated parts? In the element of form, for example, does it develop the theme in a variety of ways (A^1, A^2, etc.), and does it have contrast (A or B)?

"Fittingness-Intensity"

Unity and variety lead to the next norm for aesthetic excellence. "**Fittingness-intensity**"[3] is a strong correlation between patterns in a work and patterns of human experience (emotional, sensory, mental, and other patterns, i.e., tension, climax, and release).

In emotional patterns of human experience, a major key with a faster *tempo* fits more closely to joy, whereas a minor key with a slower tempo fits more closely to sorrow (and a host of other qualities of human experience). [Recall FRÉRE JACQUES at a fast *tempo* in major and a slow *tempo* in minor (Mahler, *Titan* Symphony, movement III)]. As another example, soul music has been variously defined as "intensity of feeling," "intense sensitivity," and "emotional fervor" reflecting Suzanne Langer's idea that "music is the tonal analogue of the emotive life."[4]

In sensory patterns of human experience (sound, sight, touch, taste, smell, and balance), expressive sounds can strongly correlate with expressive sights; expressive sights can strongly reflect vivid mental images, and so on. With practice, it is possible to correlate sounds, colors, textures, tastes, smells, and verbal images.[5] For example, the expression "he was wearing a *loud* tie" means "he was wearing a *bright* tie." In the realm of touch, a person who is mentally bright is sharp, and a person who is mentally dull is blunt. In the realm of pace, fast is *allegro* (cheerful, bright), and slow is *lento* (slow, dull). Perhaps the easiest way to experience cross-sensory patterns is to discover how something might fit across the arts—painting a poem or setting a poem to music or vice-versa, for example.

Other patterns of human experience include tension, climax, and release—struggle, victory, and joy, and a host of other patterns. When the arts are combined, imag*e*inative excellence means that all the arts involved fit well together by strongly reflecting similar patterns of human experience. In an excellent song, the music fits the

---

[1] Samuel Taylor Coleridge calls this "multeity in unity" [*On the Principles of Genial Criticism* (1814)].
[2] Leonard B. Meyer calls this "relational richness." Nicholas Wolterstorff calls it "internal richness."
[3] The term "fittingness-intensity" is taken from Nicholas Wolterstorff (*Art in Action*, Grand Rapids: Eerdmans, 1980), pp. 96–121. Leonard Bernstein calls this "expressivity" (*Norton Lectures* at Harvard University, 1973); and Calvin Seerveld calls this "allusiveness" (*Rainbows for the Fallen World*, Toronto: Tuppence Press, 1980).
[4] Suzanne Langer, *Feeling and Form* (New York: Charles Scribner's Sons, 1953), p. 27.
[5] Persons in which this skill is highly developed are called *synaesthetes*.

poetry, and the poetry fits the music. In an excellent dance, the music and dance fit foot to foot and hand in hand, and so on. [Also, recall the 2nd movement of Haydn's *Creation* moving from soft minor to a sudden loud, full C major chord closely fitting the words from the creation story moving from darkness to the creation of brilliant light, and its correlation to the use of *chiaroscuro* in art.] Two intriguing examples of cross-perceptual exploration may be found in 1) Sid Caesar's rendition of the 1st movement of Beethoven's 5th symphony (*YouTube* keywords: Sid Caesar Beethoven Argumento), and 2) in the correlation between the music of Pink Floyd's *Dark Side of the Moon* and the original movie for *The Wizard of Oz* (*YouTube* keywords: wizard dark side synced glidman3).

For further discussion of "fittingness," "fittingness-intensity" and of studies relating to it, see Nicholas Wolterstorff, *Art in Action*, pp. 96–121 ("fittingness") and pp. 166–167 ("fittingness-intensity"), excerpts of which are quoted below. He writes,

> Consider these lines:
>
> Everybody in my experience judges that the former fits better with restlessness and the latter with tranquility....
>
> ...
>
> Consider Gustave Flaubert's statement that 'The story, the plot of a novel is of no interest to me. When I write a novel I aim at rendering a color, a shade.... In Madame Bovary, all I wanted to do was to render a grey color, the mouldy color of a wood-louse's existence.' On first hearing, this may strike one as fanciful nonsense. To see that it is not nonsense consider a counterpart example from a work more familiar to most of us—say, Shakespeare's *Hamlet*. Does *Hamlet* fit better with purple or with yellow, with green or with burgundy? In my experience everyone offers purple and burgundy as the answers.
> In music too we perceive fittingness. Everyone in my experience judges that tones an octave apart fit better with tranquility, tones a seventh apart with restlessness....[1]

Is this "fittingness" or "cross-modal similarity" culturally conditioned, or does it hold across cultures? Nicholas Wolterstorff concludes:

> ...in the results of the cross-cultural studies, we have an answer to another question. To what extent is the perception of cross-modal similarities shared across cultures? The answer is *massively*. Of course the agreement is not total. But then neither is the agreement total within a culture on many *intra*-modal similarities. Yet it is hard to imagine anyone in any

---

[1] Nicholas Wolterstorff, *Art in Action* (Grand Rapids: Eerdmans, 1980), pp. 97–98.

culture thinking that a jagged line fits better with tranquility and an undulating line with restlessness.[1]

Aesthetic Excellence Summarized

Sustained interaction with the form and other aesthetic elements of a work in the arts will help us to create and discover **aesthetic excellence**—*unity, diversity, and fittingness-intensity*. [Recall the definition: Form is the structure of a work with central theme (**A**), development (**A**^{1}, **A**^{2}, **A**^{3}), contrast (*B*, *C*), and dramatic shape (*rising tension, climax, and release*).] The following poem in long meter (can be sung to OLD HUNDREDTH on page C5) summarizes our previous discussion.

> The goal: aesthetic excellence
>   through form and other elements
> With unity, diversity,
>   and fittingness-intensity.

Creating, Discovering, and Practicing Aesthetic Excellence

The question then occurs, "How can we create, discover, and practice aesthetic excellence?" Aesthetic excellence may be created, discovered, and practiced by active participation in and by energetic attention to all the perceptual elements of a particular work. This process may take place individually or in community over a period of hours, days, weeks, months, and even years. The best way to learn about the arts is to participate actively in the experience of recreating them (reading and playing them aloud, memorizing and performing them, copying them, imitating them, and even rearranging them). Without our active participation, a work in the arts lies dormant. The discovery and creation of aesthetic excellence rewards the diligent. In assessing aesthetic excellence, we may ask the following questions: Does my work or someone else's work hang together over the long haul (unity)? Does it hold my attention and the attention of others over the long haul (diversity)? Does it closely reflect qualities of shared human experience (fittingness-intensity)?

Becoming Part of a Practicing Community

How do we know which works and artists to pay attention to? There are so many possibilities that we will never have time to discover and use every work on our own (even over many lifetimes). We can usually trust the judgment of a practicing community of connoisseurs who have had extensive and thoughtful experience with a particular area of the arts (called critics), especially those who are creating in that area. For example, when considering what to play or listen to in jazz, it is wise to get to know people in the jazz community who have developed discriminating taste (jazz critics) in order to

---

[1] Ibid., p. 108.

determine which pieces we should pay attention to, especially if jazz is not something that we appreciate initially. Finding those who have enjoyed and experienced particular areas of the arts over a number of years will give us many good clues as to where to begin. When we find works that intrigue others that we trust, we can begin to experience them ourselves. Aesthetic responsibility leads to the joy of continued discovery and delight.

The Aesthetic Excellence of a Performance and the Aesthetic Excellence of a Work

There is a distinction between the aesthetic excellence of a work in the arts and the aesthetic excellence of its performance. It is important to distinguish between the work and its re-creation in performance, although sometimes it is difficult to separate the two. One of the best ways to do this is by considering different performances of the same work. An excellent performance does not necessarily indicate an aesthetically excellent work. Even a brilliant performance cannot completely paper over an aesthetically weak work. On the other hand, an aesthetically excellent work may be re-created poorly, but its aesthetic excellence will still shine through.

Face to Face with *Combatooka, Thi,* and *Jabberwocky*

As examples, consider three poems that differ in their aesthetic excellence—two short poems and one longer one. Read the poems aloud a number of times and let them percolate in your mind as you consider the aesthetic excellence mediated through the elements of poetry, beginning with the form (central image [A], development [A^1, A^2, etc.], contrast [B, C], rising tension, climax [*volta*], and release) and working through the packed word pictures (IMSSP) and packed word sounds (HMEW), noting unity, diversity, and fittingness-intensity. What is the difference in the aesthetic excellence of these poems?

Poem 1 *Combatooka*	Poem 2 *Thi*
Combatooka gine dee	Thi thi thi thi thi thi thi
Anzo ar gan	Thi thi thi thi thi thi thi
Zif eldonarad expi	Thi thi thi thi thi thi thi
Nadokona ami boelo verdifadimaniku	Thi thi thi thi thi thi thi
Keetoe	Thi thi thi thi thi thi thi
Arbi qlkt	Thi thi thi thi thi thi thi
Pryd	Thi thi thi thi thi thi thi
K	Thi thi thi thi thi thi thi[1]

---

[1] Poems 1 and 2 by Allen Schantz.

Poem 3 (in Original Context from *Through the Looking-Glass*)
(*Naxos* keywords: Jabberwocky Comic Poetry [1])

There was a book lying near Alice on the table, and while she sat watching the White King (for she was still a little anxious about him, and had the ink all ready to throw over him, in case he fainted again), she turned over the leaves, to find some part that she could read, "—for it's all in some language I don't know," she said to herself.

It was like this.

YKCOWREBBAJ

sevot yhtils eht dna, gillirb sawT'
:ebaw eht ni elbmig dna eryg diD
,sevogorob eht erew ysmim llA
.ebargtuo shtar emom eht dnA

She puzzled over this for some time, but at last a bright thought struck her. "Why, it's a Looking-glass book, of course! And if I hold it up to a glass, the words will all go the right way again."

This was the poem that Alice read.

JABBERWOCKY

'Twas brillig, and the slithy toves
  Did gyre and gimble in the wabe:
All mimsy were the borogoves,
  And the mome raths outgrabe.

'Beware the Jabberwock, my son!
  The jaws that bite, the claws that catch!
Beware the Jubjub bird, and shun
  The frumious Bandersnatch!'

He took his vorpal sword in hand:
  Long time the manxome foe he sought—
So rested he by the Tumtum tree,
  And stood awhile in thought.

And as in uffish thought he stood,
  The Jabberwock, with eyes of flame,
Came whiffling through the tulgey wood,
  And burbled as it came!

One, two! One, two! And through and through
  The vorpal blade went snicker-snack!
He left it dead, and with its head
  He went galumphing back.

'And has thou slain the Jabberwock?
  Come to my arms, my beamish boy!
O frabjous day! Callooh! Callay!'
  He chortled in his joy.

'Twas brillig, and the slithy toves
  Did gyre and gimble in the wabe:
All mimsy were the borogoves,
  And the mome raths outgrabe.[1]

---

[1] Carroll, Lewis, *Through the Looking Glass and What Alice Found There* (1872) taken from the annotated version by Martin Gardner, *More Annotated Alice* (New York: Random House, 1990), pp. 176, 178.

148   12—THE GOAL: AESTHETIC EXCELLENCE

Evaluating the Aesthetic Excellence of Three Works of Art

In a similar way, compare the following three paintings. Begin by looking at the form (noting central theme [A], development [A^1, A^2, etc.], contrast [B, C], and dramatic shape (*rising tension, focal point, and release*) and working through the colors, textures, shapes, lines and spaces noting unity, diversity, and fittingness-intensity. What is the difference in the aesthetic excellence of these paintings?

Frank Stella (b. 1936) *Hyena Stomp* (1962), oil on canvas, 198.2 x 198.1 x 9.1 cm. (5ft. 5 in. x 5 ft. 5 in. x 3.5 in.), Tate Modern, London. [Stella translated musical syncopation into visual form, taking the title, *Hyena Stomp*, from a jazz piece by Jelly Roll Morton.]

12—The Goal: Aesthetic Excellence 149

Agnes Martin (1912–2004), *On a Clear Day* (1973), one of a portfolio of 30 screenprints, 12 in. x 12 in., pencil on Japanese rag paper, Craig F. Starr Gallery, New York.
Tretyakov Gallery, Moscow.

Joseph Stella (1877–1946) *Old Brooklyn Bridge* (ca. 1941) oil on canvas, 194 x 173 cm (6 ft. 4¼ in. x 5 ft. 8¼ in.) Museum of Fine Arts, Boston, Gift of Susan Morse Hilles in memory of Paul Hellmuth, 1980.

Three Selections of Music

Now evaluate the following three selections of music in terms of their aesthetic excellence or lack of it. Listen to all three pieces in sequence (about 12 minutes altogether). Then, listen again for the form (noting central theme [A], development [A^1, A^2, etc.], contrast [B, C], and dramatic shape (*rising tension, climax, and release*), noting unity, diversity, and fittingness-intensity. All pieces are in a style called **musical minimalism** (in music, a reductive style characterized by the progressive transformation of repetitive structures).

1) *Short Ride in a Fast Machine* (*Naxos* playlist Arts Key 12A [1] or keyword: 8.559031 [1]);
2) *Einstein on the Beach, Act III, Trial, Prison, Ensemble* (*Naxos* playlist Arts Key 12A [2] or keyword: 075597932362 [11].
3) *Für Anna Maria* (*Naxos* playlist Arts Key 12A [3] or keyword: 8.572525 [17].

Beethoven's Fifth

Most people have heard the first movement of Symphony No. 5 in C Minor (1807–1808) by Beethoven (1770–1927) many times, but have never heard the remainder. It is a rewarding experience to listen to it with new ears. (It is difficult to appreciate Beethoven's Symphony No. 5 by listening while operating a jackhammer.) A listening guide for each movement is provided at the end of this chapter (pages 157–161), *Naxos* playlist Arts Key 12B Beethoven 5th [1] or keywords: Beethoven 5 Leibowitz Leonore [6,7,8,9]). Extended time with this work will help you to appreciate its full aesthetic excellence. E. M. Forester in his novel *Howard's End* gives a wonderful description of its fittingness-intensities.

> It will be generally admitted that Beethoven's Fifth Symphony is the most sublime noise that has ever penetrated into the ear of man. All sorts and conditions are satisfied by it. Whether you are like Mrs. Munt, and tap surreptitiously when the tunes come—of course, not so as to disturb the others—; or like Helen, who can see heroes and shipwrecks in the music's flood; or like Margaret, who can only see the music; or like Tibby, who is profoundly versed in counterpoint, and holds the full score open on his knee; or like their cousin, Fraulein Mosebach, who remembers all the time that Beethoven is "echt Deutsch"; or like Fraulein Mosebach's young man, who can remember nothing but Fraulein Mosebach: in any case, the passion of your life becomes more vivid, and you are bound to admit that such a noise is cheap at two shillings. It is cheap, even if you hear it in the Queen's Hall, dreariest music-room in London, though not as dreary as the Free Trade Hall, Manchester; and even if you sit on the extreme left of that hall, so that the brass bumps at you before the rest of the orchestra arrives, it is still cheap.[1]

---

[1] E. M. Forester, *Howard's End* (1910) from Great Novels of E. M. Forster: Where Angels Fear to Tread, The Longest Journey, A Room with a View, Howard's End (New York: Caroll & Graff Publishers, Inc., 1992), Chapter 5, pp. 587–589, available online at http://www.hti.umich.edu/cgi/p/pd-modeng/pd-modeng-idx?type=header&idno=ForstHowar.

Perhaps the best way to begin to think about this symphony is to consider its overall form. The unity, diversity, and fittingness-intensities of Beethoven's Symphony No. 5 range from the *majestic* rhythms of its fourth movement to the *knocking* rhythm of its first four notes (short, short, short, long). This first *knocking* rhythm or **motive** (central theme cell) serves as the basis for much of the first movement (including the first theme) and is reiterated at strategic points throughout the symphony, providing extraordinary structural unity and diversity. It is sandwiched between contrasting sections of longer material in movement three, occurs in a much different guise as the second theme of movement four, and then comes back in a mysterious and unexpected way to provide the prelude to a powerful climax. (Movements three and four are played together with no break between them.) The melodies using this motive are outlined on the following page, with accompanying chords.

The motive of this symphony was associated with the letter V in Morse Code (dot-dot-dot-dash) to stand for "V for Victory" by the Allies during World War II. This symphony is traditionally associated with Beethoven's grappling with his growing deafness (C minor movements) and his victory over "his fate" as he moves to the final movement in C major. Beethoven began to lose his hearing in 1798 and wrote his famous Heiligenstadt Testament (letter) in 1802, five years before his Fifth Symphony. In this letter, he struggles with his growing deafness:

A page from Beethoven's Heiligenstadt Testement, **Staats-und Universitatsbibliothek** [State and University Library], Hamburg.

"But what a humiliation for me when someone standing next to me heard a flute in the distance and *I heard nothing*, or someone heard a *shepherd singing* and again I heard nothing. Such incidents drove me almost to despair, a little more of that and I would have ended my life—it was only *my art* that held me back. Ah, it seemed to me impossible to leave the world until I had brought forth all that I felt was within me."[1]

---

[1] *Thayer's Life of Beethoven* translated by Henry Edward Krehbiel (1921), rev. and ed. Elliot Forbes (Princeton: Princeton University Press, 1967), p. 305.

Central Motive and Other Themes for Beethoven's Fifth Symphony

Unity—Four-note central idea (knocking motive)—Movement I, theme **A** (I**A**) theme I**A** in minor

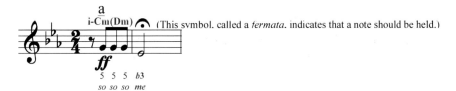

Structural Unity and Development—more of the first part of minor theme I**A**

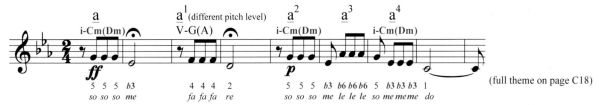

*Diversity, Contrast, and Fittingness-Intensity—Movement I, contrasting theme I*B

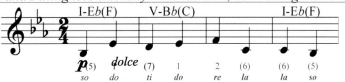

Unity, Diversity, and Fittingness-Intensity—original four-note central idea reappears in odd meter in movement III, theme *B* (III*B*); also comes in as a surprise in movement IV.

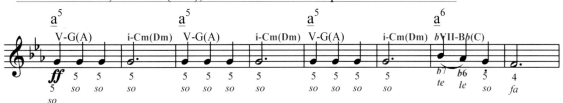

Diversity, Contrast and Fittingness-Intensity —Joyful Movement IV, theme A (IV**A**) in Major

Unity and Diversity—Original four-note central idea (motive) appears in triplets in movement IV, theme *B* (IV*B*).

Whatever the specific association, the journey from *C* minor to *C* major in this symphony expressively fits the human qualities of struggle and victory (as well as many similar qualities),[1] providing a fitting conclusion to this chapter.

---

[1] In considering fittingness-intensity, most people tend to associate minor with cooler, less stable, darker, sourer, sadder, smaller, and more mysterious qualities of human experience, whereas major tends to be associated with warmer, more stable, lighter, sweeter, happier, larger, and clearer qualities.

Actions for Practice and Delight

12/1. Memorize the four-line poem on page 145 summarizing aesthetic excellence (you may wish to sing it to the tune of OLD HUNDREDTH on page C5), and then expand the meaning of each line of the poem in your own words, so that you are able to use the poem to recall what you have learned about aesthetic excellence.

12/2. Evaluate the three poems on pages 146 and 147. Read the poems aloud a number of times and let them percolate in your mind. In writing, discuss the 1) form [central image, development, contrast, and dramatic shape], 2) packed word sounds, and 3) packed word pictures, noting their unity, diversity, and fittingness-intensity. Based on your discussion, rate each poem on a scale of 1 to 10 (ten being the highest) in terms of their aesthetic excellence.

12/3. Compare the three paintings on pages 148, 149 and 150 of this chapter. First, look at the paintings a number of times. Then, try to recreate them from memory. In writing, discuss the 1) form [central image, development, contrast, and dramatic shape], 2) colors, 3) textures, 4) spaces, 5) shapes, and 6) lines for each of these paintings, noting their unity, diversity, and fittingness-intensity. Based on your discussion, rate each of these paintings in terms of their aesthetic excellence on a scale of 1 to 10 (ten being the highest).

12/4. Compare the three musical selections below in terms of their aesthetic excellence or lack of it. Listen to all three pieces in sequence several times. In writing, discuss the 1) form (central theme, development, contrast, and dramatic shape), 2) sound colors, 3) textures (layers), 4) rhythm, 5) harmony, and 6) melody, noting unity, diversity, and fittingness-intensity. Based on your discussion and your copious notes, rate each of these selections in terms of their aesthetic excellence on a scale of 1 to 10 (ten being the highest).

4) *Short Ride in a Fast Machine* (*Naxos* playlist Arts Key 12A [1] or keyword: 8.559031 [1]);
5) *Einstein on the Beach, Act III, Trial, Prison, Ensemble* (*Naxos* playlist Arts Key 12A [2] or keyword: 075597932362 [11].
6) *Für Anna Maria* (*Naxos* playlist Arts Key 12A [3] or keyword: 8.572525 [17].

12/5. Consider (sing and/or play if you can) themes I**A** in minor and I*B* in major as shown on page 153 (full themes on page C18). Then, listen to movement I of Beethoven's Fifth Symphony (a number of times distributed over several hours and days, *Naxos* playlist Arts Key 12B Beethoven 5th [1] or keywords: Beethoven 5 Leibowitz Leonore [6]) as you interact with the following listening guide (page 158, sometimes using it and sometimes just listening). Master this movement so that you can recognize each of the sections when they come in, with and without the listening guide: 1) Theme I**A**, 2) Bridge, 3) Theme I*B*, 4) Closing, 5) Development, and 6) Theme IA when it enters after the development, with the long oboe solo at the end. Write about your experience and your progress in listening. Be able to identify any of the six sections by listening only.

12/6. Consider (play and/or sing if you can) *all* the principal themes for Beethoven's Fifth Symphony as shown on page 153 (full themes on page C18). Then, listen to the entire symphony (*Naxos* playlist Arts Key 12B Beethoven 5th [1, 2, 3, 4] or keywords: Beethoven 5 Leibowitz Leonore [6,7, 8, 9]) and work on hearing the unifying motive. Then, listen to a little of each movement of Beethoven's Fifth Symphony (a number of times distributed over several hours and days). When you are ready, listen to the entire symphony (more than once, if time permits). Review the listening guides provided on the following pages before, after, or while you listen. In writing, describe your experience and what strikes you the most about the aesthetic excellence of this symphony.

12/7. Study the material in this chapter on fittingness-intensity (pages 143–145). Then, watch the following two clips on *YouTube*: 1) Sid Caesar's rendition of the 1st movement of Beethoven's Fifth Symphony (*YouTube* keywords: Sid Caesar Beethoven Argumento), and 2) Pink Floyd's *Dark Side of the Moon* correlated with the original movie for *The Wizard of Oz* (*YouTube* keywords: wizard dark side synced glidman3). In writing, discuss your experience and thoroughly explain how each of these clips illustrate fittingness-intensity.

Listening Guides

for

Beethoven's Symphony No. 5

(*Naxos* playlist <u>Arts Key 12B Beethoven 5th</u> [1, 2, 3, 4] or keywords: <u>Beethoven 5 Leibowitz Leonore</u> [6, 7, 8, 9])

Listening Guides—Beethoven's Symphony, No. 5 in C Minor

Movement I

Rhythm: Meter, 2/4 (even), Tempo (*Allegro con brio* [with vigor])
Melody: reiterates motive for theme A, lyrical for theme B
Harmony: Principal keys of C minor, E♭ major, and C major
Texture: split between polyphonic and homophonic
Dynamics: Ranges from *fortissimo* to *pianissimo*
Instrument Range/Timbre: 2 *Flauti* [flutes], 2 *Oboi* [oboes], 2 *Clarinetti* (B♭) [clarinets], 2 *Fagotti* [bassoons], 2 *Corni* (E♭) [French horns], 2 *Trombe* [trumpets], timpani (C, G), strings
Sonata Form: Exposition | Repeat Exposition | Development | Recapitulation | 2nd Development|Coda
(Alternating) |A Bridge B Closing |A Bridge B Closing | Development | A Bridge B Closing | 2nd Development|Coda

Exposition Theme IA, knocking motive in C minor	*fortissimo* unison strings/clarinet state motive, repeat a step lower *piano* strings develop "short, short, short, long" motive in C minor *crescendo* motive in full orchestra introduces 3 *forte* chords, then high, long held note
Bridge	*piano* descending violins develop motive, modulate from Cm to E♭ major *fortissimo* horn call of motive extended sets up the key of E♭ major
Theme IB (contrast) in E♭ major	lyrical theme in E♭ major played by violins, echoed by clarinet, then flute—"short, short, short, long" motive as ground rhythm in low strings. 4-note fragment of lyrical theme in strings enters 4 times full orchestra with gradual crescendo to fortissimo chord
Closing	strings with motive descending begin closing, repeated motive downward in winds, answered by strings, repeated 3 statements of the motive, 2-bars of rest
REPEAT EXPOSITION!	Entire first part (A | Bridge | B | closing) repeated.
Development (Variety and Contrast with Rising Tension) Climax!	*fortissimo* horns/clarinets begin motive, echoed in strings *piano* motive developed as at beginning, winds and strings toss motive back and forth *crescendo* to rapidly repeated, hammered chords violins play motive answered by low descending strings, repeated shortened to 2-note fragment echoed between winds/strings, shortened to 1-note echo *fortissimo* interruption by motive in full orchestra continued by 1-note echo, *diminuendo* to *pianissimo* sudden *fortissimo* motive repeated 8 times leads into
Recapitulation (Release) Theme IA, knocking motive in C minor with long oboe solo at the end	*fortissimo* full orchestra states motive, repeats a step lower *piano* strings develop motive but now with oboe countermelody *crescendo* motive to 3 chords with the last chord *forte*, **high held note now in oboe—oboe continues with a cadenza-like melody**
Bridge	*piano* strings build motive and modulate from C minor to C major bassoon call (not horns now) motive extended sets up the key of C major
Theme IB (contrast) now in C major	8-note lyrical theme **B** in C major now echoed between violins and flute—motive as background rhythm in low strings, violins, then flute 4-note fragment of theme **B** developed between violins and flute, then full orchestra with gradual crescendo to fortissimo chord
Closing	strings with motive descending begin closing, repeated motive in strings, downward in winds, repeated, 3 statements of the motive
2nd Development 2nd Climax!	statements of the motive tossed between winds and strings *fortissimo* rapidly repeated, hammered chords *piano* motive, answered *fortissimo*, hammered chords, motive horn call motive in bassoon/low strings twice against violin countermelody full orchestra in descending pattern, new rising theme in strings, legato and staccato gradually shortened and echoed between winds and strings in 4-note fragments, 2-notes and 1-note, 2-notes and 1-note; rhythmic motive leads to hammered chords
Coda (Release)	*fortissimo* motive stated twice similar to beginning *pianissimo* strings develop motive in C minor as at beginning *fortissimo* motive stated 3 times, then powerful V-i chords 5 times end this movement

Movement II

Rhythm: Meter, 3/8 (Odd), Tempo, *Andante con moto* (*con moto* means "with motion")
Tune: 2 tunes, **A** and *B*
Accompaniment/Harmony: Tune **A** in A*b*, [for theory *cognoscenti*, tune *B* modulates from A*b* to C via German 6th]
Texture: Homophonic
Dynamics: range from *pianissimo* to *fortissimo*
Instrument Range/Timbre: Same instruments as movement I except French horns are now in C
Form: Theme and variation form with two themes (thus a type of alternating form as well):
    A *B* **A**^{1} *B*^{1} **A**^{2} *B*^{2} **A**^{3} Coda

A, Flowing Theme **2 Themes (IIA and IIB)**	*piano* violas/cellos with flowing theme over bass background rhythm with 4-note rising and falling response rising and falling response repeated by the full strings and bassoon, echoed and extended by the woodwinds, varied by strings followed-up by winds and then strings plus woodwinds
II*B*, Dancing theme	dancing theme in Ab [modulates to C (V^7/IV=Gr^6) in Bar 7] ascending 1-bar chords modulate from C back to Ab
II**A**^{1}, Flowing Theme **Variation of Themes**	Variation of flowing theme with added notes in the melody
II*B*^{1}, Dancing theme **Rising Tension**	Variation of dancing theme with added notes in the ground rhythm
II**A**^{2}, Flowing Theme in 3 variations ending with development	8 bars with melody in cello 8 bars with melody in viola 9 bars with melody in bass beginning fragment of flowing theme developed for 24 bars
II*B*^{2}, Dancing theme, fanfare only	Fanfare only
Transition	8 bars of transition beginning fragment of flowing theme developed similar to end of **A**^{2}
II**A**^{3}, Flowing Theme **Climax**	Violins state theme but leave out repeat of 4-note rising and falling response (2 bars) and last part so theme **A** is now only 21 bars
Coda based on Flowing Theme **Release**	Flowing theme developed to close using beginning and ending fragments

Movement III

Rhythm: Meter, 3/4 (Odd), Tempo, Allegro
Melody: A—mysterious theme; B—short, short, short, long motive; C—chase theme
Harmony: C*m*, B*b*, B*b*m, C, repeated
Texture: Homophonic and polyphonic
Dynamics: range from *pianissimo* to *fortissimo*
Instrument Range/Timbre: 2 *Flauti* [flutes], 2 *Oboi* [oboes], 2 *Clarinetti* (Bb) [clarinets], 2 *Fagotti* [bassoons], 2 *Corni* (C) [French horns in E*b*], 2 *Trombe* (C) [trumpets], timpani (C, G), strings
Form: (three-part form):   **A**   *B*   **A**^{1}
                            A   *B*   *A*^{1} *B*^{1} *A*^{2} *B*^{2} *C*   *C*   *C*^{1} *C*^{2} *A*^{3} *B*^{3} *A*   *B*   *B*

Form		Comments
A	IIIA¹, central mysterious theme (C minor)	cello and bass play question phrase (mono.)|violin plays answer (homophonic) theme repeated and extended in the middle
	IIIB¹, "short, short, short, long" <u>knocking motive</u>	horns play <u>motive</u> melody; strings provide harmony on the beat orchestra extends <u>motive</u> melody; woodwind/strings provide harmony
	IIIA², mysterious theme now in Bb minor	cello and bass play question phrase (mono.)|violin plays answer (homophonic) first phrase of theme expanded to 18 measures
	IIIB², <u>knocking motive</u>	clarinets, horns, violins, violas play <u>motive</u> melody *forte*; harmony then *fortissimo* as <u>motive</u> melody is extended
	IIIA³, mysterious theme	cellos and basses play question (mono.) |flutes/oboes answer (homophonic) |violins with <u>motive</u> counterpoint second phrase of theme repeated and developed extensively
	IIIB³, <u>knocking motive</u>	*fortissimo* in full orchestra |*piano* without clarinets/horns
B	IIIC¹, chase theme (C major)	monophonic in basses/cellos, then polyphonic with violas/bassoons repeated exactly
	IIIC², chase theme with two false starts	(*forte*) monophonic in basses/cellos, then polyphonic to full orchestra
	IIIC³, chase theme again with two false starts	(*forte*) monophonic in basses/cellos, then polyphonic to full orchestra
	Bridge	down through woodwinds to *pizzicato* (strings plucked) in basses
A¹	IIIA⁴, mysterious theme	cello and bass play question (monophonic)|clarinets/bassoons answer (homophonic) bassoons/*pizzicato* violas repeat (m) |*pizzicato* violins answer (homophonic)
	IIIB⁴, <u>knocking motive</u>	(*pianissimo*) in clarinets |answered by violins strings provide background rhythm/harmony, bassoons join in answer repeated in oboes, everything else the same as before extended for 10 bars
	IIIA⁵, <u>knocking motive</u> overlaps end of mysterious theme **Rising Tension**	bassoons, cellos on question phrase (mono.) |violins answer (homophonic) "short, short, short, long" <u>motive</u> overlaps answers and extension
	IIIB⁵, <u>knocking motive</u>	8 bars, ends on a deceptive cadence in C minor (V-VI)
	IIIB⁶, <u>knocking motive</u> transition	timpani reiterate "short, short, short, long" <u>motive</u>; other instruments join to lead directly into the fourth movement with no break

LISTENING GUIDES FOR BEETHOVEN SYMPHONY NO. 5

Movement IV (No break from movement III)
Rhythm, Meter: 4/4 (even), Tempo (*Allegro*), 3/4; Melody/Harmony: C, G, Cm, C; Dynamics: range as before;
Instrument Range/Timbre: Piccolo and 3 trombones [*tromboni*] added; clarinets, French horns, and trumpets now in C
Sonata Form: Exposition Section | Development | **Surprise** | Recapitulation | 2nd Dev. 2nd Clim. | Coda
(Alternating) | A *Bridge* **B** Closing | *Development* | Climax | A *Bridge* **B** Closing | 2nd Development | Coda

Exposition—IV**A**, Triumphant theme	*fortissimo* full orchestra emphasizing trumpets arpeggiates a C major chord, answering upward staccato notes developed; scale with off-beat accents leads to
IV Bridge theme	*fortissimo* melody and thrusting 3-chord response; melody extended by violins leading to a conversation between woodwinds and strings leading to
IV**B**, Joyful theme—from "short, short, short, long" motive	"short, short, short, long" rhythm repeated in 12-note, then 16-note phrase now in G major; *fortissimo* energetic scale passage followed by two *forte* staccato chords leads to
IV Closing theme	six-note downward scale repeated, sequenced, and answered forms the closing theme; *forte* repeat by full orchestra, repeated chords and ascending *fortissimo* motive in the strings leads directly into
Development (of *B* theme) [rising tension] Re-transition	the development of theme **B** in all sorts of combinations followed by a development of the countermelody of theme **B** first in contrabassoon, then trombone, then strings and trombones in imitation, and finally by full orchestra; transition leads to
IV **Surprise** insertion of "short, short, short, long" motive Climax!	SURPRISE! *Pianissimo* strings, clarinets, and oboes repeating the "short, short, short, long" motive from the *scherzo* *crescendo* directly into
Recapitulation—IV**A**, Triumphant theme	*fortissimo* theme A in full orchestra again arpeggiates C major chord, again answering upward staccato notes developed; scale with off-beat accents again leads to
IV Bridge theme	*fortissimo* melody and thrusting 3-chord response; again melody extended by violins leading to a conversation between woodwinds and strings leads to
IV**B**, Joyful theme derived from knocking motive	"short, short, short, long" motive of joyful theme again repeated in 12-note, then 16-note phrase now back in C major with fuller accompaniment *fortissimo* energetic scale passage followed by two *forte* staccato chords leads to
IV Closing theme	six-note downward scale repeated, sequenced, and answered forms the closing theme with different instruments; *forte* repeat by full orchestra, repeated chords and ascending *fortissimo* figure in the strings leads directly into
2nd Development 2nd Climax!	more development of theme B and its countermelody; six staccato chords lead to a woodwind development of the bridge theme in imitation followed by rising scales in the piccolo, then more development of theme B now in the strings with countermelody and trills in the piccolo, accelerando to a development of the closing theme in violins and then full orchestra; crescendo and parts of the closing theme lead to
Coda (Release)	fortissimo and presto theme A in full orchestra; theme A quickly developed followed by a very, very long ending of hammered chords, ending finally on a single C played by all the instruments of the orchestra

PART II—AESTHETIC AND EXTRA-AESTHETIC INTERACTION

13. AESTHETICS, **F**UNCTION, **E**THICS, AND **W**ORLDVIEW ▪ 165

14. A SHORT **H**ISTORY OF **S**TYLE ▪ 179

15. IT'S **Y**OUR **M**OVE ▪ 195

Neo-classical (1750–1825)—Jacques-Louis David (1748–1825) *Napoleon Crossing the Alps* (1801) oil on canvas, 261 x 221 cm (102 1/3 x 87 in), Château de Malmaison, Rueil-Malmaison, France.

Chapter 13

Aesthetics, Function, Ethics, and Worldview

"It is amazing how complete is the delusion that beauty is goodness." Leo Tolstoy

Notice the aesthetic excellence of the painting on the preceding page. All the lines point upward to the invisible summit on the left—the rider's right arm and hand, the horse's nose and face, the riders' left arm mirroring the slope of horse and the ridge, the underbelly of the horse mirroring the slope of the rocks below and the French troops hauling a cannon up the mountain. The foreground shapes of the horse and the rider are deftly drawn in perspective against the sky, mountains, troops, and rocks below. The bold colors of orange, blue, and green in the rider's clothing are softly reflected in the background sky. The white of the horse contrasts with the black in the face, the tail, and the chest and the boots of the rider. The blended and smooth textures of the paint give the painting a fine and finished feel. The central theme of the rider on the horse (A) is finely detailed and developed, set off against the contrasting background (B) of sky, mountains, troops, and rocks. The eye of the viewer is drawn toward the face of the rider leading to the climax in the upraised hand of the rider and the horse's head straining forward. The eye gradually relaxes and releases as it moves to other parts in the background of the painting. Jacques-Louis David has successfully portrayed a hero. [David signed and dated the painting on the horse's breastplate yoke.]

It is easy to mistake beauty for goodness, to equate moral excellence with aesthetic excellence. Artistic excellence must include aesthetic excellence, but it is a broader category that includes extra-aesthetic excellence as well.

The painter, Jacques Louis David, impacted the world with his aesthetically excellent art in the service of various political causes. Before the French Revolution, David's paintings fit the moral climate of the Old Regime of Kings and Queens. During the Revolution (1789–1799), David was a member of the

> Jacobins, a group of revolutionary extremists, and the patrons of David's painting, which served contemporary political events. David himself was elected to the National Convention and voted to send Louis XVI to the guillotine. When Robespierre, the minister who presided over the Reign of Terror, fell, David was imprisoned twice. But he regained favor under Napoleon, who appointed him to be his imperial painter…[1]

The Painting of a Hero

In 1800, Napoleon led his troops across the Alps hoping to surprise the Austrians. Although he did not surprise them, he defeated the Austrians in the Battle of Marengo. The French victory over the Austrians in Italy paved the way for talks to re-establish

---

[1] Laurie Schneider Adams, *A History of Western Art*, third edition (New York: McGraw-Hill, 1994) p. 376.

French diplomatic relations with Spain. The Spanish King, Charles IV, commissioned the painting of *Napoleon Crossing the Alps* as part of the traditional gift exchange for re-establishing diplomatic relations. The painting was hung in the Royal Palace of Madrid reflecting the restored relationship between France and Spain. In response, Napoleon commissioned Jacques-Louis David to paint three additional versions: one for the palace Château de Saint-Cloud about 3 miles west of Paris, one for the library of *Les Invalides* (Veteran's Hospital) in Paris, and one for the palace of the Cisapline Republic in Milan, Italy. These four versions of the same event fulfill their purpose admirably as works of fine-art symbolizing Napoleon's role in the rapprochement between France and Spain.

Equestrian portraits were the rage for royalty. In the paintings by David, Napoleon is pictured astride an Arabian stallion. (Actually, Napoleon did not lead his troops; he followed them several days later on the back of a mule rather than on a horse.) Although Napoleon himself suggested the idea of his portrait on a horse, he refused to sit for the portrait, so one of Jacques-Louis David's sons dressed in Napoleon's uniform and, atop a ladder to simulate the height on a horse, filled in for him. The inscriptions on the bottom of the painting portray Napoleon (BONAPARTE) as a general comparable to HANNIBAL (247–ca.182 B.C.) and Charlemagne [KAROLVS MAGNVS IMP] (ca. 747–814) who had both crossed the Aps in military campaigns. David's painting supported the political ambitions of Napoleon (and his own as well).

A Symphony Picturing a Hero

Like many others, Beethoven was impressed with Napoleon, regarding him as bringing liberty, equality, and brotherhood (*liberté, egalité, fraternité*) to the common person. Legend has it that the French ambassador to Vienna suggested to Beethoven that he write a work to honor Napoleon. By 1804, Beethoven had completed his work, which he titled *Sinfonia grande Intitolata Bonaparte* [*Grand Symphony Titled Bonaparte*]. However, when he learned that Napoleon declared himself emperor in 1804, he was so incensed that he violently tried to erase the name and ended up tearing a hole in the page, although it appears that he later relented. When the symphony was published in 1806, it was titled *Sinfonia Eroica* (*Heroic Symphony*).

A FEW Critera for Artistic Excellence

Our journey now takes us to the interaction of aesthetics (#4 on the chart), social function (#6 on the chart), ethics (#2 on the chart), and worldview (#1 on the chart). **A FEW** criteria for artistic excellence are 1) *Aesthetic excellence*, 2) *Functional fit*, 3) *Ethical integrity*, 4) *Worldview fit*. These may be judged independently of one another, but all must be present in order to have *artistic* excellence.

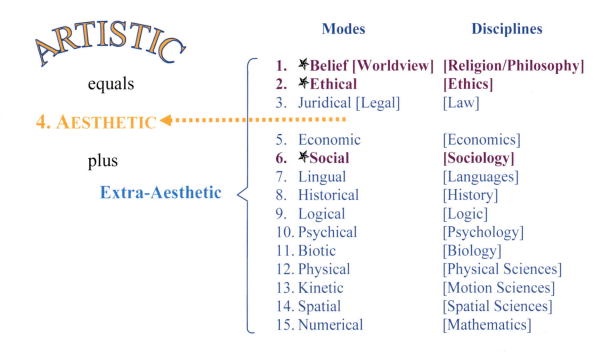

Aesthetic Excellence as the First Criterion for Artistic Excellence

The first criterion and *sine qua non* for artistic excellence is *aesthetic excellence*. Does a work possess unity, diversity, and fittingness-intensity in form and other elements (previous chapter), or is it aesthetically shoddy? If it is aesthetically shoddy, it cannot be artistically excellent.

Functional Fit as the Second Criterion for Artistic Excellence

The second criterion for artistic excellence is *functional fit*. Does a work function well for the purpose for which it is intended, used, or distributed? Does it suit the occasion? Recall the Chapter 2 discussion of function and the broad categories of folk function, fine-art function, and popular/commercial function. An aesthetically excellent symphony does not work effectively as a marching band piece without some major changes, nor does a marching band piece work effectively in a concert hall. A good hymn (folk music) is intended to enable everyone in the congregation to worship God effectively through music. In addition to its aesthetic excellence, a good hymn is eminently singable. The *Star-Spangled Banner* is an excellent solo that works effectively at ball games but difficult for the average person to sing because of its wide range.

Ethical Integrity as the Third Criterion for Artistic Excellence

The third criterion for artistic excellence is *ethical integrity*. Is the purpose for which the work is used honest and honorable? In addition to the three broad uses of the arts (fine, folk, and popular/commercial), there are a plethora of other possible uses. As just a few examples, a work may be made or used to please one's teacher, to give praise to God, to glorify oneself, to be therapeutic, to be a palliative (drug), to set a mood, or to build camaraderie. The Pied Piper of Hamelin lured the rats away from the town with his musical piping (an ethical use), but when the town refused to pay him for his services, he used his music to lure the children away from the town never to return (a sadly unethical use of music). In a similarly unethical use of music, the Nazis used familiar music to serve as a palliative to lure those taken to the gas chambers into a false sense of security.

Worldview Fit as the Fourth Criterion for Artistic Excellence

The fourth criterion for artistic excellence is *worldview integration*. In contrast to **absolute music** (instrumental music not intended to represent or illustrate something else) and non-representational art and dance, deeded and worded works (deeded art and dance, worded-music, poetry, story, theatre, and musical theatre) present a world that is intended to be part of the artistic experience. Nicholas Wolterstorff calls this "world-projection."[1] This artistic world is not intended to photocopy reality, but to provide an alternative world for our consideration. In addition to its aesthetic and functional aspects, the story projected by this alternative world usually presents a perspective on the actual world. Artistic action is always part of a larger **worldview** [*weltanschauung* in German], "a set of presuppositions (assumptions which may be true, partially true or entirely false) which we hold (consciously or subconsciously, consistently or inconsistently) about the basic make-up of our world." James W. Sire gives seven helpful questions to ask in understanding worldviews:[2]

1) What is prime reality—the really real?
2) What is the nature of external reality—the world around us?
3) What is a human being?
4) What happens to a person at death?
5) Why is it possible to know anything at all?
6) How do we know what is right and wrong (ethics)?
7) What is the meaning of human history?

The following steps help in evaluating the story of projected worlds in all the arts and understand how they relate to worldview. (In all these steps, it is important to remember that, whatever their extra-aesthetic purpose, an essential part of projected worlds and stories is to encourage us to use our aesthetic *imag*e*i*nation.)

A. Observation—What does the story say? Look and listen for the story of the projected world with eyes and ears wide open. Let it carry you to a different dimension,

---

[1] Nicholas Wolterstorff, *Art in Action* (Grand Rapids: Eerdmans, 1980), p. 122.
[2] James W. Sire, *The Universe Next Door* (Downer's Grove, Illinois: Intervarsity Press, 1999), p. 7.

time, and space. Take time to experience the entire work *over* time, being careful not to read into the work something that is not there. In this regard, it may be helpful to make an exact paraphrase, retelling the story from memory in one's own words in order to get the story straight. A story may deal with things that have actually happened (a historical event), things that could occur but have not actually happened (a fiction that is possible), or things that could not possibly happen (a fiction that is logically impossible).

B. Interpretation—What is the point of the story? Determine the perspective of the story (the attitude that the story invites you to take toward the actual world). Be careful to distinguish the overall perspective from the perspectives of particular characters in the story. These attitudes are not necessarily the same. For example, the creator of the work may present attitudes of particular characters that she or he actually wishes us to avoid. We may be encouraged to emulate the wittiness of a villain or to eschew the mistakes of a hero (as in the story of *Samson*, for example). It is also important to understand that the creator of a work may not intend just one specific point. Often, works in the arts are used to evoke different reactions and to allow for exploration of multiple perspectives, perhaps even points that the artist did not foresee. An artist may also project a world purely for its aesthetic possibilities rather than to present any particular point of view. This is always true in absolute music and non-representational art, where there is no story with a point of view.

C. Application—How does the point relate to worldview? In step *C*, decide to which of the seven aspects of worldview (on the previous page) the point relates. It is not the subject matter *per se*, but the *attitude* that we are invited to take toward the subject matter that is the determining factor. Stories filled with sex and violence are not unethical *per se*. It is the *attitudes* and *actions* that these stories invite us to take toward sex and violence that are crucial rather than the subject matter itself. As an example of something in the ethical dimension, consider the lyrics of a song about someone who has chosen suicide as a solution. The artist may present the story with the intent of giving positive alternatives, dissuading us from considering suicide, or the artist may present the story with the intent of inviting us to consider suicide as an option for escaping an intolerable situation. The ethical value of the *attitudes* and *actions* that a work invites us to take may be judged by how well they fit the norms of a Christian worldview.

Francis Schaeffer (philosopher, theologian, and author of *How Should We Then Live*) believes that *Christian* art should have both a "*major theme*—the meaningfulness and purposefulness of life" and a "*minor theme*—the abnormality" of a world revolting against God.

> Christian art is the expression of the whole life of the whole person who is a Christian. What a Christian portrays in his art is the totality of life… Every artist should build up an entire body of work as well as individual works of art… Therefore, we cannot judge an artist's work from one piece.[1]

---

[1] Francis A. Schaeffer, *Art & the Bible* (Downers Grove, Illinois: InterVarsity Press, 1973), pp. 56–57, 61–62.

Examples of Observation, Interpretation, and Application. At the beginning of the chapter, we experienced the projected world of *Napoleon Crossing the Alps*. We discussed its aesthetic excellence, its functional fit, and began to discuss its ethical integrity and worldview implications. We observed the actual story of this world (step A), and interpreted its main point (B) to be—presenting Napoleon Bonaparte as the quintessential hero for all time. In step C, we applied the point to worldview question 6: "How do we know what is right and wrong?" We noticed that Jacques-Louis David used this work to promote Napoleon Bonaparte's political fortunes and his own political and personal fortunes as well by stretching the truth, an ethical choice clearly counter to a Christian worldview. Beethoven, on the other hand, had no ulterior motive other than to write an aesthetically excellent work of art music to honor someone he considered a hero. His point is more consistent with a Christian worldview.

In chapters 8 and 10, we experienced the stories of the *Nutcracker Ballet*, the *Samson and Delilah* story, and the play *Much Ado About Nothing*. In step *A*, we paraphrased the stories of these worlds using viewing and reading guides. (In doing this, we uncovered the aesthetic excellence and functional fit of each of these stories.) Now we are ready to consider step *B*, the point of these stories. As a preliminary thesis, we might posit the main points to be the following:

- *Nutcracker*: "Fairy tales can come true."
- *Samson and Delilah*: "With repentance, there can be redemption even for those who make miserable mistakes."
- *Much Ado About Nothing*: "The aesthetic aspects of male-female interaction are to be relished and savored."

In the *Nutcracker*, we are motivated to cheer on and participate in the dreams of children. In *Samson and Delilah*, we learn the tragic consequences of failure and the redemption that comes from repentance. In *Much Ado About Nothing*, we are encouraged to laugh, and to explore the relationship between men and women through the aesthetic use of words. Words *do* matter. Do the points in the stories above fit biblical norms (step *C*)? Indeed they do, for imag*e*ining is part of what it means to be a human being (worldview area 3), repentance and redemption are not only possible, but are biblical imperatives (worldview area 6), and laughing/loving are part of our humanity (worldview area 3).

Trying Your Hand at Evaluating Two Paintings

Consider first the aesthetic excellence or shoddiness of the two paintings on the next page. How would you rate them in terms of unity, diversity, and fittingness-intensity for the form and other elements of art? Next, consider function, the ethics, and the world presented by these paintings. Although the following two paintings refer to actual historical incidents during the time of Napoleon, it is important to understand that real art is not a photocopy of reality. Rather, it is a nuanced interpretation that presents a world for our consideration.

13—Aesthetics, Function, Ethics, and Worldview 171

Top: Jacques Louis David (1748–1825), *Le sacre de l'empereur Napoléon 1ᵉʳ et couronnement de l'impératrice Joséphine dans la cathédrale Notre-Dame de Paris, le 2 décembre 1804* [*The Consecration of Emperor Napoleon I and Crowning of Empress Josephine in the Cathedral of Notre Dame in Paris*] (1806–1807, Paris), oil on canvas, 621 x 979 cm (20 ft. 4½ in. x 32 ft. 1½ in.), Louvre. Photograph © 2004 by Allen P. Schantz. All rights reserved.

Bottom: Francisco de Goya y Lucientes (1746–1828), *Los Fusilamientos del 3 de Mayo* [*The Executions of the Third of May*] (1814–1815), Oil on canvas, 267 x 345 cm., 8 ft. 9 in. x 11 ft. 4 in., Prado, Madrid.

Painting 1. The top painting on the previous page by Jacques Louis David dominates a gigantic wall in the Louvre. It portrays in detail the portraits of the people who attended the historical ceremony in the cathedral of Notre Dame during which Napoleon Bonaparte crowned his wife Josephine as empress after his own consecration (see title above). A consummate painter in the neo-classic style, David uses his painterly talents to make the point that Napoleon was the legitimate heir to the crown of the Holy Roman Empire, blessed by God, adored by his mother, and sanctioned by Pope Pius VII. (Notice Napoleon's mother in the center of the box seat on the upper left and the Pope seated on the right raising his hand in blessing.) Artist Jacques-Louis David served and survived three very different regimes in French political history as an artist who was always *politically correct*: 1) as a patriotic neo-classicist before the Revolution (*The Oath of the Horatii, The Death of Socrates*), 2) as producer of the great national festivals and the art that supported the Revolution (a close friend of Robespierre and painter of *Death of Marat*), and later as 3) an artist who

> embraced with equal enthusiasm the imperial dreams of Napoleon Bonaparte… David, it appears, always needed a hero and a cause, while Napoleon needed a painter of David's stature to commemorate the glories of his rule. The alliance between them was inevitable and mutually satisfying. It was especially so since Napoleon, the hero risen from the Revolution, combined his professions of liberty and equality with Classical personal tastes. David was showered with Napoleonic honors, and it was of course he, as First Painter, who was commissioned to memorialize Napoleon's accession to imperial rank in 1804. The result was the great canvas of *le Sacre,* or *The Consecration,* usually known in English, inaccurately but handily, as *The Coronation of Napoleon*…
>
> The ceremonial moment portrayed had to be changed from that in David's original sketch, for it was not thought wise to show the historic gesture of Napoleon proudly placing the crown on his own head while the pope sat helplessly by. Rather, against the Classical stage-set that had been specially installed in Gothic Notre Dame for the ceremony, the pope now was depicted with his arm raised in blessing as the emperor lifted high the crown to be placed on the head of the kneeling Josephine. The effect of the whole is remarkably naturalistic, most notably the handsomely luminous figure of the empress.[1]

---

[1] Henry Vyverberg, *The Living Tradition,* 2nd ed. (Ft. Worth: Harcourt Brace Jovanovich College Publishers, 1988), p. 408.

Painting 2. The response of Francisco de Goya to the accession of Napoleon was different. Goya, at first, considered France the center of enlightenment and reform. He was sympathetic when Napoleon began moving troops into Spain around 1807. However, it soon became clear that Napoleon's goal was conquest rather than reform; a fierce resistance soon sprang up, and a series of bloody events ensued from 1808–1814. Goya now began to see Napoleon as a tyrant and the enemy of freedom and liberty. Goya chronicled the fighting in a series of paintings including *The Executions of the Third of May, 1808* painted in 1814–1815. Laurie Schneider Adams interprets the world presented by Goya as follows:

> The raised arms of the central, illuminated victim about to be shot recall Christ's death. His pose and gesture, in turn, are repeated by the foremost corpse. The lessons of Christ's Crucifixion, Goya seems to be saying, are still unlearned.[1]

Take some time to get into these paintings aesthetically, functionally, ethically, and worldviewishly. Then evaluate them, using the steps outlined in chapter 12 for aesthetic evaluation and the steps outlined in this chapter for functional, ethical, and worldview evaluation. Remember that it is not the subject matter (consecration or violence) that is important in evaluating worldview fit, but rather the viewpoint taken toward that subject matter.

"Going the Extra Mile" with a Christian View of Ethics

In the Christian view, it is not enough to abhor violence, or to refrain from it. It is not enough to toe the line. It is not even enough to love our neighbors as we love ourselves. Rather, the extra mile means loving even our enemies (see Insight 13-1 on the next page). Arvo Pärt has attempted to capture this idea in his work *Credo*, combining violent 12-tone music with the serene prelude in C major by J. S. Bach. He writes:

> In the 1960s I became so fascinated by that central idea of Christianity 'Love your enemies' that it gave birth to my composition *Credo*. The work comprises two musically opposing, colliding worlds: one serial and aleatoric, the other an arrangement of a prelude by Bach.
>
> What I wanted to show through the work's unfolding—inexorable like a chain reaction—is how the postulate "**An eye for an eye, a tooth for a tooth**," harmless as it may seem in its initial stage, only gradually displays the full destructive dimensions of its true face: and escalation of power that, like an avalanche, eventually comes up against its own limits. What at first we perceive as human justice finally turns into its opposite. "**Do not resist an evildoer**"... "**Love your enemies**"—there is nothing more radical than these words of Christ, which nearly burst the bounds of our reason."[2]

---

[1] Laurie Schneider Adams, *A History of Western Art.* 3rd ed. (New York: McGraw-Hill, 2001), p. 394.
[2] Quoted by Michael Church in Liner Notes for the album titled *Credo* as performed by Hélène Grimaud (© 2003 by Deutsche Grammophon GmbH, Hamburg, p. 11).

> **Special Insight 13-1—*An Eye for an Eye, the Ten Commandments, and the Radical Ethics of Jesus* (*Going the Extra Mile and Loving Your Enemies*)**
>
> <u>An eye for an eye</u>. *An eye for an eye* is an ethical principle that limits retaliation for a crime that has been committed. The punishment should not be greater than the crime as described in the Code of Hammurabi and the Law of Moses: "But if there is harm, then you shall pay life for life, eye for eye, tooth for tooth, hand for hand, foot for foot, burn for burn, wound for wound, stripe for stripe" (Exodus 21:23–25).
>
> <u>The Ten Commandments</u>. The Ten Commandments (which summarize the laws of many cultures and play a fundamental role in Judaism, Islam, and Christianity) expand this principle to do no harm:
> a) You shall have no other Gods before me;
> b) You shall make no carved images;
> c) You shall not take the name of the Lord your God in vain;
> d) Remember the sabbath day, to keep it holy;
> e) Honor your father and mother;
> f) You shall not murder;
> g) You shall not commit adultery;
> h) You shall not steal;
> i) You shall not bear false witness against your neighbor; and
> j) You shall not covet what belongs to your neighbor.
>
> The first four of these commandments are summarized in Deuteronomy 6:4–5: "Love the Lord your God with all your heart and with all your soul…" and the last six in Leviticus 19:18 "Love your neighbor as yourself."
>
> <u>The Radical Ethics of Jesus</u>. Jesus reiterates this summary (Mark 12:28–31) and takes this idea of loving God even further. He draws a stark contrast between "***an eye for an eye and a tooth for a tooth***" and the ethics of "***loving your enemies***."
>
>> You have heard that it was said, '***An eye for an eye and a tooth for a tooth***.' But I say to you, ***Do not resist an evildoer***. But if anyone slaps you on the right cheek, turn to him the other also. And if anyone wants to sue you, and take your shirt, let him have your coat also. And if anyone forces you to go one mile, go also the second mile. Give to the one who asks of you, and do not turn away from the one who wants to borrow from you. You have heard that it was said, '*You shall love your neighbor* and hate your enemy.' But I say to you, ***Love your enemies*** and pray for those who persecute you. (Matthew 5:38–44)

Guide to the Words of Pärt's *Credo*
(*Naxos* playlist Arts Key 13 [2] or http://youtu.be/yYWpfNi9h4c and http://youtu.be/3QUuq5Cf5Fs)

Credo, Credo, Credo *Credo in Jesum Christum, in Jesum Christum* [Bach C major prelude begins; breaks off at the following words.]	I believe, I believe, I believe I believe in Jesus Christ, in Jesus Christ
Audividistus dictum *oculum pro oculo, dentem pro dente* [Tension continues to build through an extended section.]	You have heard that it was said An eye for an eye, A tooth for a tooth
oculum pro oculo, dentem pro dente *oculum pro oculo, dentem pro dente* *oculum pro oculo, dentem pro dente* [Whispers followed by more violent music; tension increases exponentially.]	An eye for an eye, A tooth for a tooth An eye for an eye, A tooth for a tooth An eye for an eye, A tooth for a tooth
Antem ego vobis dico: *non esse resistendum injuriae…* [Prelude returns, with a few interjections.]	But I say to you Do not resist an evildoer…
non esse, non esse resistendum *non esse, non esse, non esse resistendum* *non esse resistendum* [Prelude breaks off before the final note.]	Do not, Do not resist Do not, Do not, Do not resist Do not resist
CREDO CREDO [Final note of prelude comes in and repeats at different octaves.]	I BELIEVE I BELIEVE

This is an intense work requiring many hearings to fully digest, but it is well worth chewing on! Before you listen to this selection, you may find it helpful to listen to the Prelude in C Major by J. S. Bach (*Naxos* playlist Arts Key 13 [1] or *YouTube*: http://youtu.be/PXMVkQ70I88).

Arthur Lubow describes the impact of this work:

> In 1968, [Pärt] caused an uproar when his choral piece "Credo" was premiered. This time, the Latin text — it proclaims, "I believe in Jesus Christ" — is what outraged the devoutly atheistic authorities. Neeme Järvi, who conducted the sole Soviet performance, told me: "The law was that you first had to show the score to the composers' union. I didn't. I thought they wouldn't let us. The Estonian Philharmonic organization said, 'Let's do it.' Next morning it was a big scandal in the Politburo of Estonia. Then the pressure starts. Some people were sacked from the Philharmonic organization." He says that he retained his position because no one was available to replace him, but that the scandal dried up Pärt's

official commissions, forcing him to rely on writing film scores to earn a living.[1]

With his combination of two different radically contrasting styles, Arvo Pärt effectively introduces us to mixed style and to the next chapter.

Artistic Excellence Summarized

Artistic excellence begins with *aesthetic* excellence. It is because of the *aesthetic* excellence of Pärt's music that he is able to effectively communicate the words of his extra-aesthetic ethical worldview. In the case of Jacques Louis David's painting of Napoleon at the beginning of the chapter, the *aesthetic* excellence of David's art enables him to effectively communicate his unethical, opportunistic worldview.

In the case of absolute music (or non-representational art and dance) used for aesthetic delight, artistic excellence begins *and ends* with aesthetic excellence. Whatever the worldview of someone who composes aesthetically excellent absolute music (or non-representational art and dance), such works glorify God. On the other hand, anyone who composes aesthetically mediocre works dishonors God.

In summary, then, artistic excellence includes four things: **A**esthetic excellence, **F**unctional fit, **E**thical integrity, and **W**orldview integration. The key ingredient for artistic excellence is *aesthetic excellence*, which reflects faithful stewardship of God's creation by human beings, who are made in his image. Without aesthetic excellence, there can be no true functional fit, ethical integrity or worldview integration even in works that project a world: "Holy shoddy is still shoddy."[2]

---

[1] Arthur Lubow, *The Sound of Spirit* in *New York Times Magazine*, October 18, 2010. http://www.nytimes.com/2010/10/17/magazine/17part-t.html?pagewanted=all&_r=0

[2] Attributed to Elton Trueblood (1900–1994), Quaker author, philosopher, educator, theologian, and Professor of Philosophy at Earlham College.

Actions for Practice and Delight

13/1. Take a great deal of time over several days to observe the two paintings on page 171. When you have explored them thoroughly, evaluate them in writing in terms of aesthetic excellence (as outlined in chapter 12) and then functional fit, ethical integrity, and worldview fit (following each of the steps outlined in this chapter). Remember that it is not the subject matter (consecration or violence) that is important in evaluating ethical excellence, but rather the viewpoint taken toward that subject matter.

13/2. Watch and listen to the Prelude in C Major by J. S. Bach (http://youtu.be/PXMVkQ70I88 or *Naxos* playlist Arts Key 13 [1]). Then listen to Arvo Pärt's *Credo* (http://youtu.be/yYWpfNi9h4c and http://youtu.be/3QUuq5Cf5Fs in two parts or *Naxos* playlist Arts Key 13 [2]) a number of times. Notice especially the form and dramatic shape. After listening carefully and interacting with the material on pages 173–176, evaluate this in writing in terms of aesthetic excellence (as outlined in chapter 12), functional fit, ethical integrity, and worldview fit (following each of the steps outlined in this chapter). Discuss whether Pärt effectively makes his point (review his intent on page 173).

13/3. Find the best example you can of a work in any of the arts that has aesthetic excellence, but presents a world with a definite point (not absolute music or non-representational art) that does not fit a Christian worldview. Choose a work that pulls you in and makes you really consider adopting that particular point of view, not a work that you might reject without thinking about it. For your example, outline why you think your choice has aesthetic excellence in terms of its unity, diversity, and fittingness-intensity for the form and other structural elements of the particular art you have chosen. Finally, independently paraphrase and discuss the story of its projected world using the steps outlined on page 168–169 in this chapter. Explain how the point of the story tends to draw you in but why it does not fit a biblical worldview.

CHAPTER 14

A SHORT HISTORY OF STYLE

"Coming to understand a painting or a symphony in an unfamiliar style, to recognize the work of an artist or school, to see or hear in new ways, is as cognitive an achievement as learning to read or write or add." [1]

Style is the characteristic way of presenting the *elements* of an art. (**Musical style** is the characteristic way of presenting *the elements* of music; **dance style** is the characteristic way of presenting the *elements* of dance, and so on.) Style is directly related to what is happening in a particular period of history. For example, the Middle Ages emphasized meditative withdrawal, whereas the Renaissance emphasized the power and beauty of the human being. This was reflected in artistic styles of both periods. In the Middle Ages, Mary (*Madonna*, Latin for "My Lady") was painted as a childlike, unearthly figure, whereas in the Renaissance she was painted as a beautiful young woman. Notice the differences in each of the elements of art: the colors, the lines and shapes, etc.

Middle Ages (450–1450) Giovanni Cimabue (c. 1240–1302) *Madonna Enthroned*, c. 1280–1290, Tempera on wood, 384 x 224 cm., 12 ft. 4 in. x 7 ft. 4 in., Galleria degli Uffizi, Florence.

Renaissance (1450–1600) Raphael (1483–1520), *Small Cowper Madonna*, ca. 1505, Oil on wood, 59.5 x 44 cm, 23 3/8 x 17 3/8 in., The National Gallery of Art, Washington, D.C.

---

[1] Nelson Goodman, *Of Mind and Other Matters* (New Haven: Harvard University Press, 1984), p. 147.

Our journey through the aesthetic dimension has brought us to the interaction with aesthetics and style throughout history. Aesthetics is independent from historical style. *There can be aesthetic excellence in any style.*

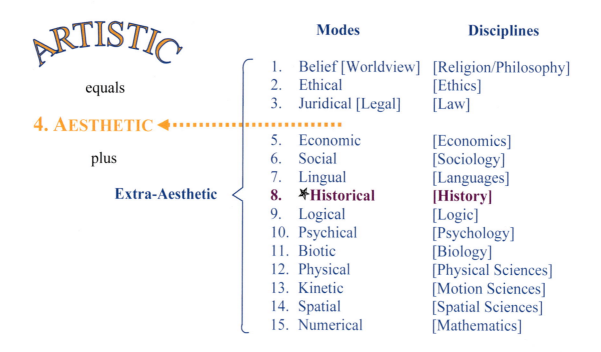

Walter Wiora in his classic volume, *The Four Ages of Music*,[1] provides a helpful division of music history as follows: *The First Age*—Pre-Historic and Early Period, *The Second Age*—High Civilizations of Antiquity and the Orient, *The Third Age*—the Special Position of Western Music (from the Middle Ages to the 20th century), and *The Fourth Age*—the Age of Techniques and Global Industrial Culture. These may be used as a general outline for artistic style and for the three broad categories of *artistic* styles in history as shown in the chart on the following page: 1) Ancient Styles, 2) Common-Practice Styles, and 3) Avant-Garde Styles.

---

[1] Walter Wiora, *Die vier Weltalter der Musik* [*The Four Ages of Music*], translated by M. D. Herter Norton (New York: W.W. Norton, 1965), 233 pp. (originally published by W. Kohlhammer, Stuttgart).

Artistic Styles in History[1]

FOLK-ART FUNCTIONS

The Beginning

Abraham ca. 2000 BC
Joseph   ca. 1776 BC
Moses   ca. 1492 BC
David   1000 BC

Ancient Styles (*The First Age: Prehistoric and Early Period*)
(*The Second Age: High Civilizations of Antiquity and the Orient*) Ancient world styles on every continent including Mesopotamian, Egyptian, Greek, Roman, Hebrew, Early Christian, Indian, Indonesian, Chinese, Japanese, and Arabic-Islamic including the Middle Ages.   (*to 1450 AD*)

Hinge—Jesus 1 AD
Lief Erikson 1000

    Middle Ages   ca. 450–1450

FINE-ART FUNCTIONS (*FOLK-ART FUNCTIONS continue on a separate track*)
(*The Third Age: the Special Position of [the Western Arts]*)

Columbus 1492

Common-Practice Style   (*1450–1900*)

    Renaissance (*Transition to Common-Practice Style in Music*)   ca. 1450–1600[2]

Decl. of Indep. 1776
Popular/Commerical
Functons in America

    Baroque (*Common-Practice Style Fully Functional in Music*)   ca. 1600–1750

    Classical (Neo-classical)[3]   ca. 1750–1825

    Romantic   ca. 1825–1900

(*The Fourth Age: Techniques and Global Industrial Culture*)   (*ca. 1900-present*)

Avant-Garde [Modern] Styles   ca. 1900–1975

Avant-Garde Styles went beyond Common-Practice Styles, incorporating mathematical, scientific, and non-Western influences to offer new and radical styles in the arts. In the search for novelty, Avant-Garde Styles often incorporated ancient styles. [On a separate track from Avant-Garde Styles, folk and popular arts continued in Common-Practice Styles.]

FOLK-ART, FINE-ART, AND POPULAR/COMMERCIAL-ART FUNCTIONS MIX

Mixed [Postmodern] Styles[4]   ca. 1975–Present

(The late twentieth and early twenty-first centuries prized all styles and cultures of the world including Ancient, Common-Practice, and Avant-Garde styles. The Western tradition in music became a standard throughout the world. The world became a global village with coexistence and hybridization of all styles previous and present.)

ME! 2000

The Consumation

---

[1] Adapted from Walter Wiora, *The Four Ages of Music* (New York: Norton, 1965); Milo Wold and Edmund Cykler, *An Outline History of Music,* 6th ed. (Dubuque, Iowa: Wm. C. Brown, 1985); and Allen P. Schantz, *A New Statement of Values for Music Education* (Boulder, Colorado: University of Colorado doctoral dissertation, 1983).

[2] 1400–1600 in many historical treatments.

[3] Called "neo-classical" in poetry (ca. 1660–1760) and in art. In poetry, "classical poetry" refers to the Roman poetry of Virgil, Horace, and Ovid. In art, "classical art" refers to ancient Greek art.

[4] I have used the term "mixed" rather than "postmodern" because of the prevalent confusion regarding its precise meaning. The term "postmodern" was first used in architectural criticism of the 1960s describing the end of the unified International style typical of *Modern*ism. It has been co-opted to cover a multitude of diverse and somewhat related concepts in a variety of fields (now including all of the arts, philosophy, and even theology).

Ancient Styles (to 1450)

Ancient world style systems use artistic techniques developed prior to the Common-Practice Style System. The arts were tied to faith, family, and community functions. Music had not yet actualized the major-minor tonal system; painting had not yet delineated linear perspective; and poetry had not yet concretized accentual rhythm.

Common-Practice Style (ca. 1450–1900)

Several things contributed to the striking evolution of Common-Practice Style and the primary focus on aesthetic aspects of the arts. The invention of movable type (1436) fostered literacy. Works of poetry, prose, and drama could now be disseminated widely. In painting, the use of linear perspective paralleled scientific discoveries in optics. In music, the development of instruments and the major-minor tonal system paralleled scientific discoveries in acoustics. Walter Wiora provides a perspective worth considering:

> Western music has done for mankind something similar to what Greek sculpture, architecture, logic, and mathematics did: it strongly set forth classic fundamentals of universal character… Pregnance of this sort, as in geometrical figures, no less than rationality in simple numerical relations, is one aspect of universal validity. This above all explains the diffusion of Western music today in all parts of the earth. Its "world empire" rests essentially upon its immanent universality.[1]

Avant-Garde [Modern] Styles (ca. 1900–1975)

The Early 20th Century developed altogether new styles and mixed evolving styles (such as abstract cubism in painting) with components of non-western styles (including Medieval, Oriental, Indian, and African styles).

Mixed [Postmodern] Period (ca. 1975–Present)

The Late 20th and Early 21st Centuries put Common-Practice Styles back into the mix for the elite, thus mixing and matching all previous styles. (In music, for example, the elite accepted jazz and other world styles as legitimate art forms.)

---

[1] Walter Wiora, *Die vier Weltalter der Musik* [*The Four Ages of Music*], translated by M. D. Herter Norton (New York: W.W. Norton, 1965), pp. 127–128 (originally published by W. Kohlhammer, Stuttgart).

14—A Short History of Style   183

Art History in Six Paintings

Examples in art allow us to consider the growth of artistic style (the characteristic way of presenting the elements of art) from ancient times to the present. Can you discover the characteristics of each period for each element in the paintings below? Notice especially the similarities between the ancient and avant-garde paintings on the left. Both lack linear perspective, whereas all four paintings in Common-Practice style have linear perspective. Notice also the similarities between the Renaissance and Neo-Classical paintings in the middle, as well as the similarities between the Baroque and Romantic paintings on the right. The paintings in the middle are more restrained and refined, whereas the paintings on the right are more extravagant and flamboyant. From this, can you identify the period for each of the six paintings on the following two pages?

Ancient Style: Middle Ages (450–1450)
Detail from *Court of Theodora*, ca. 547, apse mosaic, 2.64 x 3.65 m (8 ft. 8 in. x 12 ft.) San Vitale, Ravenna, Italy.

Common Practice: Renaissance (1450–1600)
Raphael (1483–1520) *Lady with a Unicorn*, ca. 1505, oil on wood, 65 x 51 cm (2 ft. 1½ in. x 1 ft. 8 in.), Galleria Borghese, Rome.

Common Practice: Baroque (1600–1750)
Vermeer (1632–1675), *The Girl with the Red Hat*, ca. 1665, oil on panel, 22.8 x 18 cm (9 x 7 1/16 in.), National Gallery of Art, Washington.

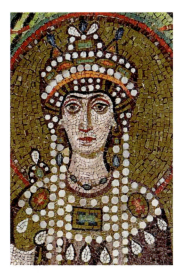

Avant-Garde (1900–1975)
Pablo Picasso (1881–1973), *Young Girl in Front of a Mirror* (1932), oil on canvas, 162 x 130 cm (5 ft. 4 in. x 4 ft. 3¼ in.), Museum of Modern Art, New York.

Common Practice: Neo-Classical (1750–1825)
Ingres (1780–1867), *Caroline Riviere*, 1806, oil on canvas, 100 x 70 cm (3 ft. 3 1/3 in. x 2 ft. 3½ in.), Musée du Louvre, Paris.

Common Practice: Romantic (1825–1900)
Delacroix (1798–1863), *Young Orphan in the Cemetery*], 1824, oil on canvas, 65.5 x 54 cm (2 ft. 1¾ in. x 1 ft. 9¼ in.), Musée du Louvre, Paris.

184   14—A Short History of Style

14—A Short History of Style 185

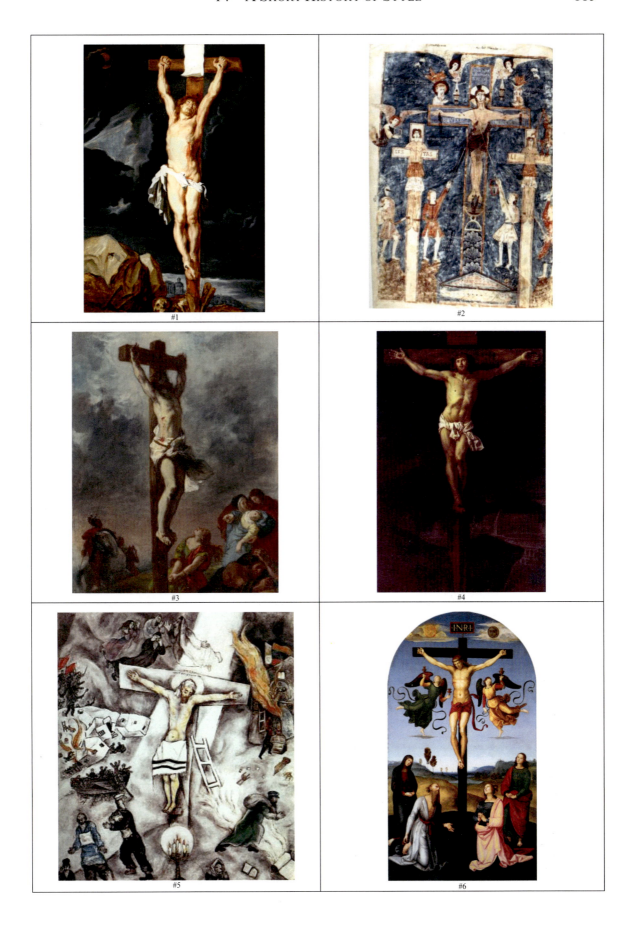

Poetic History in Six Poems

Language (and especially poetry) may be understood as making *music* with spoken words. Thus, we will use poetry as our paradigm for considering historical style in languages. When one listens to poetry in a language one does not understand, it is easy to isolate the *musical* aspects of that poetry (line, packed word sounds, rhythm/meter, volume, vocal instrument range, timbre, form). When one reads or listens to poetry in a language that one understands, packed word pictures are added to the mix. As you read aloud the following poetry (written or translated into English), concentrate on the aesthetic elements of the poetry rather than on the extra-aesthetic ideas and meanings. Notice especially the similarities between the ancient and avant-garde poems below. Both lack regular meter, whereas all four poems in Common-Practice style have regular meter. Notice also the similarities between the Renaissance and Neo-Classical poems (tighter and more refined), as well as the similarities between the Baroque and Romantic poems (more exaggerated and extravagant). Can you discover other differences and similarities?

Ancient Style: Hebrew Poetry in English David (ca. 1000 B.C.) 2 Samuel 22:2–3a, 7–11 (cf. Psalm 18:2a, 6-10)	**Avant-Garde [Modern] (1900–1975)**— T. S. Eliot (1888–1965), excerpt from *Choruses from the Rock* (1934)

The Lord is my rock, my castle and my deliverer.
  God is my strength, and in him will I trust…
I called to the Lord,
  and cried to my God.
And he heard my voice out of his temple,
  and my cry entered into his ears.
And the earth trembled and quaked,
  and the foundations of heaven moved
  and shook, because he was angry.
Smoke went up out of his nostrils,
  and consuming fire out of his mouth,
  that coals were kindled of him.
And he bowed heaven and came down
  and darkness underneath his feet.
And he rode upon a Cherub and flew:
  and appeared on the wings of the wind…
(trans. William Tyndale)
	The Eagle soars in the summit of Heaven,
	The Hunter with his dogs pursues his circuit.
	O perpetual revolution of configured stars,
	O perpetual recurrence of determined seasons,
	O world of spring and autumn, birth and dying!
	The endless cycle of idea and action,
	Endless invention, endless experiment,
	Brings knowledge of motion, but not of stillness;
	Knowledge of speech, but not of silence;
	Knowledge of words, and ignorance of the Word.
	All our knowledge brings us nearer to death,
	But nearness to death no nearer to God.
	Where is the Life we have lost in living?
	Where is the wisdom we have lost in knowledge?
	Where is the knowledge we have lost in information?
	The cycles of Heaven in twenty centuries
	Bring us farther from God and nearer to the Dust.
	…

Common-Practice: Renaissance (1450–1600)— Shakespeare (1564–1616), Sonnet 18 (between 1592/1609)
 	
Shall I compare thee to a summer's day?
  Thou art more lovely and more temperate.
Rough winds do shake the darling buds of May,
  And summer's lease hath all too short a date.
Sometime too hot the eye of heaven shines,
  And often is his gold complexion dimmed;
And every fair from fair sometime declines,
  By chance or nature's changing course untrimmed;
But thy eternal summer shall not fade
  Nor lose possession of that fair thou ow'st;
Nor shall death brag thou wander'st in his shade,
  When in eternal lines to time thou grow'st:
    So long as men can breathe, or eyes can see,
    So long lives this, and this gives life to thee.
	Common-Practice: Baroque (1600–1750)— Milton (1608–74), Sonnet 19 (between 1652/1655)
	
	When I consider how my light is spent,
	  Ere half my days in this dark world and wide,
	  And that one talent which is death to hide
	Lodged with me useless, though my soul more bent
	To serve therewith my Maker, and present
	  My true account, lest He returning chide;
	  "Doth God exact day-labor, light denied?"
	I fondly ask. But Patience, to prevent
	That murmur, soon replies, "God doth not need
	  Either man's work or His own gifts. Who best
	  Bear His mild yoke, they serve Him best. His state
	Is kingly: thousands at His bidding speed,
	  And post o'er land and ocean without rest;
	  They also serve who only stand and wait."

Common-Practice: Neo-Classical (1750-1800)— Alexander Pope (1688–1774), *Sound and Sense* (1711)
 	
True ease in writing comes from art, not chance,
  As those move easiest who have learned to dance.
'Tis not enough no harshness gives offense,
  The sound must seem an echo to the sense:
Soft is the strain when Zephyr gently blows,
  And the smooth stream in smoother numbers flows;
But when loud surges lash the sounding shore,
  The hoarse, rough verse should like the torrent roar;
When Ajax strives some rock's vast weight to throw,
  The line too labors, and the words move slow;
Not so, when swift Camilla scours the plain,
  Flies o'er the unbending corn, and skims along the main.
    Hear how Timotheus' varied lays surprise,
    And bid alternate passions fall and rise!
	Common-Practice: Romantic (1800-1900)— Wordsworth (1770–1850), *I Wandered Lonely* (1804)
	
	I wandered lonely as a cloud
	  That floats on high o'er vales and hills,
	When all at once I saw a crowd,
	  A host, of golden daffodils;
	Beside the lake, beneath the trees,
	Fluttering and dancing in the breeze.
	
	Continuous as the stars that shine
	  And twinkle on the milky way,
	They stretched in never-ending line
	  Along the margin of a bay:
	Ten thousand saw I at a glance,
	Tossing their heads in sprightly dance.
	
	The waves beside them danced, but they
	  Out-did the sparkling leaves in glee;
	A poet [buoyed to] be [that way],
	  In such a jocund company!
	I gazed—and gazed—but little thought
	What wealth the show to me had brought:
	
	For oft, when on my couch I lie
	  In vacant or in pensive mood,
	They flash upon that inward eye
	  Which is the bliss of solitude;
	And then my heart with pleasure fills,
	And dances with the daffodils.

14—A Short History of Style

Music History in Fifteen Minutes

In a similar way, examples in music allow us to consider the growth of musical style from ancient times to the present. Listen to each of the musical examples below to get a feel for the characteristic way of presenting each element in each period.

	Ancient World Styles *Folk-Art Functions*		Western Common-Practice Styles (Major-Minor Tonal System) *Fine-Art Functions*			Avant-Garde	Mixed
	Veni Emmanuel Middle Ages (450–1450)	***The Cricket*** Renaissance (1450–1600)	***Spring, I*** from *The Four Seasons* Baroque (1600–1750)	***A Little Night Music, III*** Classical (1750–1825)	***Ride of the Valkyries*** Romantic (1825–1900)	***Scene III: The Moor's Room*** Avant-Garde [*Modern*] (1900–1975)	***Credo*** and ***One Small Child*** Mixed [Postmodern] (1975–present)
Elements of Music	*Veni Emmanuel* (*O Come Emmanuel*) 15th-century French Processional (Playlist Arts Key 14A Style [1]) or http://youtu.be/tId6ePj7Zpo	*The Cricket Is a Good Singer* [*El grillo*] (pub. 1505), attr. Josquin des Prez (ca. 1450–1521)—(Playlist Arts Key 14A Style [2]) or http://youtu.be/62-aBOZrqh8?t	Antonio Vivaldi (1678–1741) *Spring* [*La Primavera*] 1st movt. from *Four Seasons* (1725)—(Playlist Arts Key 14A Style [3]) or http://youtu.be/cQgd0vx3nYM	Wolfgang Amadeus Mozart (1756–1791) *Eine kleine Nachtmusik*, III Menuetto (Playlist Arts Key 14A Style [4]) or http://youtu.be/en6MzTZuiVQ	Richard Wagner (1811–1886) *Feuerzauber,* last scene of *Die Walküre* (1854–1856), 2nd opera in *The Ring* (Playlist Arts Key 14A Style [5]) or http://youtu.be/P73Z6291Pt8?t	Igor Stravinsky (1882–1971), *Scene III: The Moor's Room* from *Petrushka* (1911), (Playlist Arts Key 14A Style [6]) or http://youtu.be/esD90diWZds?t=14m3s [to 17:01]	Pärt—*Credo* (1968) [mix of Avant-Garde/Common-Practice Styles] Arts Key 13 [2] and Meece—*One Small Child* (1971) [mix of Ancient/Common-Practice Styles] Arts Key 14B [2]
Melody	F Aeolian (♭7)	G Mixolydian, 7th raised at times	E Major/C# Minor	G Major/D Major	B Minor/B Major	D Aeolian (♭7)	
Harmony	None	Non-functional Harmony	Functional Harmony	Functional Harmony	Chromatic Harmony	Dissonance (♭VII)	
Rhythm	Follows words	2/2	4/4 *Allegro*	3/4 *Allegretto*	9/8 *Lebhaft* [lively]	Mixed Meters/Tempos	
Texture (Layers)	monophonic	homophonic, unlike most Renaissance music	homophonic/polyphonic	homophonic	homophonic	Homophonic	
Colors of Sound	voices	4 voices superius altus tenor bassus	solo violin 1st violins 2nd violins violas cello/harpsichord	1st violin 2nd violin viola cello double bass	2 piccolos 3 flutes 3 oboes English horn 3 clarinets bass clarinet 3 bassoons 8 horns 3 trumpets bass trumpet 4 trombones 4 Wagner tubas, tuba timpani 6 harps cymbals glockenspiel snare drum triangle tam-tam	2 piccolos 4 flutes 4 oboes English horn 4 clarinets bass clarinet 4 bassoons contrabassoon 4 Horns 2 trumpets 2 cornets 3 trombones tuba timpani 2 harps piano celesta bass drum cymbals glockenspiel snare drum tambourine triangle xylophone tam-tam offstage snare drum offstage tambourine 1st violins	
Form	abcda	AAA¹A¹BBA	AB♣¹C♣¹D♣²B¹♣³B²♣⁴	A B A ‖:a:‖:ba:‖:b:‖:cd:‖:c:‖:a:‖:ba:‖	A Ride theme throughout in major and minor	Intro-A-B-A¹	

Study carefully how each historical period is distinctive and how each expands the size and scope of each of the elements of music: melodies, rhythms, textures, dynamics, instrument ranges, etc. Notice also how music grew out of folk music into music that focuses primarily on its aesthetic aspects. Take some time to really enjoy each selection, and to pick a favorite or two. Once you have become familiar with these pieces, listen to the similarities between the selections from the Middle Ages and the Avant-Garde [Modern] period. Notice that both are modal (*b*7 scale degree) whereas the selections in Common-Practice style (from Baroque through Romantic) use the major-minor tonal system (with the raised 7th scale degree). [The Renaissance provides a transition with both *b*7th and raised 7th scale degree in most works]. Memorize the name of each work, the period, and the composer.

Mixed [Postmodern] Style

Mixed [Postmodern] styles in the arts include all previous styles singly and in combination. Music illustrates this well. Perhaps the best example of the mixture of Common-Practice Style and Avant-Garde Style in fine-art music is the *Credo* by Arvo Pärt (see last chapter). Avant-Garde Style in folksongs is rare. [However, it is easy to find strong avant-garde flavor in popular music, for example, in *heavy metal*, *punk*, and *screamo*[1] styles.] Folk tunes (including hymns) are usually in Common-Practice Style and sometimes in Ancient Style.

Two folk tunes illustrate the differences between Ancient Style and Common-Practice Style, and how these come together in Mixed Style. As noted above, ancient style uses a modal system with a lowered seventh scale degree a whole step below the keynote with a corresponding major *b*VII chord, whereas Common-Practice Style uses the major-minor tonal system with the raised seventh scale degree half a step below the keynote with a corresponding major V chord. The first tune (in ancient style ca. 1450) is the Latin song VENI IMMANUEL (page C20). The next tune (page C21) by David Meece (1971) is in mixed style, alternating between modal and major-minor styles, modal in the first part **A** and major in the second *B* (form—**AABABA**). Recordings of these songs are found on *Naxos* playlist <u>Arts Key 14B</u>, and the first lines of both are given below. Sing (and play) both in the key of D Aeolian (chords in parentheses) and F major (chords in parentheses) for the second half of *One Small Child*.

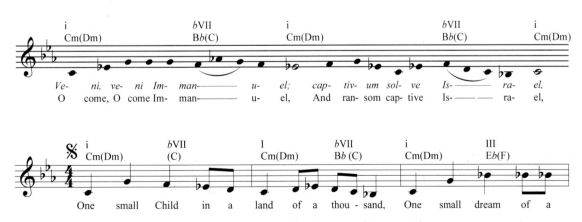

---

[1] *Screamo*—a dissonant, screaming style influenced by hardcore punk.

Special Insight 14-1: *Natural Harmonic Series—The Key of Joy*

The **natural harmonic series** (a series of tones consisting of a fundamental tone (1) and the consecutive harmonics produced by it, related by an exact fraction—1/2, 1/3, 1/4, 1/5, etc.) grows out of the way that natural objects produce sound. If you strike a metal pipe with a mallet, you will hear a particular frequency of sound, which serves as a fundamental (1). If you cut that pipe in half and strike that half, you will hear the frequency that is an octave (eight notes) higher. If you take the same length of pipe and cut it in thirds and strike one of those thirds, you will hear the frequency an octave and a fifth higher. Cut in fourths, you will hear the note two octaves higher, cut in fifths two octaves plus a third higher, cut in sixths two octaves plus a fifth, cut in sevenths two octaves plus a sixth, cut in eighths three octaves higher, cut in ninths three octaves plus a second, and cut in tenths three octaves plus a third. The fundamental note (1) may be any length of pipe and begin on any note. The natural harmonic series below is built on C^2.

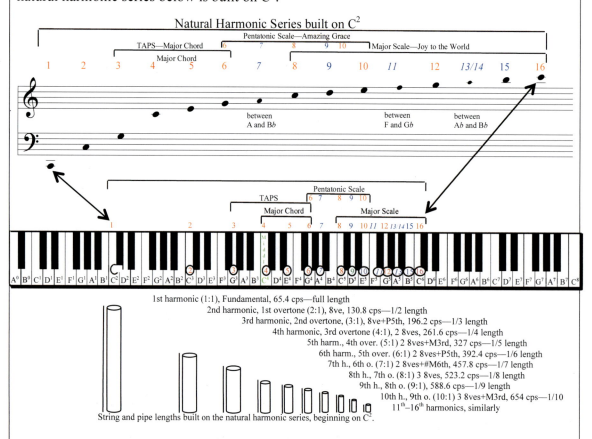

String and pipe lengths built on the natural harmonic series, beginning on C^2.

Harmonics (1, 2, 3, 4, 5, 6, 8, 10, 12, and 16) combine to outline the major chord. Pipes 3, 4, 5, and 6 outline the notes for TAPS. Harmonics 6, 7, 8, 9, 10 produce the **pentatonic** (five-tone) or wind-chime scale. Harmonics 8, 9, 10, *11*, 12, *13/14*, 15, and 16 produce the major scale. The minor, chromatic, and 12-tone scales clash with this harmonic series and introduce dissonance that cries for resolution. *Credo* by Arvo Pärt (Playlist Arts Key 13 [2] or Arvo Pärt *Credo* Wenn [11]) summarizes the whole development of western music by contrasting unbearable 12-tone dissonance against Bach's serene, Prelude in C Major, which begins and ends the work. Listen to this work to experience the struggle of fittingness-intensities that release ultimately with the major scale, its major chord, and its fundamental—the **key of joy**!

The Amazing Pentatonic

The connection of the arts to our common human identity may be illustrated by music. From common roots in the natural harmonic series (Insight 14-1), ancient musical styles of the world gradually developed and diverged. Recall the overtone[1] singing from Tuva in central Asia (Playlist Arts Key 14C [1]) and the playing of the pipe from the Middle East (Playlist Arts Key 14C [2]) both using the harmonic series. Harmonics 3, 4, 5, and 6 outline the major chord as illustrated by the natural trumpet (for example, TAPS, Playlist Arts Key 14C [3]). The pentatonic scale (5-note scale using harmonics 6, 7, 8, 9, 10) also appears across traditions. The American folk tune NEW BRITAIN (with words *Amazing Grace*), based on the pentatonic scale, illustrates this connection (Playlist Arts Key 14C [4]).

Joy to the World!

In the Baroque period, tuning systems made it possible to go even farther up the harmonics series ladder, leading to Common-Practice Style. The major scale is generated by harmonics 8–16, as in the first eight notes of the tune ANTIOCH (*Joy to the World*, Playlist Arts Key 14C [5]).

In the twentieth century, many non-western cultures assimilated the major-minor tonal system of Common-Practice Style while retaining their distinctive flavors and/or traditions. In turn, western cultures incorporated traditions from all over the world. This cross-pollination of styles continues its crescendo in the twenty-first century. Common-Practice Style now belongs not just to the west but to the World!

Is the natural harmonic series the connection between all musical languages of the world however diverse they may seem at first? Leonard Bernstein thought so, and developed this idea in his six *Norton Lectures* at Harvard University in 1973.[2] Bobby

---

[1] Overtones are harmonics *above* the fundamental.
[2] Leonard Bernstein, *Norton Lectures* at Harvard University in 1973 (Video Music Education, Inc. 1992).

McFerrin also develops this idea in his lecture to the World Science Festival: *YouTube* keywords: Bobby McFerrin Pentatonic worldsciencefestival.

Like music, could it be that ultimately the diverse styles of *all* the arts are simply different facets of the same sparkling diamond? The methods of architect Daniel Libeskind[1] emphasize this possibility:

> The interconnectedness of music, architecture, and other art forms is a recurring theme in Daniel Libeskind's work. He has designed not only structures such as the [Denver Art] Museum's new Frederick C. Hamilton Building, but the sets and costumes for operas and even a grand piano. All art forms are sources of his inspiration. "Sometimes my thoughts are triggered by a piece of music or a poem, or simply by the way light falls on a wall," he says… Libeskind is himself a musician. He was a child prodigy on the accordion… He often uses musical metaphors to talk about the Hamilton Building, calling the atrium the building's "overture." He even prefers to sketch his architectural ideas on blank music paper.[2]

Is there a connection between all the arts that is built into our world? Is our longing for aesthetic and artistic excellence hard-wired into our humanity and our world?

---

[1] The architect chosen for the master plan of the the World Trade Center Memorial Complex who is also responsible for Jewish Museum Berlin and the Denver Art Museum's Frederick C. Hamilton Building.
[2] "hot dam: arts at altitude" in *Denver Art Museum On & Off the Wall* (July/August 2006), p. 8.

Actions for Practice and Delight

14/1. Thoroughly study the chart on page 181 and memorize the periods and dates that are reiterated below. Notice that as an aid to memory, the first period is 1000 years, the next two periods are 150 years each, and the last four are 75 years each.

FOLK-ART FUNCTIONS

Ancient Styles *(to 1450 AD)*
   Middle Ages   ca. 450–1450

FINE-ART FUNCTIONS join FOLK-ART FUNCTIONS

Common-Practice Style *(1450–1900)*
   Renaissance *(Transition to Common-Practice Style in Music)*   ca. 1450–1600[1]
   Baroque *(Common-Practice Style Fully Functional in Music)*   ca. 1600–1750
   Classical (Neo-classical)[2]   ca. 1750–1825
   Romantic   ca. 1825–1900

Avant-Garde Styles   ca. 1900–1975

FOLK-ART, FINE-ART, AND POPULAR/COMMERCIAL-ART FUNCTIONS MIX

Mixed Styles   ca. 1975–Present

14/2. Make and fill out a chart for the paintings in this chapter on page 183 similar to the one below using the categories to compare styles in each of the six paintings. Then, identify the period for each of the six paintings on page 184 and the period for each of the six paintings on page 185 without looking at the answers. Check your answers at the bottom of the following page and grade yourself on this part for your first try.

	Ancient Style: Middle Ages	Avant-Garde Style	Common-Practice: Renaissance	Common-Practice: Baroque	Common-Practice: Neo-Classical	Common-Practice: Romantic
Line						
Shape						
Perspective						
Space						
Texture						
Colors of Light						
Form						

14/3. Read aloud the six poems given in this chapter on pages 186 and 187. Then, make a chart for poetry similar to the one outlined below to compare styles of each of the six poems.

	Ancient Style: Hebrew Poetry	Avant-Garde Style	Common-Practice: Renaissance	Common-Practice: Baroque	Common-Practice: Neo-Classical	Common-Practice: Romantic
Packed Word Pictures (ISSMP, etc., list specifics)						
Packed Word Sounds (HMEW, end rhyme—abab, etc.)						
Rhythm/Meter iambic, etc.)						
Form (central theme [**A**], development [**A**^{1}, **A**^{2}, etc.], contrast [*B, C*], rising tension, climax [Volta], and release)						

---

[1] 1400–1600 in many historical treatments.
[2] Called "neo-classical" in poetry (ca. 1660–1760) and in art. In poetry, "classical poetry" refers to the Roman poetry of Virgil, Horace, and Ovid. In art, "classical art" refers to ancient Greek art.

14/4. As suggested in this chapter on pages 188 and 189, listen to each of the examples outlined in the chart. Listen for the differences between the three Common-Practice Style pieces (Baroque through Romantic) and the Renaissance/Avant-Garde selections. Think carefully about how the works from each period differ for each element of music, and create a chart similar to the one on page 188. See if you can fill in the main characteristics of each selection for each element of music without looking at the answers. Then, grade yourself and write comments on your experience. Which is your favorite selection, and why? Be able to identify the period to which each work belongs, the title of the work, and the composer of that work by listening only.

14/5. Listen to *Naxos* playlist <u>Arts Key 14B</u> several times, and then learn to sing the following two folk songs (accompanying them with the bass line and chords). Discuss how your understanding of the lowered and raised seventh scale degree (and the corresponding bVII and V chords) helps you to sing (and play) these songs in Ancient Style and Mixed Style (Ancient in the **A** sections plus Common-Practice in the *B* sections) respectively: VENI IMMANUEL (page C20) and ONE SMALL CHILD (page C21). [The first line of each song is also on page 189.]

14/6. After a thorough review of pages 190-192, listen to *Naxos* playlist <u>Arts Key 14C</u> several times, and then explore the video clip with Bobby McFerrin and the pentatonic scale (*YouTube* keywords: <u>Bobby McFerrin Pentatonic worldsciencefestival</u>) as you interact with the final part of this chapter. In writing, discuss your experiences with the material above, and then attempt to answer the two questions posed by the World Science Festival, *Notes & Neurons—In Search of the Common Chorus*: 1) Is our response to music hard-wired or culturally determined? and 2) Is the reaction to rhythm and melody universal or influenced by environment?

Answers for page 184
1—Avant-Garde [Modern]: Picasso, *Harlequin on Horseback* (1905), 100 x 69.2 cm (39.37 x 27.25 in.), oil on cardboard, Print, Various Locations.
2—Baroque: Peter Paul Rubens (1577-1640), *Equestrian Portrait of Giancarlo Doria* (ca. 1606), oil on canvas, 188 x 265 cm (74 x 104.33 inches), Galleria Nazionale di Palazzo Spinola, Genoa, Italy.
3—Renaissance: Raphael Sanzio (1483-1520), *St. George and the Dragon* (1504-1505), oil on wood, 28.5 x 21.5 cm (11.2 x 8.5 in) National Gallery of Art, Washington, D.C.
4—Ancient, Upper Paleolithic: Lascaux Caves, Prehistoric Painting of Horse, Lascaux, France.
5—Romantic: Francisco de Goya y Lucientes (1746-1828), *General José de Palafox* (1814), 248 x 224 cm (97.6 x 88.2), Museo del Prado, Madrid.
6—Neo-classical—Jacques-Louis David (1748-1825) *Portrait of Count Stanislaw Potocki* (1781), oil on canvas, 304 x 218 cm (120 in × 86 in), Museum of King John III's Palace at Wilanów, Warsaw.

Answers for page 185
1— Baroque: Peter Paul Rubens (1577-1640), *Christ on the Cross*, c. 1610, oil on panel, 114.3 x 78.1 cm (45 x 30.75 in.), The Bob Jones University Museum and Gallery, Greenville, South Carolina.
2— Middle Ages: Beatus of Girona 976. Folio 16v. *Crucifixion*. Codex from the monastery of San Salvador de Tábara to the Commentary on the Apocalypse of St. John (776-786), work of Beatus of Liébana. Copy ordered by Abbot Dominicus, written by the escribe Senior and illustrated by the nun En, Ende or Eude and the presbyter Emeterius. Visigothic art, Miniature Painting. SPAIN. CATALONIA. Gerona. Cathedral's Treasure-Capitular Museum.
3— Romantic: Eugene Delacroix (1798-1863), *Christ on the Cross* (1853), oil on canvas, 73.5 x 59.7 cm (28.9.x 23.5 in.), The National Gallery, London.
4— Neo-Classical: Jacques-Louis David (1748-1825), *Christ on the Cross* (1782), oil on canvas, 188 x 276 cm (74 x 108.66 in.), Church of St. Vincent and Alexander, Pontenicsa, Italy.
5—Avant-Garde [Modern]: Marc Chagall (1887-1985). *The White Crucifixion* (1938), oil on canvas, 154.6 x 140 cm (60.87 x 55.12 in.), Art Institute of Chicago.
6—Renaissance: Raphael Sanzio (1483-1520), *Crucifixion* (1502-1503), oil on poplar, 83.3 x 167.3 cm (52.8 x 65.87 in.), The National Gallery, London.

CHAPTER 15
IT'S YOUR MOVE

"Now this is not the end.
It is not even the beginning of the end.
But it is, perhaps, the end of the beginning."[1]

    What a ride! Our trek has taken us through the arts (**M**usic, **A**rt, **D**ance, **P**oetry, **S**tory, and **T**heatre) to aesthetic excellence and beyond. We have taken time to understand and use our aesthetic *image*ination. We now savor aesthetic excellence wherever it may be found, whatever the social function, worldview, or style. Nonetheless, we realize that aesthetic excellence may be used for good or for ill—*artistic* excellence includes both aesthetic and extra-aesthetic diligence. We are faced with a choice in the arts and in every area of life. We may choose not to act, we may act irresponsibly, or we may choose to act and be motivated by the transforming power of love. Artistic excellence unites truth and beauty, justice and love, responsibility and joy. It's your move!

---

[1] Winston Churchill, *The End of the Beginning* (Speech at the Lord Mayor's Luncheon, Mansion House, November 10, 1942) http://www.churchill-society-london.org.uk/EndoBegn.html.

APPENDIXES

APPENDIX A—A CREATIVE PROJECT IN THE ARTS ▪ A3

APPENDIX B—GUIDE TO *JOSEPH AND HIS BROTHERS* ▪ B1

APPENDIX C—TUNES AND TEXTS ▪ C1

APPENDIX A
A CREATIVE PROJECT IN THE ARTS

For a creative project in the arts, choose from one of the following (concentrating on the aesthetic aspect) with a suggested form of **A** *B* **A**^{1} *B*^{1} **A**^{2}.

1) Original[1] instrumental music with contrasting themes (maximum 3½ minutes)
2) Original[2] carving, colored drawing, or painting with contrasting foreground/ background (minimum 18 x 24 in. for colored drawing or painting)
3) Original cycle of five poems, contrasting themes (12 to 24 lines each)
4) Original short story, contrasting themes, (max. 1000 words, 3½ minutes)
5) Original fictional play, contrasting themes (max.1000 words, 3½ minutes)
6) Original dance, contrasting movements (maximum 3½ minutes)

A. <u>Brainstorm your project</u>. First, brainstorm your project. Using elements of the particular art you have chosen, generate as many ideas as you possibly can by sketching (if art), playing (if music), speaking out loud (if poem, story, or play), or dancing. In the first stage of creation, it is never productive to reject any idea no matter how crazy it may seem. Record it, draw it, and/or write it down, so you do not lose it. Keep all of your ideas so that you can demonstrate your process.

B. <u>Develop ideas into an overall theme</u>. Next, choose one of your best ideas to repeat, vary, and develop into small sections (phrases in music) that then combine to make an overall theme with a climax (focal point in art) and release. Repeat this with another idea so that you have another possible theme, and repeat the process again so that you have three or four different possibilities for your work.

C. <u>Contrast primary (foreground) and secondary (background) themes, and begin writing listening or viewing outline</u>. Next, choose one of the themes above to serve as your primary theme and another to serve as your secondary theme. Using the elements of the particular art you have chosen, *generate as much contrast as you can between your primary and secondary themes*. For example in music you might use the following for first theme/second theme: low/high, mellow/piercing, soft/loud, even/odd, slow/fast, minor/major, dissonant/consonant, thin/thick, etc. Record, draw, and/or write all of your ideas, so you can demonstrate your process. Begin writing a listening or viewing outline, first listing the general characteristics of all the elements in order and then outlining the form in a column on the left and what is happening with each element on the right as you go through the form of your work. (See *Outline* of *Samson and Delilah* [page 116] and *Vivaldi's Spring,* I [pages 132 and 133] as models.)

D. <u>Work on development, rising tension, climax (focal point), and release</u>. Next, work on development of your primary theme and contrasting secondary or background theme) to generate rising tension, come to an appropriate climax (focal point), and provide release. Play/play/play, sketch/sketch/sketch, read/read/read, and/or dance/

---

[1] Original music means music that can be performed live (without editing or recording manipulation).
[2] Original painting means using an object, scene, or live subject (not working from a photograph) or an original idea for an abstract work.

dance/dance. Record all of your ideas so that you can remember them later. Work in short sessions and distribute your time over days or weeks. Your objective is to generate reams and reams of recorded (or sketched) material (and keep it as part of your process).

E. <u>Pare down your ideas to the absolute essentials</u>. Next, begin to pare down your project to the absolute essentials to give the project a sense of integrated unity. Again, practice and distribute your work over time. It is important to enjoy the process! You will find that if you do not work your brain too hard, it will work on these ideas on its own while you are doing something else. Your brain may even wake you up in the middle of the night with a thought that may provide just the right inspiration.

F. <u>Revise/revise—cut/cut—revise/revise—cut/cut—revise/revise</u>. The next part of the process is to practice and record your project, reading it out loud, dancing it, or sketching it on a sample paper. Revise and cut, revise and cut, and revise again until you complete the first draft of your final project at just the right size—about 2½ to 3½ minutes in length. (If a drawing or painting, your work should be detailed enough to cover the foreground and background themes, but simple enough to be interesting.) Then, put your project to bed for several days and forget about it.

G. <u>Wake up your project and getting to know it again and finishing your listening or viewing outline</u>. Next, wake up your project and listen to your recording of the first draft (or look at your painting sample or the videotape of the first draft of your dance), imagining that someone else had created it. Critique it as if it is their work—not yours! Check it for unity, diversity, and fittingness-intensity in all its elements, and punch as many holes in it as you can. Then revise/revise/revise and come up with a final draft and a finished listening or viewing outline. Put it to bed again, and then wake it up, proof it, and make any corrections necessary and practice or paint your final draft. Ask these questions when evaluating your project:

1. Unity [central theme]—is there repetition, variation, and development in each element of the central theme providing integration that brings the whole work together?
2. Diversity [contrasting secondary theme]—is there contrast (using the elements) between the primary (foreground) and secondary (background) themes and in the work as a whole?
3. Fittingness-intensity—does the work state the theme and contrasting theme clearly, develop the themes thoroughly, build to a satisfying climax (focal point), and release the tension appropriately?
4. Is the work long (detailed) enough to cover the ideas but short (simple) enough to be interesting?
5. Do the reams and reams of process material reflect a thorough and detailed approach over the course of many weeks?

H. <u>Practice (finish) and record your project</u>. Now, record the final draft of your project live on tape/CD (if music, poetry, or story) or videotape/DVD (if play or dance) so you have a permanent record of what you have done. If your project is a painting, take the best digital photograph of it that you can so that you will have a record of it even if you give or sell your work to someone else. Prepare your listening/viewing guide.

APPENDIX B
GUIDE TO *JOSEPH AND HIS BROTHERS*

Characters—
- JOSEPH, father's favorite son, seventeen years old
- REUBEN, brother who tries to save Joseph
- JUDAH, leader of the brothers who sell Joseph
- OTHER BROTHERS
- JACOB, father of 12 brothers
- POTIPHAR, chamberlain, captain of the guard
- POTIPHAR'S WIFE
- BUTLER, cupbearer to the Egyptian pharaoh
- BAKER, for the Egyptian pharaoh
- PHARAOH, king of Egypt

Word Choice: coat of many colors, dream—sheaves, sun/moon/11 stars; dream—3 branches of a vine, 3 baskets of baked food; dream—fat cows/thin cows, plump ears of grain/thin ears of grain; pun on lift up your head/lift up your head from you; Egyptian loan words in the Hebrew narrative: Nile, soothsayers [magicians], reed grass, ring, fine linen.

Setting—physical: lands of Canaan and Egypt; historical: ca. 1776? B.C.; cultural: the values of a nomadic family culture of shepherds and herdsman in Canaan are set against the royal court in Egypt.

Colors of Sound: (Dynamics, voice pitch range, timbre)—change according to specific characters and narrative

Form: Alternating A B A^1 B^1 A^1 A^2 A^3 B^2 A^4 B^3 A^5 A^6 A^7

Chapter	Form	Setting	Story
37	A B	Canaan—Hebron Valley (tent), Shechem, Dothan	**Themes**—A (17-year-old Joseph's <u>dream</u>—word pictures of sheaves and stars/sun/moon) B (the jealousy of his brothers) **Rising Tension**—Joseph flung into a pit and later sold by his brothers
39	A^1 B^1 A^1	Egypt—Potiphar's house and in prison	Joseph's success—The LORD was with Joseph... [Potiphar] put him in charge of all that he had." Potiphar's wife tries to seduce Joseph, and Joseph is flung into prison. "The LORD was with Joseph... The chief jailer put him in charge" of everything. Chapter in symmetrical $a^1b^1a^1$ form[1]
40	A^2	Egypt—Prison	Joseph interprets cupbearer's <u>dream</u> (word pictures of 3 branches, grapes, cup) and baker's <u>dream</u> (word pictures of 3 baskets, pastries, birds) with pun: $^{40:13}$ Pharaoh will *lift up your head* and restore you to your office $^{40:19}$ Pharaoh will *lift up your head*—from you—and hang you on a pole
41	A^3	Egypt—King's Court	Joseph interprets king's <u>dream</u> (images of 7 fat/7 thin cows; 7 fat/7 thin ears of grain). Made Ruler of all Egypt
42	B^2 A^4	Canaan—Hebron valley to Egypt—Joseph's Court and back again to Canaan	Jacob sends his sons (Joseph's brothers) for food; Flashback—Joseph's <u>dream</u> comes true: recognizes brothers; they don't recognize him; Benjamin requested/Simeon detained Joseph weeps for the 1st time (away from his brothers). Joseph returns silver in brothers' packs. Dramatic irony (reader knows something characters don't know) when brothers discover silver: ^{28} "What is this that God has done to us?"
43	B^3 A^5	Back to Egypt—Joseph's Court	Food runs out. Brothers return with Benjamin/take double silver. Joseph weeps for the 2nd time (away from brothers).
44	A^6	Joseph's Court	Joseph puts silver back in packs and puts his cup in Benjamin's pack to test his brothers. Finds cup and finds brothers repentant; they won't do to Benjamin what they did to him.
45	A^7	Joseph's Court Canaan	Joseph weeps for the 3rd time (now in the presence of his brothers) and reveals himself. **Climax** Joseph forgives his brothers! "So it was not you who sent me here, but God." **Release** Jacob finds his favorite son is alive.

---

[1] "...the most elegantly symmetrical episode in Genesis. It comprises an introductory narrative frame (verses 1–6), a closing frame (20–23) that elaborately echoes the introductory verses, and the central story of the failed seduction, which is intricately linked to the framing verses by a network of thematic key words" (all, hand, house, blessing, succeed). [Robert Alter. *The Five Books of Moses* (New York: Norton, 2004, p. 221)].

Food for Thought

Could Vincent Van Gogh have had the story of Joseph in mind when he painted *Starry Night*? Count the number of stars and notice the moon blocking the sun below. Recall the following passage from the story of *Joseph and His Brothers*:

> [9] And he dreamed yet another dream and recounted it to his brothers, and he said, "Look, I dreamed a dream again, and, look, the sun and the moon and eleven stars were bowing to me." [10] And he recounted it to his father and to his brothers, and his father rebuked him and said to him, "What is this dream that you have dreamed? Shall we really come, I and your mother and your brothers, to bow before you to the ground?" [11] And his brothers were jealous of him, while his father kept the thing in mind. (Genesis 37:9-11)

Vincent van Gogh (1853–1890) *Nuit étoilée à Saint Remy* [*Starry Night at St. Remy*] (1889), oil on canvas, 73 x 92 cm. (28¾ x 36½ in.) Museum of Modern Art, New York.

Can you correlate the painting with the passage from the story above? Did you count eleven stars? Joseph had eleven brothers. Could the moon and the sun represent Joseph's mother and father? What do you think?

Appendix C
Tunes and Texts

[Tunes and texts on facing pages from C2–C11 are interchangeable.]

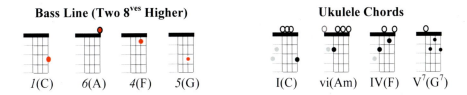

HEART AND SOUL (1938) [excerpt]
Hoagy Carmichael (1899–1981)

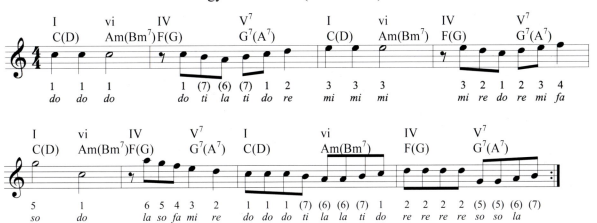

Chord Chart for Soprano/Concert/Tenor Ukulele
[Chords a Fifth Higher for Guitar—Extra Strings in Gray Print]

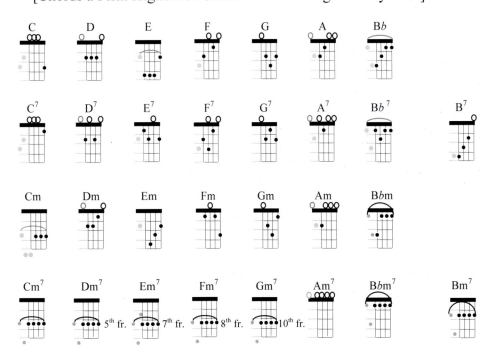

Amazing Grace CM (8.6.8.6.Iambic)
John Newton, 1779 (based on Eph. 1:3–14, 2:8)

Amazing grace! How sweet the sound
That saved a wretch like me!
I once was lost, but now am found,
Was blind, but now I see.

'Twas grace that taught my heart to fear,
And grace my fears relieved;
How precious did that grace appear
The hour I first believed!

Through many dangers, toils, and snares,
I have already come;
'Tis grace hath brought me safe thus far,
And grace will lead me home.

The Lord has promised good to me,
His word my hope secures;
He will my shield and portion be
As long as life endures.

Yes, when this flesh and heart shall fail,
And mortal life shall cease,
I shall possess, within the veil,
A life of joy and peace.

The earth shall soon dissolve like snow,
The sun forbear to shine;
But God, who called me here below,
Will be forever mine.

Joy to the World CM (8.6.8.6.Iambic)
Isaac Watts, 1719 (vers. Ps. 98/Gen. 3:17–18)

Joy to the world! the Lord is come!
Let earth receive her King;
Let every heart prepare him room,
And heav'n and nature sing.

Joy to the earth! the Savior reigns!
Let men their songs employ,
While fields and floods, rocks, hills, and plains,
Repeat the sounding joy.

No more let sins and sorrows grow,
Nor thorns infest the ground;
He comes to make his blessings flow
Far as the curse is found.

He rules the world with truth and grace,
And makes the nations prove
The glories of his righteousness,
And wonders of his love.

Gilligan's Island CM (8.6.8.6.Iambic)

Just sit right back and you'll hear a tale,
A tale of a fateful trip
That started from a tropic port,
Aboard this tiny ship.
…

APPENDIX C: TUNES AND TEXTS

NEW BRITAIN (8.6.8.6.Iambic) American Folk Tune (*Amazing Grace*) [with drone on C(D)]

ANTIOCH CM (8.6.8.6. Iambic with Refrain) Lowell Mason, 1848

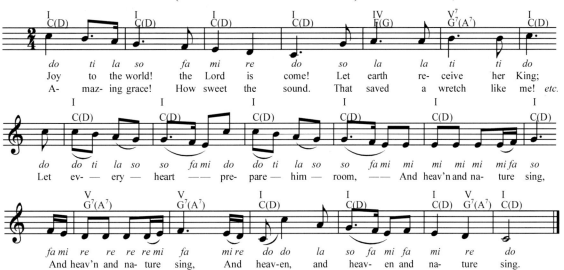

GILLIGAN'S ISLAND CM (8.6.8.6.Iambic) [Aeolian mode]

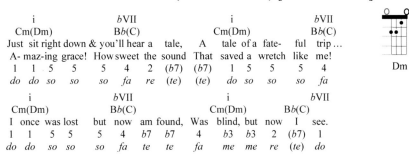

Now Come, You Servants of the Lord LM [Long Meter, 8.8.8.8.Iambic] (original words for this tune) Psalm 134, vers. Theodore of Beza, 1551, Genevan Psalter, trans. Allen Schantz

Or sus, serviteurs du Seigneur,
Vous, qui di nuit en son honneur
Dedans sa maison le servez,
Louez le, et son nom elevez.

Now come, you servants of the Lord,
Who honor him with one accord
Within his house by day and night,
And praise the Lord with all your might.

All People That on Earth Do Dwell LM [Long Meter, 8.8.8.8.Iambic] (later words for this tune) Psalm 100; vers. William Kethe, 1561, alt.

All people that on earth do dwell,
Sing to the Lord with cheerful voice;
Him serve with joy, his praises tell,
Come ye before him, and rejoice.

The Lord, ye know, is God indeed,
Without our aid he did us make;
We are his folk, he doth us feed,
And for his sheep he doth us take.

O enter then his gates with praise,
Approach with joy his courts unto;
Praise, laud, and bless his name always,
For it is seemly so to do.

For why? The Lord our God is good:
His mercy is forever sure;
His truth at all times firmly stood,
And shall from age to age endure.

Praise God from Whom All Blessings Flow LM [Long Meter, 8.8.8.8.Iambic] (even later words for this tune) Thomas Ken, 1674

Praise God, from whom all blessings flow;
Praise him, all creatures here below;
Praise him above, ye heavenly host;
Praise Father, Son, and Holy Ghost

In Christ Alone LMD [Long Meter Doubled, 8.8.8.8.D.Iambic] Stuart Townend, 2001, Copyright © 2001 Kingsway Thankyou Music. Used by permission. License #508184

In Christ alone my hope is found
He is my light my strength my song
This Cornerstone, this solid Ground
Firm through the fiercest drought and storm
What heights of love, what depths of peace
When fears are stilled when strivings cease!
My Comforter my All in All
Here in the love of Christ I stand.

In Christ alone! - who took on flesh
Fullness of God in helpless babe!
This Gift of love and righteousness
Scorned by the ones He came to save
Till on that cross as Jesus died
The wrath of God was satisfied –
For every sin on Him was laid:
Here in the death of Christ I live.

There in the ground His body lay
Light of the world by darkness slain
Then bursting forth in glorious Day
Up from the grave He rose again!
And as He stands in victory
Sin's curse has lost its grip on me
For I am His and He is mine –
Bought with the precious blood of Christ.

No guilt in life no fear in death
This is the power of Christ in me
From life's first cry to final breath
Jesus commands my destiny
No power of hell no scheme of man
Can ever pluck me from His hand
Till he returns or calls me home
Here in the power of Christ I'll stand!

OLD HUNDREDTH (GENEVAN 134) LM (8.8.8.8.iambic)
Louis Bourgeois, 1551

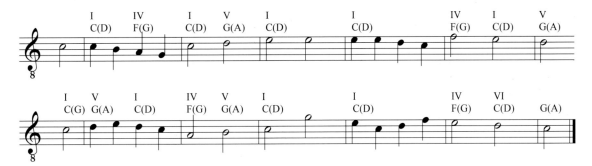

IN CHRIST ALONE LMD (8.8.8.8.D.iambic)
Keith Getty, 2001, Copyright © 2001 Kingsway Thankyou Music. Used by permission. License #508184

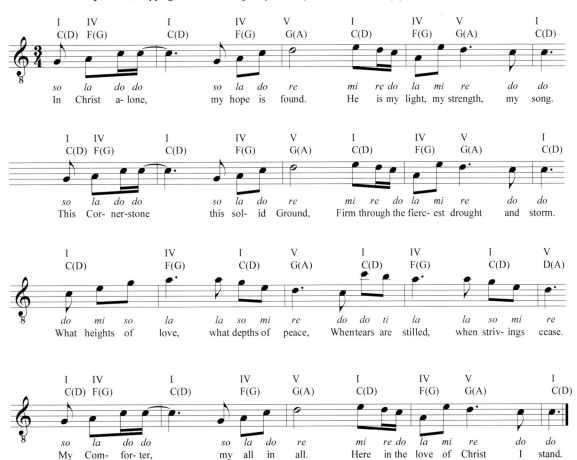

Les Anges Dans Nos Campagnes (based on Luke 2:10–20)
Angels We Have Heard on High 7.7.7.7. with refrain (trochaic)
Traditional French, 18th Century, trans. by James Chadwick (1813–1882), *alt.*

Les anges dans nos campagnes Ont entonné l'hymne des cieux Et l'écho de nos montagnes, Redit ce chant mélodieux *Glo- - - - - - - ria* *in excelsis Deo!* *(bis)*	Angels we have heard on high Sweetly singing o'er the plains, And the mountains in reply Echoing their joyous strains. *Glo- - - - - - - ria* *in excelsis Deo!* *Repeat*
Bergers, pour qui cette fête Quel est l'objet de tous ces chants ? Quel vainqueur, quelle conquête Mérite ces cris triomphants ? *Gloria in excelsis Déo! (bis)*	Shepherds, why this jubilee? Why your joyous strains prolong? What the gladsome tidings be Which inspire your heavenly song? *Gloria in excelsis Deo! (repeat)*
Cherchons tous l'hereux village Qui l'a vu naître sous ses toits Offrons lui le tendre hommage Et de nos cœurs et de nos voix ! *Gloria in excelsis Déo! (bis)*	Come to Bethlehem and see Christ whose birth the angels sing; Come, adore on bended knee, Christ the Lord, the newborn King. *Gloria in excelsis Deo! (repeat)*

Ah ! vous dirai-je, Maman (English translation)

Ah ! vous dirais-je, Maman, Mother, may I tell you why
Ce qui cause mon tourment? I'm upset enough to die?
Papa veut que je raisonne, Father wishes me to reason
Comme une grande personne. Like a grown-up, in one season.
Moi je dis que les bonbons Me, I say that candy is
Valent mieux que la raison. Worth far more than reason is.[1]

Morgen kommt der Weinachtsmann (English translation)

Morgen kommt der Weihnachtsmann, Santa comes tomorrow morn,
Kommt mit seinen Gaben. Comes with all his presents,
Trommel, Pfeifen und Gewehr, Drum and fifes and gun for war,
Fahn und Säbel und noch mehr, Flag and sabre and still more
Ja ein ganzes Kriegesheer, Yes, a total army corps
Möcht' ich gerne haben. That's my wish for presents.[1]

Twinkle, Twinkle, Little Star

Twinkle, twinkle, little star.
How I wonder what you are.
Up above the world so high,
Like a diamond in the sky.
Twinkle, twinkle, little star.
How I wonder what you are.

Alphabet Song

A, B, C, D, E, F, G,
H, I, J, K, L-M-N-O, P,
P, Q, R, S, T, U, V,
W, X, and Y, and Z.
Now I know my ABC's.
Next time will you sing with me?

Baa, Baa, Black Sheep

Baa, baa, black sheep, have you any wool?
Yes sir, yes sir, three bags full.
One for my master and one for my dame,
One for the little boy who lives down the lane.
Baa, baa, black sheep, have you any wool?
Yes sir, yes sir, three bags full.

Hallelujah, Praise the Lord 7.7.7.7.7.7
Psalm 150, vers. Marie J. Post. © 1988 CRC Publications, (alt.). Used by permission.

Hallelujah, praise the Lord. Praise him in his holy place. Praise him with the plucking string, Praise with instruments of wood,
Praise him with each note and word. Shout his power through outer space. cymbal clang and trumpet ring, for the Lord is just and good.
Praise him for his mighty ways, Everything that breathes, proclaim tapping foot and clapping hand; Praise with unison and chord.
who with love exalts our days. praise and honor to God's name. praise the Lord through all the land. Hallelujah, praise the Lord!
Hallelujah, Hallelu, Hallelujah, Hallelu, Hallelujah, Hallelu, Hallelujah, Hallelu,
Hallelujah, praise the Lord! Hallelujah, praise the Lord! Hallelujah, praise the Lord! Hallelujah, praise the Lord!

---

[1] Translation by Allen Schantz and Sam and Nora Richardson.

APPENDIX C: TUNES AND TEXTS

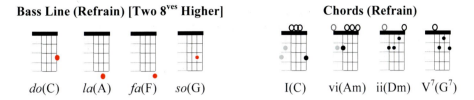

GLORIA 7.7.7.7.ref. (Trochaic)
French Folk Tune, 18th cent.; arr. Edward S. Barnes, 1937

AH, VOUS DIRAIS-JE MAMAN 7.7.7.7.7.7. (Trochaic)
French Folk Tune (variations by Mozart, 1778)

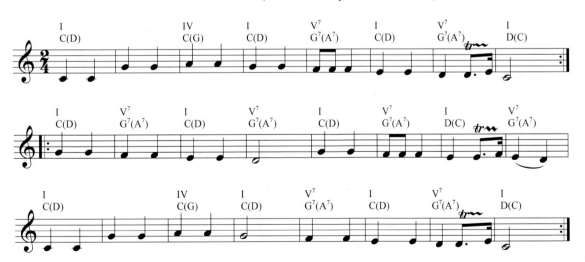

ODE TO JOY 8.7.8.7 D (Trochaic)—*Joy, You Glorious Spark/Joyful, Joyful, We Adore Thee*!

"'Where were you when I laid the foundation of the earth?
…when the **morning stars** sang together and all the *angels* shouted for **joy**?'"—Job 38:4, 7

"All thy works with **joy** surround thee; earth and heav'n reflect thy rays
Stars and *angels sing* around thee…
Mortals join the mighty chorus
Which the **morning stars** began"—Henry Van Dyke

Tune: ODE TO JOY 8.7.8.7.D. (Trochaic) from Beethoven's 9th Symphony, 4th movement (1822–1824)
Text: Top stanzas (Schiller's 1st and last stanzas) from 9th Symphony; remaining stanzas by Henry Van Dyke (1907)[1]
Tune also used for European Union Anthem (no words) and various hymns

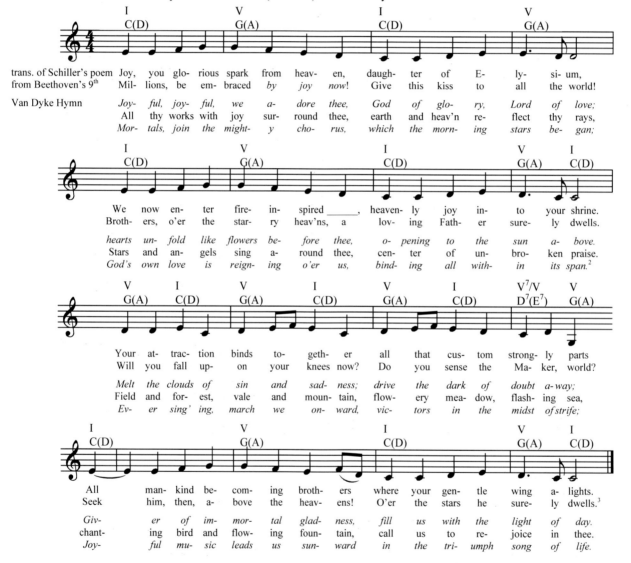

---

[1] Henry Van Dyke (1852–1933) wrote *Joyful, Joyful, We Adore Thee* in 1907 while he was a guest preacher at Williams College in Massachusetts. Inspired by the Berkshire Mountains, he presented the manuscript to Williams College President Harry Augustus Garfield "one morning at the breakfast table suggesting that it be sung to Beethoven's HYMN TO JOY." Henry Van Dyke was an "American preacher, author, and educator," with degrees from Brooklyn Polytechnic Institute, Princeton University, and Princeton Theological Seminary. Among many other accomplishments, he was Murray Professor of English Literature at Princeton University for 23 years, served as US minister to the Netherlands and Luxembourg, and an American Lecturer at the University of Paris. One of his well-known stories is *The Story of the Other Wise Man* [from *Dictionary Handbook to Hymns for the Living Church* by Donald P. Hustad (pp. 29–30, 331) and other sources].
[2] Original: "Father love is reigning o'er us, brother love binds man to man."
[3] Translation from German by Allen Schantz.

AUSTRIAN HYMN 8.7.8.7 D (Trochaic)—*German National Anthem/Apostles' Creed*

Tune: AUSTRIAN HYMN composed by Haydn for Emperor's birthday, 1797, also 2nd movt. of his *Emperor* String Quartet.
Text: Last stanza of Hoffman's poem, German National Anthem today; Apostles' Creed, versified anonymously; tune also used to set various hymns including *Glorious Things of Thee Are Spoken*.

Gott erhalte Franz, den Kaiser
Lorenz Haschka (1797) set to music by Haydn [above]

Gott erhalte Franz, den Kaiser,
[God save Franz our Emperor]
Unsern guten Kaiser Franz!
[Our good Emperor Franz!]
Lange lebe Franz, der Kaiser,
[Long live Franz, the Emperor]
In des Glückes hellstem Glanz!
[In bright, splendid happiness!]
Ihm erblühen Lorbeerreiser,
[Sprigs of laurel, may they bloom for him]
Wo er geht, zum Ehrenkranz!
[Hon'ring him where e'r he goes!]
|: Gott erhalte Franz, den Kaiser,
Unsern guten Kaiser Franz! :|

Das Lied der Deutschen August Heinrich Hoffmann (1821), adopted as National Anthem of Germany in 1922

Deutschland, Deutschland über alles,
Über alles in der Welt,
Wenn es stets zu Schutz und Trutze
Brüderlich zusammenhält.
Von der Maas bis an die Memel,
Von der Etsch bis an den Belt,
(Repeat first two lines twice)

Deutsche Frauen, deutsche Treue,
Deutscher Wein und deutscher Sang
Sollen in der Welt behalten
Ihren alten schönen Klang,
Und zu edler Tat begeistern
Unser ganzes Leben lang.
(Repeat first two lines twice)

Einigkeit und Recht und Freiheit
Für das deutsche Vaterland!
Danach lasst uns alle streben
Brüderlich mit Herz und Hand!
Einigkeit und Recht und Freiheit
Sind des Glückes Unterpfand;
|: Blüh' im Glanze dieses Glückes,
Blühe, deutsches Vaterland! :|

[All stanzas were used when Hitler was in power. Only the last stanza is used today.]

O Danny Boy 11.10.11.10.11.10.11.12 (Iambic)
Frederick Weatherly, 1910

O Danny boy, the pipes, the pipes are calling
From glen to glen, and down the mountain side.
The summer's gone, and all the leaves are falling.
'Tis you, 'tis you must go and I must bide.
But come ye back when summer's in the meadow,
Or when the valley's hushed and white with snow.
'Tis I'll be here in sunshine or in shadow.
O Danny boy, O Danny boy, I love you so.

And when ye come, and all the flow'rs are dying.
If I am dead, as dead I well may be.
Ye'll come and find the place where I am lying,
And kneel and say an "Ave" there for me.
And I shall hear, tho' soft you tread above me,
And oh, my grave shall warmer, sweeter be,
For ye will bend and tell me that you love me,
And I shall sleep in peace until you come to me.

We Rest on Thee 11.10.11.10.Iambic
Edith G. Cherry, ca. 1695

We rest on Thee, our Shield and our Defender!
We go not forth alone against the foe;
Strong in Thy strength, safe in Thy keeping tender,
We rest on Thee, and in Thy Name we go.
Strong in Thy strength, safe in Thy keeping tender,
We rest on Thee, and in Thy Name we go.

Yes, in Thy Name, O Captain of salvation!
In Thy dear Name, all other names above;
Jesus our Righteousness, our sure Foundation,
Our Prince of glory and our King of love.
Jesus our Righteousness, our sure Foundation,
Our Prince of glory and our King of love.

We go in faith, our own great weakness feeling,
And needing more each day Thy grace to know:
Yet from our hearts a song of triumph pealing,
"We rest on Thee, and in Thy Name we go."
Yet from our hearts a song of triumph pealing,
"We rest on Thee, and in Thy Name we go."

We rest on Thee, our Shield and our Defender!
Thine is the battle, Thine shall be the praise;
When passing through the gates of pearly splendor,
Victors, we rest with Thee, through endless days.
When passing through the gates of pearly splendor,
Victors, we rest with Thee, through endless days.

Sonnet 18 10.10.10.10 (Iambic)

Shall I compare thee to a summer's day?
Thou art more lovely and more temperate.
Rough winds do shake the darling buds of May,
And summer's lease hath all too short a date.

Sometime too hot the eye of heaven shines,
And often is his gold complexion dimmed;
And every fair from fair sometime declines,
By chance or nature's changing course untrimmed.

But thy eternal summer shall not fade
Nor lose possession of that fair thou ow'st;
Nor shall death brag thou wander'st in his shade,
When in eternal lines to time thou grow'st:

    So long as men can breathe, or eyes can see,
    So long lives this, and this gives life to thee.

Be Still, My Soul 10.10.10.10.Iambic, Katharina A.
von Schlegel, 1754; tr. Jane L. Borthwick, 1855

Be still, my soul: the Lord is on thy side.
Bear patiently the cross of grief or pain.
Leave to thy God to order and provide;
In every change, He faithful will remain.
Be still, my soul: thy best, thy heavenly Friend
Through thorny ways leads to a joyful end.

Be still, my soul: thy God doth undertake
To guide the future, as He has the past.
Thy hope, thy confidence let nothing shake;
All now mysterious shall be bright at last.
Be still, my soul: the waves and winds still know
His voice Who ruled them while He dwelt below.

Be still, my soul: the hour is hastening on
When we shall be forever with the Lord.
When disappointment, grief and fear are gone,
Sorrow forgot, love's purest joys restored.
Be still, my soul: when change and tears are past
All safe and blessèd we shall meet at last.

Be still, my soul: begin the song of praise
On earth, believing, to Thy Lord on high;
Acknowledge Him in all thy words and ways,
So shall He view thee with a well pleased eye.
Be still, my soul: the Sun of life divine
Through passing clouds shall but more brightly shine.

APPENDIX C: TUNES AND TEXTS   C11

LONDONDERRY AIR 10.10.10.10.D. (Iambic)
Irish Folk Tune

FINLANDIA [10.10.10.10.10.10] (Iambic)
Jean Sibelius, 1899

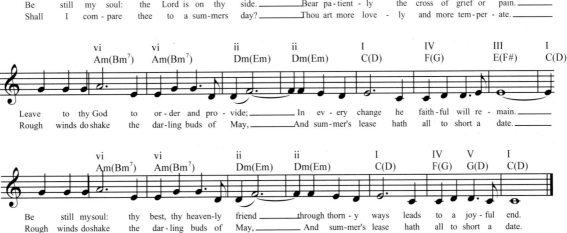

My Favorite Things (excerpt for study)
Lyrics by Oscar Hammerstein II [10.10.11.11 (Dactylic)] Music by Richard Rodgers © 1959

i
Em(Dm)
Raindrops on roses and whiskers on kittens,

VI
C(B♭)
Bright copper kettles and warm woolen mittens,

iv   VII   III   VI
Am(Gm)   D(C)   G(F)   C(B♭)
Brown paper packages tied up with strings,

III   VI   iv   V
G(F)   C(B♭)   Am(Gm)   B⁷ (A⁷)
These are a few of my favorite things.

GOD SAVE THE KING [6.6.4.6.6.6.4 (dactylic)] Attributed to John Bull, ca. 1619?

Words: *God Save the King* [*Queen*]: Traditional [6.6.4.6.6.6.4 (dactylic)]
Words: *My Country 'Tis of Thee*: Samuel F. Smith 1832, [6.6.4.6.6.6.4 (dactylic)]

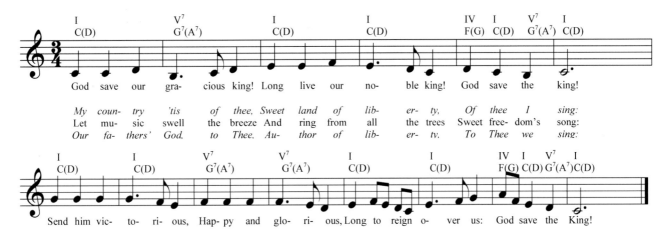

FRÉRE JACQUES [ARE YOU SLEEPING]
(*Naxos* keyword: Marianne8672248 [Disc 5, #19])

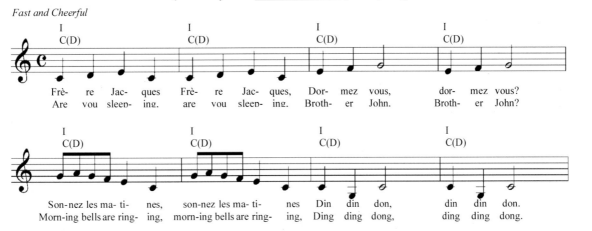

It's a Funeral [FRÉRE JACQUES in minor]
(1st part of Mahler, 1st Symphony, *Titan*, 3rd Movement) (*Naxos* keywords: Titan Cinema Classics [3])

TZENA [Irregular]
Words and Music: Issachar Miron (Stefan Michrovsky), 1941

Alternate words: *I Will Sing Unto the Lord* (from Exodus 15:1–3)

APPENDIX C: TUNES AND TEXTS

I Danced in the Morning (*Irregular*)
By Sydney Carter © 1963 Stainer & Bell, Ltd. (Admin. Hope Publishing Company, Carol Stream Il 60188). All rights reserved. Used by permission. Reprinted under license #65742.

I danced in the morning when the world was begun,
And I danced in the moon and the stars and the sun,
And I came down from Heaven and I danced on earth,
At Bethlehem I had my birth.

Refrain
Dance then, wherever you may be,
I am the Lord of the dance, said he,
And I'll lead you all wherever you may be,
And I'll lead you all in the dance, said he.

I danced for the scribe and the Pharisee,
But they would not dance, and they would not follow me.
And I danced for the fishermen, for James and John,
They came with me and the dance went on. *Refrain*

I danced on the Sabbath and I cured the lame;
The holy people said it was a shame.
They whipped and they stripped and they hung me high,
And they left me there on a cross to die. *Refrain*

I danced on a Friday when the sky turned black;
It's hard to dance with the devil on your back.
They buried my body and they thought I'd gone,
But I am the dance and I still go on. *Refrain*

They cut me down, but I leapt up high.
I am the life that'll never, never die
And I'll live in you if you'll live in me.
I am the Lord of the dance," said he. *Refrain*

Simple Gifts (*Irregular*)
Traditional Early American Hymn

'Tis the gift to be simple, 'tis the gift to be free,
'Tis the gift to come down where we ought to be,
And when we find ourselves in the place just right,
'Twill be in the valley of love and delight.
When true simplicity is gained,
To bow and to bend we shan't be ashamed,
To turn, turn will be our delight
'Till by turning, turning we come round right.

SIMPLE GIFTS irregular (American Shaker Folk Tune)

STARS AND STRIPES FOREVER (excerpt), John Philip Sousa, 1896
The music for Tune A (refrain) is given below with the original words by Sousa.[1]

---

[1] Many people know the tune of this chorus by these alternate lyrics (probably written by some *quack*).

Be kind to your web-footed friends,
   For a duck may be somebody's mother
Be kind to your friends in the swamp,
   Where the weather is cold and damp.
	You may think that this is the end.
	   Well, it is—you are right, but just remember:
	Be kind to your web-footed friends!
	   Be ever kind, yes, oh, so kind to all the duckies!

DE COLORES [ALL THE COLORS]

Beethoven 5th Symphony (1st Two Themes of I, III, and IV)

I, Theme 1

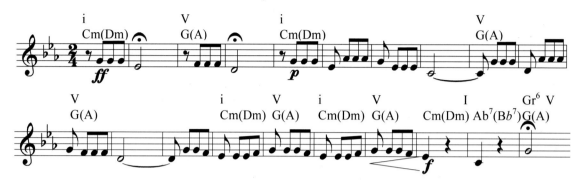

I, Theme 2

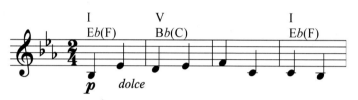

III, Theme 1

III, Theme 2

IV, Theme 1

IV, Theme 2

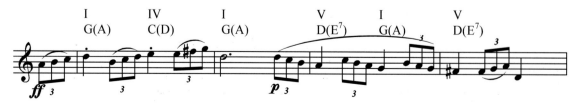

When Israel Was in Egypt's Land (*irregular*)
Traditional Afro-American spiritual

When Israel was in Egypt's land,
Let my people go,
Oppressed so hard they could not stand,
Let my people go.
Refrain:
Go down, Moses,
way down in Egypt's land,
tell old Pharaoh:
Let my people go.

The Lord told Moses what to do,
Let my people go;
to lead the Hebrew children through,
Let my people go. Refrain

As Israel stood by the waterside,
Let my people go;
at God's command it did divide,
Let my people go. Refrain

When they had reached the other shore,
Let my people go;
they let the song of triumph soar,
Let my people go. Refrain

The Lord has triumphed gloriously,
Let my people go;
thrown horse and rider in the sea,
Let my people go. Refrain

Lord, help us all from bondage flee,
Let my people go;
and let us all in Christ be free,
Let my people go. Refrain

Amazing grace—how sweet the sound,
Let my people go;
I once was lost, but now am found,
Let my people go. Refrain

GO DOWN, MOSES (Irregular Meter)
Traditional Afro-American spiritual

SANCTUS
Text: Isaiah 6:3, Matthew 21:9; Tune: Liber Usualis Sanctus XVIII

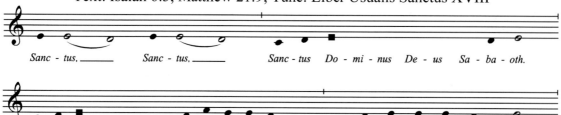

VENI IMMANUEL
Text: Isaiah 7:14, Matthew 1:23; Tune: from a 15th-century French *Processional*

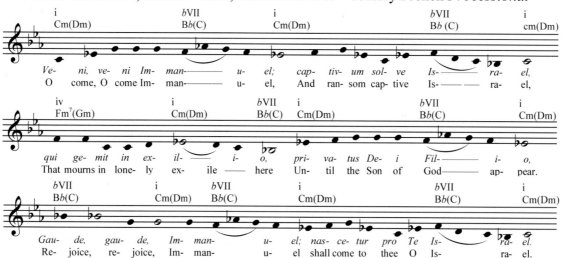

NON NOBIS DOMINE
Text: Psalm 113:9 (Latin), Psalm 115:1 (Hebrew and English)
Tune: Patrick Doyle, 1989, for Shakespeare's *King Henry V*

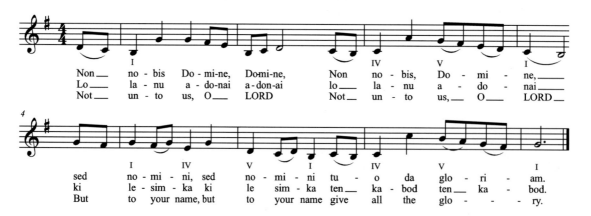

ONE SMALL CHILD (Irregular)

Text and Music: David Meece
© Copyright 1971 by Word Music (a division of WORD MUSIC). All rights reserved. Used by permission.

Song of Praise 19 (David)

Text: Psalm 19, poetic translation by Helen Otte, 1987
© 1987, CRC Publications. Used by permission.

Tune: NEW 19th, Allen Schantz
© 2010. All rights reserved.

The spacious heavens tell the glory of the LORD;
  the skies his work proclaim.
Each day and night is heard their voice in all the earth;
  they glorify God's name.
Each day the mighty sun rejoices in its run,
  arising in the morning—
a bridegroom coming forth, a runner on the course—
  bright shining in its glory.

God's perfect law is good, for it revives the soul
  and makes the simple wise.
The precepts of the LORD give joy unto the heart
  and light unto the eyes.
All God's commands are sure— the fear of God is pure—
  forevermore enduring
more precious than pure gold or honey from the comb;
  to keep them is rewarding.

Who can discern their wrongs? Forgive my hidden faults.
  Keep me from willful sins.
May they not rule my life; then I will blameless be,
  not guilty of great sin.
All of these words and thoughts, [melodies from] my heart,
  in praise to you I offer.
May this my sacrifice, be pleasing in your sight,
  my Rock and my Redeemer.

Chord Chart for Soprano/Concert/Tenor Ukulele
[Chords a Fifth Higher for Guitar—Extra Strings in Gray Print]

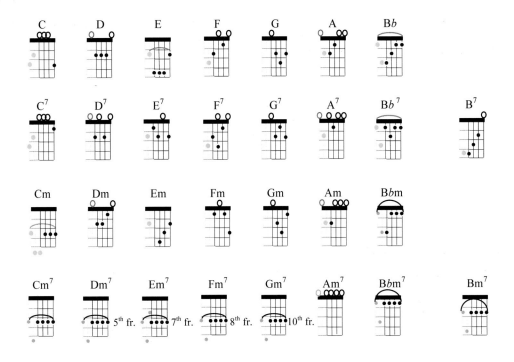

Playlists. The following playlists are keyed to each chapter in the text. For example, Arts Key 01 correlates to Chapter 1 in the text, Arts Key 02 correlates to Chapter 2, etc. These playlists are available through *Naxos Music Library* (a streaming internet music service) that may be accessed free of charge through the university. To log in to Naxos, paste the following into your internet browser: http://ezproxy.ccu.edu:2150/. Then type in your CCU user name and password. Once *Naxos Music Library* comes up, click on Playlists. Then click on Colorado Christian University Playlists. Then click on *Arts in the Key of Joy*. (*Naxos* playlists are also available on your iPhone, iPad, or a phone with Android by downloading the free *Naxos* app. Contact your professor for the username and password.) You can also access each recording individually by using the underlined keywords below [with the track number in brackets]. The underlined keywords will also work on *iTunes* (*Apple Music*) or *Spotify* {in brackets where different from *Naxos*}.

Arts Key 01 Tasting Aesthetic Excellence
1. Josquin *El Grillo* Amarcord [22]
2. Vivaldi *Four Seasons Spring* I Tafelmusik Santo [1]
3. Mozart *Nachtmusik* III divertimento G Harnoncourt [3]
4. Wagner *Ride of the Valkyries* 5099974197750 [1]
   {*Spotify*: Wagner *Ride of the Valkyries* Klemperer 100 Best}
5. Stravinsky *The Moor's Room* Boulez [5]

Arts Key 02 Folk, Fine, and Popular Uses
1. Overtone Singer 8.570316 [17]
   {*Spotify*: Overtone Singer}
2. Chupani Song of the Ney [9]
   {*Spotify*: Omoumi Song of the Ney [9]}
3. Shofar Blessings [1]
   {*Spotify*: Shofar Calls Wosk}
4. Amazing Grace Folk Mushet [14]
5. Gat Kirwani Portrait of Genius [6]
6. Bohemian Rhapsody Relaxing Pan Pipes [1]

Arts Key 03 God Save the King [America]
1. God Save the Queen original languages [13]
2. Beethoven Variations on *God Save the King* Uhlig [7]
3. Ives *Variations on America* 8.559651 [5]
   {*Spotify*: Ives *Variations on America* Schwarz [1]}

Arts Key 04A Layers
1. Beatles *Lucy in the Sky with Diamonds* Boreades [15]
2. Rodgers *My Favorite Things* saxophone quartet [14]
3. *My Favorite Things* Air Force Band Mid-America [4]
4. Beethoven, *Ode to Joy* Breiner [5]

Arts Key 04B Major and Minor
1. *Wolferl's Schmankerl* Opera Swing Quartet [12]
2. Mozart *Ah vous dirai* 6 Tewes [26]
3. 074646073223 [8, Mahler Symphony No. 1 III]
   {*Spotify*: Mahler Symphony No. 1 in D Major III Bernstein Adagio}
4. Marianne8672248 [Disc 5, Track 19, *Frère Jacques*]
   {*Spotify*: *Frère Jacques* Manfred Mann}
5. Beethoven *God Save the King* I Scherbakov [42]
6. Beethoven *God Save the King* V Scherbakov [46]
7. Beethoven *God Save the King* VII Scherbakov [48]
8. Kremer *Happy Birthday* Ragtime [11]
9. Kremer *Happy Birthday* Tango [12]
10. Kremer *Happy Birthday* Czardas [13]

Arts Key 05A Vocal Sound Colors
1. Lewis Carroll *You Are Old, Father William* Comic [10]
2. Rameau, *Le Nuit* Night Choristes [13]
3. Mantyjarvi *Double, Double, Toil Trouble* Chicago [5]
4. *Tzena* Male Choir [13]

Arts Key 05B Instrumental Sound Colors
1. Sousa *Stars and Stripes Forever* Greatest Royal Brion [17]
2–7. Britten *Guide* Pesek Very Best [1–6]
   {*Spotify*: Britten *Guide* Pesek Orchestral [1–6]}

Arts Key 07 Chiaroscuro in Music
Handel *Messiah, Glory to God* 0077776378459 [16]
{*Spotify*: Handel *Messiah, Glory to God* Willcocks}

Arts Key 08 Dance
1. *Tzena* Male Choir [13]
2. *The Lord of the Dance* McLoughlin Pub [3]

Arts Key 09 Poetry and Music
1. *Favorite Things* Casserole [5] from *The Sound of Music*
2. *Psalm 104* Monaco [43]
3. *The Proud Horse* Monaco [17]
4. *The Eagle* Monaco [13]
5. *Amazing Grace* Jul Harmony [19]
6. *Shall I Compare* Antiqua [15]
7. *Let Me Not to the Marriage* Antiqua [13]

Arts Key 11A Dramatic Shape and Variation Form
1. Beatles *A Day in the Life* Egan [20]
2. and 3. Copland *Appalachian Spring* Ainsworth [1, 24]

Arts Key 11B Four Seasons
1. Vivaldi *Four Seasons Spring* Tafelmusik Santo [1–3]
2. Vivaldi *Four Seasons Summer* Tafelmusik Santo [4–6]
3. Vivaldi *Four Seasons Autumn* Tafelmusik Santo [7–9]
4. Vivaldi *Four Seasons Winter* Tafelmusik Santo [10–12]

Arts Key 12A Three Music Selections
1. Adams *Short Ride in a Fast Machine* Alsop Shaker [1]
2. Glass *Einstein on the Beach* Prison 075597932362 [11]
   {*Spotify*: Glass *Einstein on the Beach* Scene I Train}
3. Pärt *Für Anna Maria* van Raat [17]

Arts Key 12B Beethoven 5th Symphony
1. Beethoven Symphony 5 Op. 67 I Leibowitz [6]
2. Beethoven Symphony 5 Op. 67 II Leibowitz [7]
3. and 4. Beethoven Symphony 5 Op. 67 III, IV Leibowitz [8, 9]

Arts Key 13 Bach Prelude and Pärt Credo
1. Bach Prelude in C BWV 846 825646316564 [1]
   {*Spotify*: Bach Prelude BWV846 Barenboim [1]}
2. Arvo Pärt *Credo* Wenn [11]

Arts Key 14A Style
1. *Veni Emmanuel* Clare Ross [1]
2. Josquin *El Grillo* Amarcord [22]
3. Vivaldi *Four Seasons, Spring* I *Allegro* Tafelmusik Santo [1]
4. Mozart *Nachtmusik* III divertimento G Harnoncourt [3]
5. Wagner *Ride of the Valkyries* 5099974197750 [1]
   {*Spotify*: Wagner *Ride of the Valkyries* Klemperer 100 Best}
6. Stravinsky *The Moor's Room* Boulez [5]

Arts Key 14B Style Ancient and Mixed
1. *Veni Emmanuel* Seoul [1]
2. Meece, *One Small Child* Ett Barn Jul Med Evie [6]

Arts Key 14C Style Harmonic Series
1. 8.570316 [17, Overtone Singer]
   {*Spotify*: Overtone Singer}
2. Chupani Song of the Ney [9]
   {*Spotify*: Omoumi Song of the Ney [9]}
3. *Day is Done* Taps Dolan [6]
4. *Amazing Grace* Folk Treasures of America Chorale [1]
5. *Kuc iwi lobo* (*Joy to the World*) [14]